EDINBURGH
EDUCATION AND SOCIETY
SERIES

General Editor: Colin Bell

Knowledge and Nation

Peter Scott

EDINBURGH UNIVERSITY PRESS

Edinburgh University Press
22 George Square, Edinburgh

Set in Linotron Palatino
by Photoprint, Torquay, and
printed in Great Britain by
The Alden Press, Oxford

British Library Cataloguing
  in Publication Data
Scott, Peter
Knowledge and nation.
1. Knowledge. Philosophical
  perspectives
I. Title
121

ISBN 0 7486 0168 6
ISBN 0 7486 0188 0 pbk

CONTENTS

PREFACE

Each summer since 1981 in *The Times Higher Education Supplement*, instead of routine editorials, I have written an essay that tries to go beyond the daily preoccupations of universities and other institutions by speculating about the wider links between knowledge and culture, education and society. These essays are one source of this book. Although they have gone through many revisions, the idea has stayed intact, to place higher education in a broader context. The other source is my earlier book *The Crisis of the University*. This was a detailed account of higher education policies, although it, too, tried to place the modern university in a historical context. The present book is an attempt to pick up where this earlier book left off, to generalise the arguments outlined there.

In writing this book my main debt is to *The THES* – to the company that publishes it, to its many friends and contributors, to the stimulating contacts it has provided and, most of all, to my colleagues. Lectures given at the universities of Birmingham, Groningen and Kent provided a stimulus to work out the arguments in Chapters 4 and 5, and an earlier version of Chapter 7 was published in the Paris journal, *Le Débat*. My thanks to Caroline Gorner and Joanna Henshaw who typed this book. It is dedicated to Cherill and Anna.

1

KNOWLEDGE AND NATION

This book begins with knowledge and ends with nation. Its purpose is to reflect upon the relationship between these two rival systems of ideas and values, beliefs and attitudes, which compete for our loyalty. On the one hand, knowledge represents the freely accepted claims of reason and science, the respect that is due to the highest intelligence of which mankind is capable in any age, the undeniable truth founded on individual experience and empirical evidence. As Galileo, perhaps apocryphally, is said to have quietly insisted even after his recantation before the Inquisition, *eppur si muove*.[1] On the other side, nation represents the compulsory claims of community, tradition, authority and faith, those unthought routines outside of which human life is a lonely and perilous enterprise, the identity that comes from matching self against selves. A contemporary of Galileo, Jacob Cats, discussing the peculiar qualities of domestic emblem literature in the seventeenth-century Netherlands, wrote of 'mute pictures which speak, little mundane matters that are yet of great weight; humorous things that are not without wisdom; things that men can point to with their fingers and grasp with their hands'.[2] Nation can as easily represent a homely ideal as a grandiose project. But in either form it denies the total claims of agnostic science and detached reason.

The relationship between, in these broad emblematic senses, knowledge and nation is not straightforward. The two patterns of thought that they imply are too different to be commensurable. Yet their respective values – reason and instinct, science and custom – must coexist. No public question is the exclusive territory of reason; no private question that of instinct or custom alone. All questions, from the most dignified interests of state to the most intimate interests of the individual, have to be shared. Yet the balance between knowledge and nation has shifted greatly over the centuries. In premodern society the powerful claims of received religion and inherited authority seemed to leave little room for the exercise of chosen beliefs or rational inquiry, although the intellectual efforts sustained through the Middle Ages and the Renaissance and Reformation to reconcile faith and reason should not be underestimated, and the rudimentary rationality which under-lay many political, social and economic customs should not be overlooked. In the nineteenth and twentieth centuries science and reason appeared to triumph. Metaphysical claims, whether the dogmas of the church or the mysteries of dynasty or estate, were overturned. It was assumed that once the clutter of *ancien régime* institutions had been swept away the nation state could be transformed into a rational organisation.[3] The whole social order could be reconstructed according to reasonable principles. Of course, there were those who feared that the democratic state might become the prisoner of primitive values and atavistic practices which an enlightened aristocratic order could safely ignore. But until close to the end of the nineteenth century such a view was uncommon. Generally, the coming of democracy and of industrialism was seen as a challenge to be overcome rather than a disaster to be avoided. The cultural strains that accompanied the transition to a mass society were regarded as the labour pains which necessarily accompanied the birth of a higher, more rational, civilisation. The confident hope was that the old elites would successfully educate their new masters.[4] Few feared that culture and reason would be swamped by a new mass irrationality, however disturbing the blood-and-soil character acquired by nationalism when it was unconstrained by the banal pragmatism of the Anglo-Saxon world and undisciplined by the Cartesian severity of French civilisation.

In the twentieth century the tension between knowledge and nation has become more apparent. There are many reasons for this. One is that the latter has demonstrated its most negative and destructive aspects. War and genocide, racial discrimination and cultural imperialism – with such barbarism the nation state has become associated in our present century. So the nation, although an inescapable category, has become more difficult to imagine as a reflection of a superior rationality. Rather, as the century has progressed the nation has been seen as an arena in which primitive pre-scientific values have re-emerged. Another reason is that the nation has increasingly employed the apparatus of rationality to serve its irrational and even immoral ends. Reason and science too often have been its servants rather than its masters or, at any rate, guides. The first consequence of this has been a frightening incongruity between reason and unreason. Technology has made possible genocide. The second is that the nation, in the narrow but powerful form of the state, has elbowed aside other, older, and more appealing interpretations of customary values, Cats's 'little mundane matters that are yet of great weight'.

A third reason is that knowledge, despite or perhaps because of the seemingly inexorable success of science and scholarship, has become less certain. The confident sureties of the nineteenth century, along with its grand all-explaining ideologies, have been dissolved. Today knowledge must also embrace the affective, the indeterminate, the unsure. A fourth reason is that human beings can no longer be regarded, or regard themselves, as entirely reasonable animals or at any rate animals capable of unrestricted reasonableness. This is not only because of Auschwitz and Hiroshima. The long arguments concerning the proper distinction to be drawn between mind and brain, an increasing awareness of the subconscious imagination, the moral conclusions that must be drawn from the continuing revolution in biological sciences and its biomedical consequences – these and similar developments have undermined our confidence in human competence. The working of the human mind, at once more powerful, seems to count for much less in moral terms.

So in the last years of the twentieth century the intersection of knowledge and nation takes place in confused and obscure territory. Knowledge has never been more imperial. Industry and employment depend increasingly on technology, which in turn depends on scientific research governed by the rules of rational inquiry. The character of modern society and the quality of our (national or international) culture are deeply influenced by developments within academic disciplines, within the hidden and private world of expert knowledge. The popularisation of science, of ideology, of intellectual fashions decisively shapes popular interests and mass values. Daniel Bell's vision of a postindustrial society in which theoretical knowledge is the central commodity is no longer futurological speculation.[5] To a large extent it is a recognisable description of our present data-driven economy and high-technology culture. Yet knowledge has largely abandoned any transcendental claims. It is content with its exploration and elucidation of the material world. It no longer attempts to explain the shape and meaning of human society; Marxism and the other great intellectual systems of the past are dead. And it no longer claims to offer a moral guide to the individual; the ethical concerns of a Matthew Arnold or an F. R. Leavis are deader still. Increasingly, science and scholarship seem to have turned their backs on the cultural consequences of their discoveries and insights. The disengagement of knowledge from morality, of course, is hardly a twentieth-century phenomenon. Perhaps Arnold's 'melancholy, long, withdrawing roar' of Christian faith made this disengagement inevitable, even if many of his contemporaries believed that an alternative and sturdier morality could be built on science and reason.[6] Frederic Myers, a Fellow of Trinity, recalled a visit by the novelist George Eliot to Cambridge in May 1873 in these much-quoted words:

> She, stirred somewhat beyond her wont, and taking as her text the three words that have been used so often as the inspiring trumpet-calls of men – the words, God, Immortality, Duty – pronounced, with terrible earnestness, how inconceivable was the first, how unbelievable the second, and yet how peremptory and absolute the third. Never, perhaps, have sterner accents affirmed the

sovereignty of impersonal and unrecompensing Law. I listened, and night fell; her grave, majestic countenance turned towards me like a Sibyl's in the gloom; it was as though she withdrew from my grasp, one by one, the two scrolls of promise, and left me with the third scroll only, awful with inevitable fates. And when we stood at length and parted amid that columnar circuit of the forest trees, beneath the last twilight of starless skies, I seemed to be gazing, like Titus at Jerusalem, on vacant seats and empty halls – on a sanctuary with no Presence to hallow it, and heaven left lonely of a God.[7]

Myer's gloomy reflections have been reproduced many times during the present century, with increasing frequency and deepening despair as it has progressed. George Eliot's Duty was too plainly a simulacrum for the evangelical Christianity that she had embraced and then rejected to be easily sustained in our secular age. Science and reason have been unwilling and unable to provide a substitute for either the discredited ethical authority of religion or the moral routines generated by the diurnal life of family, community or nation. Yet, despite everything, the suspicion remains that the complicated fabric of modern knowledge rests ultimately on a transcendental reinsurance or, better still, reassurance, which we are reluctant to acknowledge.[8] Its images, its codes, its meanings, the whole paraphernalia of science and scholarship, are grounded in ethical categories which are not susceptible to rational interrogation.

However, nation, the rival of knowledge, is also incapable of peopling the vacant halls or hallowing the empty sanctuary. Its practice, too, is contrived. Its values have lost their spontaneity. No longer an organic accumulation of lived experiences, the nation has been transformed by economies of intellectual and social scale into a scheme of abstract ideas, as austere as any scientific description of the material world. If nation and religion can be compared, a passage in George Eliot's Adam Bede may capture the character of this transformation. It comes just after Dinah Morris's preaching at Hayslope, an episode of breathless imagination that is among the greatest in the novel:

The after-glow has long faded away; and the picture we are apt to make of Methodism in our imagination is not an amphitheatre of green hills, or the deep shade of broad-leaved sycamores, where a crowd of rough men and weary-hearted women drank in a faith that was a rudimentary culture, which linked their thoughts with the past, lifted their imagination above the sordid details of their narrow lives, and suffused their souls with a sense of a pitying, loving, infinite Presence, sweet as summer to the houseless needy. It is too possible that to some of my readers Methodism may mean nothing more than low-pitched gables in dingy streets, sleek grocers, sponging preachers and hypocritical jargon.[9]

Unfair to Methodists, of course, as Matthew Arnold perhaps was to all Nonconformists in his *Culture and Anarchy*, published nine years later.[10] But, removed from this particular context and applied more widely to the customary values summed up under the heading 'nation', Eliot's words well describe the atrophying of personal, even primitive, loyalties that grew out of shared memories, needs and hopes.

This confused intersection between knowledge and nation has made it difficult to sustain a coherent cultural debate in modern Britain. Of course aesthetic, intellectual and political questions are ceaselessly debated. But the attempt to connect them up is rarely made. The bigger question, the character and quality of our culture, has been abandoned to silence. In general terms this silence is easy to understand, for reasons which have already been briefly discussed. The increasing sophistication of knowledge in the late twentieth century discourages general speculation that is not supported by detailed empirical research or painstaking scholarship. We have become the prisoners of a reductionist syllogism. Under modern conditions intelligence is rooted in expertise; expertise is achieved by pursuing the particular; so general statements can rarely be regarded as intelligent ones. At the same time, the growing artificiality of nation has undermined the foundations on which an alternative interpretation of wisdom could be built, one that rested on customary extra-scientific values. Those unthought routines, Cats's 'mute pictures', may still be as influential in shaping our culture. But they are denied any authoritative expression, except perhaps as objects to be studied.

However, these are general considerations which inhibit cultural debate in all modern societies. They do not explain the particular silence of the British who, of course, have not *always* been so silent. In the nineteenth century there was a constant chatter of cultural speculation. On the one hand was Carlyle's gloomy prognostication about the dangers of 'shooting Niagara', of plunging into the turmoil of a democratic and industrial society;[11] on the other, Arnold's glorious conclusion: 'This is the *social* idea and the men of culture are the true apostles of equality.'[12] But such speculation was not confined to those who directly addressed the cultural questions of their age. Mill and Macaulay never doubted that their scholarship was woven into a grander pattern, that politics and history were part of a more extensive intellectual civilisation. A century later, these expansive ambitions have been abandoned. The type of cultural analysis once practised by Carlyle and Arnold is now regarded as banal pamphleteering suitable only for Sunday newspapers or the flashier journals. Or it is seen as eccentric – intellectually fascinating but hardly safe academically. Perhaps the work of George Davie, the author of *The Democratic Intellect* and *The Crisis of the Democratic Intellect*, both books which offer a penetrating account of Scottish culture, has been treated in this manner.[13] A

century ago Davie would probably have been regarded as a more
central and influential figure. The elaboration of knowledge during the
last one hundred years is not sufficient to explain this change in
attitude. Rather, knowledge's studied neglect of its own cultural
consequences has withered the desire and the capacity to address the
grand questions that interest Davie.

This neglect is most pronounced in Britain. In many other countries
there is a livelier cultural debate. In the United States, books like Allan
Bloom's *The Closing of the American Mind*,[14] a deliberate polemic, and
Paul Kennedy's *The Rise and Fall of the Great Powers*,[15] a scholarly work
hijacked by polemicists, become bestsellers. Not only are such books
called upon or offered as expert witness in the making of public policy,
but in their own right they are also important interventions in the
continuing debate about the character and quality of American culture.
They influence the way in which Americans see themselves rather than
simply fuelling the discussions that take place within a closed
intellectual elite. Nor is this a peculiarly American phenomenon which
reflects the rhetorical and populist character of that culture. In France,
Emmanuel Le Roy Ladurie's *Montaillou*, published in 1978,[16] sold on a
scale not seen in Britain since Macaulay's *History of England* captured
the imagination of the Victorian middle class one hundred and forty
years ago. Politicians and industrialists as well as professors and
teachers competed to assert their enthusiasm for the book. No doubt
the picture-book quality of the inquisition into the Cathar heresy, and
the glimpse it afforded of peasant life in the medieval Mediterranean,
attracted many thousands of readers despite the forbidding anthropological apparatus of the book, the themes of which hardly seemed
relevant to late twentieth-century France. In Britain, history fails to stir
the cultural imagination to the same degree. Even books like Lawrence
and Jeanne Fawtier Stone's *An Open Elite?*,[17] which directly discusses
Britain's historical personality (and our claim to be regarded as benignly
exceptional), or Jonathan Clark's *English Society 1688–1832*,[18] a deliberate attempt to debunk liberal pieties about the British past, provoked
little interest outside the ranks of professional historians.

The question of British exceptionalism is perhaps this book's most
important secondary theme. Why, in a modern world surprisingly
reluctant to engage in cultural debate, are the British especially
diffident? One explanation may be our pragmatic intellectual tradition,
which in its worse moments is difficult to distinguish from anti-
intellectualism. But accounts of British pragmatism are generally
exaggerated. If explicit ideology seems to play a slighter part in our
national culture this may be because the unseen undertow of implicit
but powerful values makes it less necessary. In any case our pragmatism
is as likely to be a symptom as a cause of our avoidance of cultural

debate. Another explanation may be the interrupted modernisation of Britain which has allowed many anachronistic, even aristocratic, institutions, and accompanying mentalities, to survive into the late twentieth century. In an interesting sense Britain has never undergone a national revolution, although it can claim to be among the earliest nation states. Institutions have been adapted, sufficiently but minimally, to take on new roles. As a result, relationships between the individual, the group, the community and the state have become exceptionally confused. A positive aspect of this confusion may be the strong sense of fraternity which sensitive Britain-watchers like Ralf Dahrendorf have noticed.[19] A negative aspect may be our weak sense of human rights. For all our democratic paraphernalia we remain subjects, not citizens. Parliament is sovereign, not the people.

This interrupted modernisation has had two important consequences. First, its scatter of anachronistic institutions, practices and attitudes is divisive, making it difficult to generate a clear national identity and purpose. This divisiveness is compounded by the widespread but secret perception that these institutions, despite the intense loyalty they still command, are intellectually bankrupt. Because they are accepted to be indefensible, silence is the best strategy to ensure their survival. Second, there has been little opportunity to learn that powerful common language which accompanies explicit modernisation. Nation, state, justice – in most comparable societies these categories have much more precise meanings because they have had to be deliberately refined. In Britain, possibly richer but certainly vaguer meanings emerged incrementally. As a result our public vocabulary is oblique and antique.

A third explanation may be that Britain's civil religion, although strong, has remained unstated. Thus it is difficult to debate its cultural dimensions. Our public values have gone largely unexpressed, perhaps because they seemed incontestable, perhaps because they were feared to be banal. Our civil religion as a result is made up of implied rather than explicit interpretations and informal rather than stated rules. These are inherited and absorbed rather than argued and understood. The more they are talked about the less engaging they may seem. There are two aspects of the reticence, if not silence, of Britain's civil religion which are worth noting. The first is the clubbability of British culture. This is generally interpreted in negative terms, as a deep-rooted national taste for identification by exclusion rather than by inclusion. It is seen as the source of a 'them and us' mentality which reinforces class distinction and may encourage discrimination against excluded minorities, whether racial or social. But, of course, clubbability can be defined in more positive terms as a sense of 'belonging' that subsumes individual differences and in favourable conditions can serve as the ethical foundation upon which notions of social justice can be built.

Despite the apparent paradox British culture may be both exclusive and encompassing. In an article in *The Manchester Guardian* in January 1928 the poet Alfred Noyes described the burial of Thomas Hardy in language which reflects this paradox:

> From the point of view of the religion which did him the honour there was something majestic in its utter indifference to his own words and his own philosophy. It was an indifference that would have appealed to Hardy himself. In the very face of all that he had written and of all the Agnostics gathered around him there were uttered once again the sublimest words in the English language: 'I am the resurrection and the life'. The cross was carried before him, and after the Dorset earth was thrown into the grave the sure and certain hope which he had so emphatically repudiated in life was uttered again in ringing tones over his body. It was a ceremony that defied all logic, and illustrated the intellectual and religious confusion of our time as nothing else but the British Constitution itself is capable of doing. Thomas Hardy had drawn a circle around his imagination which shut out almost everything that was assumed in the ceremony, but the faith that had been shut out calmly drew a wider circle which included him in all his doubts and grief.[20]

The second aspect is that, although largely unarticulated, Britain's civil religion is far from being obscure or weak. Of course it is much easier to feel than to explain that post-Christian ideal, George Eliot's Duty, a strange conjunction of aristocratic obligation, bourgeois virtue and working-class aspiration which has shaped our society over the past two centuries. But its powerful presence remains. Its centrepiece is a commitment to balance – between aristocratic and democratic principles of government, between professional and commercial values, between capital and labour, between hierarchy and reform. Almost as important, however, is the belief that balance is more efficiently maintained by informal negotiation within a framework of flexible institutions and adaptable convictions, than through public regulation by courts and constitutions. The key dates in the formation of this civil religion can be disputed: 1642 and 1688 perhaps provided only a mythic retrospective endorsement of its principal beliefs; the years between 1760 and 1783 were probably more important than is generally assumed; 1832 was a crucial episode; and, in the present century, 1906 and 1945 were the decisive climacterics. But the gradual evolution of seventeenth- and eighteenth-century notions of balance, which looked back to the humanist ideal of a good, even godly, society and appealed to contrived antiquarian precedents, into twentieth-century corporatism, fed by the various currents of modern thought, has marked the development of Britain's peculiar civil religion. The question today is whether that religion has begun to decay. Maybe it enjoyed its finest and its final hour in mid-century. The Dunkirk evacuation, the Bletchley Park code-breakers, the Beveridge report on social security, the 1944 Education Act, the Manhattan Project for all its baleful consequences, the National Health Service – perhaps these were its last triumphs. If it is true that Britain in the 1980s is passing through a cultural counter-revolution, which is particularly intense because our peculiar corporatism is so deeply dug into the strata of our history, then the inarticulateness of our old civil religion may make its defence particularly difficult.

This book is an attempt to swim against the tide of silence. Or, more modestly, an attempt to reflect on the relationship between knowledge, the limited sureties of science and reason, and nation, the infinite but obscure patterns along which our lives run. The next chapter discusses the knowledge business in the context of its main disciplinary families – the arts, the social sciences, the natural sciences and technology. The arts receive the most extensive treatment because they seem to be most relevant to the theme of the book. But, in each case, the intention is to examine broad characteristics, which together determine what we understand academic knowledge to be. Chapter 3 attempts to trace the development of the ideas which have shaped modern society. With the exception of the first section, which discusses the particularity of the British response to these ideas, the approach is historical. The second section examines the grand ideologies which came out of the nineteenth century and the third the character of the postwar pragmatism which replaced them. The final section in this chapter looks at what is happening to those ideas today. Must we expect the triumph of neo-conservatism, or does the increasing divisiveness of academic knowledge now make it impossible to talk of the leading ideas of the age? Each section is accompanied by a sketch of a thinker whose work is emblematic rather than representative of theme under discussion. Thus, Richard Hoggart partners the particularity of the British; George Steiner is matched with the grand ideologies (as their memorialist, not their advocate); David Riesman accompanies the postwar pragmatism to which he so famously but uneasily contributed; and Thomas Kuhn's life and work are used to illustrate the character of our present intellectual age.

The next chapter begins to form a link between the book's two themes. It attempts to discuss the relationship between knowledge, culture and education, with particular reference to the university. This is done under four headings: a sketch of this relationship in a historical context; a description of the main characteristics of contemporary society; an account of the pluralism of modern higher education systems; and a discussion of the tension between givenness, accepting the world as it is, and transcendence, reimagining the world as it could be.

Chapters 5 and 6 consider education – the former, higher education, which is not only the primary producer of academic knowledge but a crucial mediator between this knowledge and notions of nationhood, and, the latter, schools which shape our secular values and modify existing social and economic hierarchies. The second of these chapters is divided into four sections. The first considers the experience of being young in the late twentieth century; the second looks at the structure of schools and the character of the teaching profession; the third discusses the purposes of schooling and how they are expressed through courses and curricula; and the fourth reflects on the relationship between education and national aspirations. Schools tell us who we think we are. The final chapter in this book is entitled 'The British Way' and is devoted largely to a discussion of the old country that is modern Britain. The first section of this chapter examines the contrast between imperial and provincial Britain (including in the latter Scotland and Wales), and considers how these geographical and political entities both sustain and contradict one another. The second section considers our perceptions of British society, particularly in terms of social class. The third argues around the overcooked concept of 'the British disease'. The suggestion that Britain's developmental difficulties have been exaggerated will be rejected by many, especially, perhaps, those who wish to believe that Britain has experienced an economic miracle in the 1980s. The final section (of the chapter and of the book) is more personal. It is organised around two places, Wallington, a Whig house in Northumberland, which is taken to represent what we were, and Wandsworth, a London borough which is taken to represent what we are. It attempts to reflect on the gap between them: what has been lost therein, what has been retained, what has been gained.

The ethos of this book is social democratic, liberal, even Whig (in late twentieth-century Britain antique categories retain a curious resonance). It is designed as an affirmation, critical but affectionate, of our historical personality, of the civil religion to which we have remained largely obedient. This is no contradiction. For it is not only by understanding but also by appreciating, and perhaps loving, the past that we can build a better future. Otherwise, we, like Titus at Jerusalem, may only gaze on vacant seats and empty halls.

2

THE KNOWLEDGE BUSINESS

Some may argue that nation rather than knowledge is a better place to begin the inquiry attempted in this book. To start with the particular, even the peculiar, the things bound by place and time and to move to the general, the universal, the values and practice freed from such constraints may seem more logical. If the opposite approach has been adopted here, it is because knowledge appears too firmly rooted in nation, because the universal so often seems to run back to the particular.

The knowledge industry, we are told, will be a key component of late twentieth-century society. Over the horizon of the next century some imagine a knowledge society. But what is knowledge? What knowlege? Whose knowledge? Knowledge and its allied categories, such as science, wisdom, learning, even truth – all these words are used promiscuously to describe aspects of the intellectual and perhaps moral inquiry that is organised in modern systems of education, and especially of higher education. These same systems also preserve and elaborate patterns of national identity. Definitions and categories of knowledge help to shape, perhaps decisively, our sense of nationhood. The link is made every day in schools and universities; it is direct and concrete, not oblique and arcane.

This chapter is about knowledge, science, wisdom, learning, truth – whichever of these semi-synonyms is preferred to describe that accumulation of experience and experiment, thought and reflection (and, of course, the technology to organise them purposively) which so many argue is the engine that powers postindustrial society. The recognition of the raw power of knowledge is hardly new, an insight only of our present century which reflects the prestige of post-bomb science, of advanced technology and of the sophisticated social engineering of the modern state. Four centuries ago Bacon expressed the same thought with great simplicity: *nam et ipsa scientia potestas est*.[1] Indeed, the same idea recurs through the pages of the Bible. In the book of *Job* 'the price of wisdom is above rubies'.[2] That wisdom, of course, was metaphysical rather than mechanical. But the transcendental ambitions of modern physics may have made this distinction unimportant.

So the words used to describe intellectual and moral inquiry are eloquent, even immanent ones, as accessible to feeling as to meaning. Yet they still reflect subtle shades of the latter. *Knowledge* is generally supposed to be more than information because it suggests the imposition of an intellectual order on disordered facts, implying *logos* rather than *data*. *Science*, taken in a broad sense, is perhaps more than knowledge because it suggests a systematic rigour designed to test the accuracy, or falsehood, of facts and the ordering of facts. *Wisdom*, if such an old-fashioned word may still be allowed, is more again. It not only suggests the ability to discriminate between more and less valuable knowledge, according to criteria that may be moral as well as scientific, but also describes the state of mind produced by the exercise of such discrimination. *Learning* may be regarded as a synonym of wisdom, for it too suggests a hierarchy of knowledge. But it may go further because it seems to emphasise the means by which wisdom is acquired. It describes the process, formal and informal, by which the individual is steered towards this desirable state of mind. As for *truth*, the prejudice of the late twentieth century, both in the rough world of politics and in the refined world of the mind, is to follow Bacon's Pontius Pilate: 'What is truth? said jesting Pilate; and would not stay for an answer'.[3]

Knowledge, therefore, does not describe a simple idea. It represents instead a confusing assembly of instinct, experience, information, experiment, technology, theory, ideology, morality. At one extreme, knowledge is the raw data luminously displayed on the green screen of the visual display unit; at the other, it aspires towards the truth 'that passeth all understanding'[4] in the Bible's eloquent but apparently illogical formula, or in Matthew Arnold's more economical phrase 'out-topping knowledge'.[5] It reaches from the routine to the religious. The power of knowledge, from its lowest to its highest forms, is recognised and even praised. But its definition remains diffuse and obscure. This difficulty raises not only philosophical questions of fundamental consequence – what can we know, and how do we know it? – but also social questions almost as difficult – how do we organise and grade what we take to be knowledge? This chapter is concerned with the latter more than the former questions. Its concern is with the social organisation of knowledge rather than its philosophical definition, although there are always echoes of the second in the first.

The segments into which a society divides the knowledge it regards as worth preserving and pursuing illuminate not only the most powerful traditions of that society but also its most resonant ambitions. The elaborate organisation of knowledge in the Middle Ages into the seven 'liberal arts', with the three arts of grammar, rhetoric and logic arranged in a preliminary *trivium*, describe both the theological and intellectual contours of medieval society and its social, political and administrative ambitions – Aristotelianism emerging out of feudalism, perhaps. Similarly, the substitution in the sixteenth century of *litterae humaniores* for these scholastic studies demonstrated the expanding political, intellectual, aesthetic and even moral horizons of the Renaissance world. Our modern four-part division of knowledge may be equally suggestive: *arts*, derived not from the medieval 'liberal arts' but from the humanism of early modern Europe; *social science*, the intellectual reverberations of the 'social question' that has agitated the nineteenth and twentieth centuries; *natural science*, an inquiry begun in the ancient world and accelerated in Renaissance Europe (and earlier in China) that has carried mankind almost beyond the edge of the knowable universe; and *technology*, the ubiquitous application of all the sciences – natural, social and even human – that surround and shape our lives. This already too simple four-part division of knowledge is often reduced to an even simpler dichotomy between arts and science. This further simplification is especially popular in the British intellectual tradition. This arts–science division is perhaps more a social than an intellectual phenomenon. It may mark the differences between old elites and new experts, between liberals and technocrats, and even between idealists and materialists. These are all themes that will be explored later in this book. The contrast between arts and science is recalled here only to justify the more extended discussion of the arts necessitated by their weighty cultural baggage. But the conventional four-part division of knowledge will provide the framework for the rest of this chapter.

ARTS

In intellectual, unlike commercial, life, labels stay the same while products change at a bewildering pace. The typical academic discipline is in a constant state of metamorphosis. Every generation it becomes something different. This is thought to be most true of the natural sciences and technology and least true of the arts. In fact it may be the other way round. Of course, the substance of physics or chemistry is being endlessly reshaped by improvements in the technical and, still more, intellectual apparatuses newly available to these disciplines. Yet, in the natural sciences and, more doubtfully, in social science, there is a flow, a continuity of priorities and techniques which in normal times is as important an influence as the ceaseless obsolescence of their content. The overarching context in which much scientific inquiry takes place, the paradigm in Thomas Kuhn's phrase, is often long-lasting and resilient.[6] Only at the great climacterics of science – the discoveries of Copernicus, Newton, Darwin, Einstein – is the continuity broken.

In the case of arts discontinuity is endemic. Instability of view is the common condition of most arts disciplines. No contextual theory is able to solidify into a seemingly objective paradigm within which intellectual inquiry can be safely marshalled. All theories are relentlessly contested. But this is not the only difficulty. Like the sciences the arts must adjust to new knowledge. Like them, they must overcome revolutionary discontinuity. The shifts in literature from romanticism through to postmodernism were as startling as those from Aristotelian to Newtonian to Einsteinian physics. But, unlike the sciences, the arts must come to terms with alarming shifts in identity and intention. Newton and Einstein thought they were addressing similar problems in physics even if they produced very different answers. But Hume's philosophy and Wittgenstein's barely touch at all, while Macaulay and Namier had such contrary views of what history was for that it is almost misleading to maintain the common label. There is a further difficulty for the arts. They must lead a double life, as the guardians and interpreters of the common stock of our culture and as vehicles for scientific inquiry. The two are inseparable in principle but often difficult to combine in practice. The validity of their scientific progress has to be judged in terms of a wider cultural project. The value of the arts cannot be determined in a private academic world and then, subsequently and independently, tested against criteria of social or economic ulility, as that of the sciences arguably can. Their definition, their intention and their value are all combined. They are aspects of each other. Moreover, the cultural project which shapes and is shaped by the arts is often interpreted in moral and even personal terms. The arts are expected to contribute to good living. They must lead to, in phrases Henry James gives to Isabel Archer in *The Portrait of a Lady*, 'the union of great knowledge with great liberty' or 'the infinite vista of a multiplied life'.[7]

The arts, therefore, have an extended and ambiguous quality not shared by the sciences whether natural, social or applied. Perhaps as a result, they are generally regarded as old, even anachronistic, disciplines and the sciences as new and vigorous ones that have evicted them from the leadership of the knowledge industry. But this view exaggerates the antiquity of the arts, in their present form at any rate, and the novelty of the sciences. Of course, our present conception of the arts can be traced back to the *litterae humaniores* of the Renaissance. In that period, philosophy escaped from the gravity of theology and the classics, which were to shape European and world civilisation so decisively in succeeding centuries, first ascended to academic glory. But, as late as the nineteenth century, philosophy still extended far beyond the moral and analytical preoccupations typical of the modern discipline. Just as medieval 'liberal arts' had included mathematics, so philosophy embraced physics. Indeed, Scottish universities still describe physics as 'natural philosophy', recalling this obsolete organisation of knowledge. As a descriptive term, *philosophy* had a century ago all the imprecise breadth typical of science today. Its relationship with the modern discipline was similar to that of political economy with the contemporary social sciences.

Other arts disciplines are even more recent creations. History was organised as a scholarly discipline, rather than as a gentlemanly antiquarianism, only in the second half of the last century. It was devised by Macaulay's children and Gibbon's great-grandchildren. English was barely established as a discipline before the beginning of this century. I. A. Richards was among the first scholars to treat literature as its own field of study rather than as an aspect of the wider literary–philosophical inquiry that had engaged Matthew Arnold or Leslie Stephen. The social sciences are often regarded as new-fangled disciplines. Yet they are as old as the arts. The foundations of modern sociology, economics and anthropology were laid down at very much the same time as those of the leading arts subjects. Both, arts and social science, are younger than chemistry, biology and many forms of engineering.

And so the antique aura of the arts may be, if not quite an illusion, at any rate highly misleading. The liberal arts with Cardinal Newman argued in *The Idea of a University*[8] should be at the heart of the university curriculum were not the arts as conceived and organised today. He wrote at a time when the older idea of the liberal arts had not been entirely displaced by the more modern and exclusive definition of the arts as humanities or even human sciences. For him they embraced mathematics certainly and, through 'natural philosophy' and 'political economy', much of what would be regarded today as natural and social science. The arts were broad synoptic disciplines that sought to integrate rather than to splinter knowledge. This was their attraction and their value as an instrument for university education. The same ideals and intentions lay behind the struggle by Scottish universities to retain a broad arts-based undergraduate curriculum later in the century and again, despairingly, in the 1920s, a struggle ably described by George Davie. The implied populism of this Scottish debate may seem to mark it off from Newman's more aristocratic project in Ireland. But both views perhaps, rested on an interpretation of the liberal arts which was already out-of-date before the nineteenth century was over. The philosophy defended by those Scottish professors and teachers so admired by Davie was commonsensical, demotic, doric. The philosophies of Moore, Russell, Wittgenstein and Heidegger, more inward, scholarly and professional, could never have provided the principles around which to organise a liberal university education. Nor, of course, would Newman have regarded the much more narrowly based arts disciplines which began to develop at the end of the nineteenth century as suitable instruments for the liberal education he desired to promote. No doubt he would have excluded them, along with other forms of technical and professional training and specialised research, from his ideal university.

The arts were by no means as dominant in the nineteenth-century university as contemporary rhetoric insisted and sentimental memory recalls. The natural sciences may have been slow to penetrate Oxford and Cambridge but science had occupied an important place in London University from the start. It was equally significant in newly-founded institutions like the civic universities in the north and midlands, and in America's land-grant colleges. In the German universities, which were rapidly emerging as a model for much of continental Europe, the natural sciences were also strongly represented. So it is misleading to present the advocates of a liberal education in Victorian Britain as an arrogant elite. Rather, they were engaged in a defensive campaign to resist the subordination of education, in particular of university education, to industrial and technical values. These battle lines were first drawn up by Coleridge and others in the 1820s. They saw a society very different from that described in retrospective luxury by Martin Wiener in *English Culture and the Decline of the Industrial Spirit 1850– 1980*.[9] They lived in the England of Merdle or Melmotte (or in America's gilded age). They saw speculation, industrialisation, mechanisation – all of which seemed to threaten the equipoise of an ordered, organic society. Their fear, so eloquently expressed by Arnold in *Culture and Anarchy*, was of a narrow Nonconformist commercial civilisation. Such an outlook cannot fairly be characterised as reactionary. Fifty years later, the novels of D. H. Lawrence expressed a similar determination to resist the stifling frustration of a narrow-minded provincial England. There are chilling echoes of the same feeling in T. S. Eliot's *The Wasteland*.[10]

A liberal education, therefore, seemed to offer the best hope for the re-creation of culture and of a cohesive elite in a troubled society and, later, for the enlightenment of citizens in a mass democracy. The arts seemed to provide the only feasible material for such an education. They appeared able to provide the intellectual beliefs and moral values which were thought appropriate for society's new leaders, many of whom were no longer selected by birth but by entrepreneurial skill or competitive examination or other forms of *la-carrière-ouverte-aux-talents* policy. With admirable anachronism these beliefs and values were imagined to reflect standards of gentlemanly cultivation to which few members of *ancien régime* elites had ever actually aspired. The arts were also taken to represent cultural traditions threatened by the growth of industrial and democratic society. In the early nineteenth century, Coleridge had proposed the establishment of a 'clerisy', a secular priesthood to defend high culture.[11] Carlyle, for his part, was concerned that a machine-like industrial society might crush to death any possibility of sustaining an organic culture. More positively, liberal educators believed that by embodying the best of the culture of the past the arts could help to form that common culture which all societies yearn for, most especially in times of rapid change and anxious crisis.

The arts also played a central role in the formation of school teachers at a time when most western nations were first developing universal systems of education with a view to maintaining social peace and facilitating democratic change. The arts formed the core of the curriculum, particularly in public and grammar schools which educated the powerful middle class. The alleged bias in favour of the arts and against the sciences in British education is long-standing and deep-rooted. The arts advanced because their intentions seemed to correspond more closely than those of the sciences to a view of education which valued 'character' more highly than skill (still an influential view, although generally disguised in modern clothes as 'transferable intellectual skills'!). Nor was the influence of the arts confined to the closed schools of the middle classes. Through the Workers' Educational Association and university extramural classes they were truly outward-bound. Indeed, it is in the latter that the strongest echoes of a peculiarly Victorian approach to the arts can still be heard.

The disjunction between the arts' wider cultural project, whether defined in conservative or democratic terms, and the particular academic direction taken by individual arts disciplines has remained. Perhaps it has widened. The victory of the natural sciences over the liberal arts in the nineteenth century, the rise of a mass society ruled by consumer rather than civic values, the cultural anxiety, pessimism and even nihilism of the modern world, the terror and horror of the twentieth century, all have made more difficult the liberal enterprise which even in Newman's and Arnold's age depended on too narrow an intellectual base. Moral generalisations are denied any scientific standing. So they are avoided. In their modern form the arts are too often timid and inward. Yet the demand for an effective liberal response to the moral relativism, the utilitarian values and the amoral collectivism of modern society is felt more urgently than ever. Of course, the liberal arts have other heirs apart from the scholarly arts which are their nominal successors. Much of their liberal impulse has been transferred to the social sciences and the caring professions. In the twentieth century Newman might have regarded sociology as a discipline as liberal as philosophy, while Arnold would surely have been sympathetic to cultural studies. Even the natural sciences and engineering have been touched by the cultural project of the old liberal arts. In a society so dependent on scientific discovery and technological innovation this is to be expected and welcomed. Liberal values can hardly afford to be confined to the arts side of C. P. Snow's two-cultures iron curtain.[12]

But it is possible to argue another way. The arts in their modern form are the true heirs of both the liberal arts of the past and new disciplines fashioned by the intellectual and political culture of the twentieth century. The present century has provided not only the opportunity for the scholarly elaboration of the arts but also the occasion to apply this scholarly apparatus to define and refine high culture. In earlier more stable centuries such a task perhaps seemed unnecessary. Today the arts are able to attempt this ambitious task because of *and* despite their academic elaboration. They have inherited from the liberal arts of the nineteenth century the urge to integrate, to exercise intellectual imagination on a scale not expected of other subjects, to try to grasp knowledge whole. Reductionism can never be an appropriate intellectual technique in the arts, however hard they are pressed into a Ph.D mould fashioned for the more specialised natural sciences.

But along with the urge to integrate, to establish meaning and value, the arts have also inherited the central dilemma that defeated the liberal educators of the nineteenth century: culture for the few or enlightenment for the many? It is apparently an even more urgent question today. But the arts find it difficult to choose. Both are their responsibility. They can never desert culture. They are stuck with their elitism because their search for meaning and value requires them to defend the high culture of the past and help articulate the most authentic of contemporary culture. On the other hand the same search demands as powerful a commitment to enlightenment, which under modern conditions must be populist. Ultimately, of course, enlightenment can only be expressed through personal experience. The individual being is at the centre of any study in the arts, whether as subject or object. The arts cannot deny their humanism any more than they can abandon their elitism; they must continue to defend hierarchies of value. The radicalism of the arts, and their conservatism, are both compounded because they remain the disciplines most likely to challenge the poverty of positivism, to assert that the true must always be related to the good and the beautiful.

So the arts today have a peculiarly Janus-like quality: they must look backwards and inward, and at the same time forwards and outward. This tension may have been increased by their simultaneous growth into both mass and scientific disciplines. No doubt their inherent humanism made the first a natural development. It has been their fate and their duty to be at the forefront of popular education. Today the arts have developed into mass disciplines enrolling very large numbers of students. As a result, far from being 'power' disciplines studied by the future great-and-good elite, they are now often regarded as residual disciplines suitable for students *without* scientific qualifications and *without* professional ambitions, lumpen subjects for mass higher education. The scientific elaboration of the arts was also an inexorable development – but again, one with ambiguous benefits. The arts have had to accommodate themselves to an academic structure designed for the natural sciences. Research rather than scholarship, the amoral accumulation of data rather than the moral interpretation (and reinterpretation) of experience, the teaching of facts rather than the learning of values – these suggestive contrasts are well understood. But despite their remorseless scientification the arts still appear less effective intellectual machines. Their knowledge, once regarded as semi-sacred, seems too tentative in a positivist world, their tools of analysis too blunt for the high-technology future. What role can the arts hope to play in the knowledge society?

One answer, of course, is to retreat into the castle of high culture and pull up the drawbridge. Coleridge and Carlyle can be summoned up to justify this pessimistic project. In our present century, Eliot and F. R. Leavis were key figures among those who saw the arts in terms of the endangered culture of a minority elite. In his *Notes Towards the Definition of Culture* Eliot argued that culture and equality could never be compatible.[13] Leavis was equally convinced of this. In *Mass Civilization and Minority Culture*, a plain-speaking title, he wrote: 'In any period it is upon a small minority that the discerning appreciation of art and literature depends. . . . It is still a minority, though a larger one, who are capable of endorsing such first-hand judgement by genuine personal response. . . . The minority capable not only of appreciating Dante, Baudelaire, Hardy (to take major instances) but of recognizing their latest successors constitute the consciousness of the race at a given time'.[14] This response has sometimes turned to resentment at those other disciplines which seem to have stolen the arts' place in the academic sun. A famous example was Leavis's ferocious assault on C. P. Snow in the early 1960s. For Leavis, Snow represented those supplanting rivals, that philistine fraternity of wartime code-breakers, atomic scientists, economic planners and social engineers who had come to dominate the postwar university.

A second answer is to emphasise the scientific qualities of the arts, to transform the humanities into the human sciences. But it is never easy to abandon the wider cultural project in which the arts have always been embroiled. The definitions, intentions and valuations of the arts are all entwined. Scientific reductionism is incapable of addressing the big questions. A third answer is to try to reassert the humanism, even populism, of the arts. But this is not straightforward. Does it require the exhumation of the liberal education tradition associated with Arnold just barely alive today in a few extramural classes? The decline and fall of Davie's Democratic Intellect suggest this is perhaps a futile ambition. Or does it mean that the populist strains to be found in most arts disciplines must be endorsed? That too may be difficult. In some eyes these strains echo too much of Marxism to be acceptable. *Radical Philosophy* and *History Workshop* are not to everyone's taste. Or does it simply mean that the arts should be eclectic in their academic elaboration, not following a narrow, scientific path but ranging across a wide intellectual territory? The arts, according to this last view, should have wide-open frontiers to other disciplines, especially social science but also science and technology, and in turn these disciplines should allow themselves to be penetrated by humanist values.

The first two views of a reasserted humanism suggest a defensive operation, awkwardly echoing of Eliot's and Leavis's minority culture. The arts are seen as providing a principled opposition to a mass society governed by amoral and technocratic values. The third intepretation is less pessimistic. The arts can fight back. This resilience can be observed in many fields. In philosophy, an interest in substantive ethical questions has superseded an earlier preoccupation with technical and procedural issues. Historians are struggling to recover the whole past, the social mentality of the poor as well as the political acts of the rich. Feminism and cultural studies are reshaping the priorities of literature. In the arts as a whole there is a new commitment to reaching out beyond the research seminar, the undergraduate lecture, the sixth form class to a broader community of students. It is not that the arts have turned their back on scientific elaboration but that they have acquired the confidence to interpret that elaboration in the context of liberal knowledge. They have no choice but to be both scientific and liberal, just as they cannot choose between culture and equality. The arts cannot claim to exist outside society. Eighteenth-century antiquarianism reflected the tastes of the gentry, particularly their concern with rank, as surely as the modern interest in women's writing and history reflects the influence of feminism. In this sense the agenda for the arts is rewritten by each succeeding generation. They are a relativist enterprise, although in a profound sense.

But there is a final question for the arts, which all other disciplines can evade. Do they civilise their students? This was the question which Newman and Arnold, Eliot and Leavis took so seriously. For them it was the nub of the arts. Perhaps it still is. Because the arts must combine the celebration of the highest culture with the enlightenment of the individual they cannot avoid this question. Of course a narrow answer can be offered. The philosopher or historian can claim that the study of their disciplines encourages rationality. But the same, or a stronger, claim can be made for mathematics, sociology or engineering.

The argument that the arts teach people to reason is compromised by the evident ability of the sciences to do the same or better. The indeterminacy of the arts enriches but also complicates their reading of rational inquiry. The claim that they teach what are today clumsily called 'transferable skills' and stimulate an intellectual flexibility which cannot easily be matched by the more rigid and determinist sciences is undermined by the fear that we live in an age that is turning away from the book, on which in some form or other all the arts depend. All subjects properly taught produce the intellectual qualities to which the arts lay particular claim. The sciences indeed have a superior claim to teach analytical skills than have the arts, because the latter's knowledge is more contextual and so less assured. And the social sciences are surely better placed to encourage fluency of communication. Their fatal attraction to jargon is more than compensated for by their relevance. Economics, business and sociology address the central issues of public policy in an industrial society.

In the past the arts were appreciated not for their own sake but because they taught rhetorical skills, the classical eloquence which was considered a proper preparation for public life and because, less categorically, it was believed they helped to inspire and sustain a common elite culture. History, the classics and literature were key components in the education of public men (and women). Today the social situation of the arts has been transformed. They have lost their political utility. The *patois* of public affairs is overwhelmingly derived from the social and applied sciences. Rhetorical skills have been displaced by managerial capacities rooted in these more modern disciplines. So the claim that the arts are well placed to inculcate forms of rationality endorsed by a classical political tradition has lost its force.

But a broader answer to the question do the arts civilise their students is even more difficult. George Steiner, of course, has argued that high culture may as easily barbarise as civilise. Its abstract speculations breed a nervous boredom, a moral *ennui*, out of which may grow a perverse fascination with violent action.[15] His favourite image is of the concentration camp guard reading Rilke or listening to Schubert. His favourite phrase is the 'cry in the poem may be more real than the cry in the street.' But even if this account is denied, even if the claim that many, or any, guards had such tastes is disputed, nevertheless it has become more difficult to root the study of the arts in the cultural urgency of our times.

There was a time perhaps, at the end of the last century and in the first half of the present century, when the dwindling of the arts' primary role as the best education for political elites was more than redressed by the growing conviction that they confronted questions not just of cultivation but of survival, of life and death for the human spirit. This conviction, of course, was not confined to the arts. It spread out across all branches of knowledge, including the sciences, in an intense belief that learning, education and culture provided the only definition of what it was to be human. The humane and the human were elided in the brilliance of Europe's pre-Holocaust civilisation. The intensity of thought and belief in Vienna, Berlin, Paris, St Petersburg came to define the modern condition with tingling accuracy.

For a while, in the 1930s and 1940s, in much of Europe humane questions actually became human ones. Literally so, for they were often matters of life and, more often, death. Perhaps in eastern Europe they have never lost the sharp edge they acquired in those years. That these questions were felt less urgently in Britain is a theme that will be taken

up in the next chapter. Behind the protection of the Channel and the
North Sea, culture remained a comfort not a challenge, reassuring
rather than threatening. The angry urgency of Leavis and the bleak
eloquence of Eliot, and the concerns of their analogues on the left,
seemed exaggerated and pointless, a mannered aestheticism at odds
with plain British common sense. So, perhaps, it has remained. As a
result the arts face a particular difficulty in Britain, because there are no
nerve ends they can jangle, no convictions they can set on edge. The
celebration of their role in culture and education is seen as a matter
of maintenance, of keeping existing values in working order, of per-
petuating social rites rather than addressing urgent and passionate
human needs. Perhaps in Britain the arts have a more conservative
colouring than in the rest of Europe and in North America. Of course,
as has already been discussed, in the arts there must always be conflict
between essence and method. Their essence is, in Arnold's phrase, 'the
best knowledge'. Even as the arts refine and define that knowledge,
they can never cease to discriminate between the more and the less
worthwhile, the more and the less authentic. Theirs is a relentlessly
elitist project. But the method of the arts is to question, criticise,
deconstruct, even subvert established values and beliefs, and so theirs
is a restlessly radical project too. In Britain, however, there may be too
great an emphasis on their former aspect, a bias that inevitably
complicates any attempt to answer the question do they civilise.

But the inability of the arts to avoid or to answer such questions may
measure their true significance. They are bound to associate thought
and conduct, ideas and being in a way that no other disciplines need
attempt. They cannot avoid a deeper commitment to truth, in a sacred
as much as scientific sense, a revealed and experienced truth that
depends on an educated moral imagination. A Kafka metaphor
perhaps sums it up best. Literature, along with all the arts, is an axe to
break up the frozen sea inside us, individuals or nations. Today science
and technology may be the most powerful and useful disciplines; social
science the most public and political; but the arts are the most personal
and the most engaged.

SOCIAL SCIENCE

'Social work, sociology, socialism – it's all the same thing, isn't it?'
When this contemptuous remark was made almost twenty years ago by
a Conservative councillor alarmed about the growth of social science in
the colleges that were soon to form the new polytechnics, it was
dismissed as an amusing example of reactionary prejudice. Inevitably it
was included in the 'This England' column of the *New Statesman*. After
all, this was the time of the Paris *événements* and the climax of protests
against the Vietnam war, of the crest of the welfare state's second wave
in Britain and the 'Great Society' in the United States. Today we are less

sure that such a view can be dismissed as a ridiculous anomaly – and not only because social science is under siege by suspicious right-wing politicians. Of course the literal absurdity of the councillor's remark remains. Not all social workers are sociologists are socialists. Yet in a looser and perhaps more allegorical sense the implied connection is not utterly false. For the social sciences are driven by the imperatives of political power; they do reflect directly the spirit of the age. They have grown out of practice towards theory, not the other way round. They are pragmatic and contemporary disciplines rooted in action rather than in contemplation. They are inside rather than outside the fabric of modern society.

So it is difficult to disentangle entirely the intellectual priorities of the social sciences from the preoccupations of the society which has developed in Europe and America over the past two centuries. The fingerprints of empire are still all over anthropology, for example, which remains biased towards the foreign and exotic rather than the domestic and familiar. Only in recent years have the insights of anthropology been applied to the various 'tribes' that inhabit modern Britain: politicians, journalists, judges, football fans. Political science is still organised around the concerns of liberal democracies. States organised on alien principles, like Iran's Islamic Republic, are impenetrable. Even those organised on aberrant principles, such as the Soviet Union (before Gorbachev?), are difficult to understand in the standard categories and contexts of political science. Psychology is still heavily influenced by psychometric notions, occasionally accompanied by disturbing undercurrents of behaviourist and even eugenicist ideology, or else by the narrow angsts of those successive psychic capitals of the Western world, Vienna and New York.

In economics, the orderly (for Keynesians, the civilised) management of capitalist free-market society remains the overarching concern. In this sense left-wing economists share the same preoccupations as Milton Friedman, although their prescriptions, of course, are different. The dominant interests remain trade, credit, production, employment. Behaviour and exchanges that do not conform to the classical rules of the market economy are often regarded as eccentric and peripheral. Even vital concerns like the impact of science and technology on economic structures are seen as fascinating but secondary questions. Most economists are preoccupied by the short-term, as Keynes advised! Sociology continues to be consumed by its efforts to understand the experiences of urbanisation and industrialisation (often still in a sentimental L. S. Lowry-like perspective). Recreating out of those experiences valid social forms and patterns of citizenship drives the discipline's preoccuaption with equality. Sociologists who are more or less unconcerned about questions of equality, are hard to find. Caring about social distress is deep in sociology's bedrock.

Of course there are exceptions – stay-at-home anthropologists, political scientists unafraid to penetrate alien states, psychologists who rise above Darwinian intelligence-testing and Freudian or Jungian controversies, economists who are not simply the facilitators of capitalism, sociologists who are interested in things other than equality. These exceptions may even be on the increase but they remain minorities within their disciplines. Certainly they do not invalidate the general rule: the shape of the social sciences has been moulded by the great social questions that have dominated nineteenth- and twentieth-century politics in the West. Their common ancestor, after all, was political economy, the first organised intellectual effort to understand and, it was hoped, modernise both state and society, an effort that reflected the values of the European enlightenment and the revolutionary changes that followed.

The contrast between the social sciences and the arts is illuminating. Three distinguishing features may be particularly significant. First, social science is interested in establishing general laws while the arts are generally content with a creative particularity. In the uncertainty of the late twentieth century these laws may have lost their earlier solidity. They may have been downgraded into models, paradigms or even metaphors. But the urge within social science to seek general explanations remains. Second, social science is rooted in pragmatic investigation while some arts subjects are still attracted by idealistic notions. Platonic metaphysics play no part in the social sciences, despite the latter's interest in general theory. Marx, it should be remembered, repudiated the Hegelian idealism of his youth. Efforts to reconstruct such idealism as the basis of a liberal Marxism have not been convincing. Third, social science aspires to action while the study of the arts leads more often to reflection and even contemplation. Most social science disciplines have utilitarian intentions. Directly through social investigation or indirectly through their influence on associated professions they seek to move the world along. Their ambition is to inform and influence public policy. Although the arts, too, aim to improve the quality of individual and social life, their approach is necessarily oblique. They cannot rival the instrumental construction of most social sciences.

Within the latter, of course, there is a great diversity – and even conflict. A favourite contrast is between 'hard' disciplines (economics?) and 'soft' disciplines (sociology?). This dichotomy is sometimes aligned with two others – that between social sciences with a strong quantitative element and those which rely more on qualitative methods of inquiry, and that between those with a strong positivistic tradition and others which regard knowledge as more provisional. A fourth contrast is between those social sciences that aspire to political neutrality, and are sometimes dismissed as 'technocratic', and those that regard political engagement, although not necessarily commitment, as an essential component of the search for truth. But the more these broad contrasts are explored the more unreliable they seem as an explanatory framework within which to describe the social sciences. All have 'hard' and 'soft' aspects; all depend on qualitative judgements as well as quantitative techniques; all combine an attachment to positivism with an acknowledgement of intellectual indeterminacy; and the most neutral social sciences are built into a bedrock of ideology while the most political are compromised by pragmatism. Far from distinguishing between the different disciplines, these contrasts may simply demonstrate an ambiguity in which all social science shares. Pulled in one direction by its desire to arrive at general explanations, social science is pushed in the other by its commitment to pragmatic investigation, its distrust of metaphysical idealism and its affinity with public policy.

So these hard–soft, quantitative–qualitative, philistine–philosophical, neutral–political contrasts are not as sharp as they seem. They describe not straightforward dichotomies that can be aligned with different disciplines, periods, or schools of thought, but spectra along which these various characteristics are expressed with increasing or diminishing force. This does not mean that such contrasts have no suggestive value. The data used by anthropologists are of a different quality than those available to economists. Also, to take another example, the two decades after 1945 can be characterised as a period of pragmatism and seeming neutrality in social science (without accepting everything implied in Daniel Bell's book title, The End of Ideology,[16]) certainly compared with the ideological exuberance of the New Left in its brief moment of intellectual glory. But these contrasts should not be pushed too far. For the desire to combine general explanations with social action, or practical theory with theoretical practice, has always been well developed in social science. In its dawning, Jeremy Bentham was the apostle of utilitarianism as a self-balancing ideology. But he was not afraid to try his hand at designing new model prisons which expressed in brick his views about the nature of crime and how to prevent it. A little later, the New Poor Law and other, more humane, reforms of public administration that laid the foundations (often literally) of Victorian Britain were informed by the same utilitarian spirit. Marx may have produced the most abstract, even the most metaphysical, of all social theories. But his analysis was built on the laborious study of Government Blue Books in the British Museum library. That tradition has been maintained. The modern state is staffed by experts, many of whom are social scientists. Thus in social science a simple division between thinkers and doers is impossible. The same desire to bind theory and practice has passed over into the professions allied to social science. Indeed, it is the explicit ambition of teachers and social workers. The title of a recent book by Donald Schön sums up this mentality: *The Reflective Practitioner*.[17] In this respect, social science may have more in common with technology than with either the arts or the natural sciences.

Some will dispute this emphasis on the practical engagement of social science. Certainly in Britain, which is influenced, perhaps, by the intellectual habits of continental Europe, the attractions of theory, of abstraction, even of idealism have always been felt. The unadorned empiricism of America has failed to establish such deep roots on this side of the Atlantic. One proof is that here sociology and social administration have remained distinct disciplines. The ethnographic tradition associated with Everett Hughes in mid-century Chicago has often been looked down on as a form of elaborate reportage.[18] An example of this distaste for pragmatism in British social science may be the evolution of political science away from the systematic intellectual training of citizen–legislators it was imagined to be in the nineteenth century to the eclectic and perhaps inchoate modern discipline with which we are familiar.[19] But social science has never had as much academic room in which to manoeuvre as the arts. It could not become too detached from its empirical roots. Despite short-lived escape bids in the radical excitement of the 1960s, medical and legal sociology, to take two examples, have never quite freed themselves from the gravity of social medicine and criminology, older disciplines with more pragmatic intentions.[20]

Indeed, social science has always found it difficult to liberate itself from the expectations of its clients or customers. Today the sovereignty of the customer is especially difficult to challenge, but as early as the mid-1950s Ralf Dahrendorf wrote: 'The sociologist certainly is a debtor of the society in which he lives in a way unparalleled in most other disciplines of scholarship. But his debt merely forces him to choose the subjects of his research in such a way that its results – if any – might contribute to informing society about itself. This is all. . . . But if an ill-advised public does not understand the process of scientific inquiry and demands more, the sociologist may and must be sufficiently proud and confident to define his scholarly responsibility in face of a misconceived obligation to society which is all too often informed by little more than a desire to please'.[21] While the arts have had to battle to relate their values to those of the practical world, social science has had to struggle to free itself from that world's suffocating embrace and so gain the intellectual room in which to breath.

There is yet another contrast, that between subjectivity and objectivity, that cannot be applied easily to social science. This is far more than the simpler contrasts between quantification and qualification, or between pragmatic neutrality and political engagement. Despite its enthusiasm for grand theory, social science has never abandoned pragmatism. In social science, abstractions, ideas and beliefs are actualised as solid objects, ideology and consciousness. In the arts, by contrast, real events and actual movements are sometimes idealised in terms of their historical meaning or cultural significance. This is an important difference, occasionally clouded by the leaden language used by some social scientists and the crisp eloquence of many scholars in the arts. But the social-science way to knowledge is a secular road. No mystery; no hermeneutics. Its truth is hewn out of common-sense descriptions of this world, not contrived from pale reflections of a shadowy ideal world beyond. But neither can social science easily accept the reductionism and determinism that are now entrenched in the natural sciences. Sociologists, economists and even anthropologists cannot hope to achieve the detachment that is taken for granted by physicists and biochemists. Social phenomena must be investigated from the inside. As a result, they may be modified by these acts of investigation. Noble savages are tainted by anthropological inquiry, financial markets are influenced by fashionable economic theories, attitudes to social hierarchy and equality may be changed by socio-logical speculation. Nor is it easy for social scientists to divide up their inquiry into digestible portions. The tentacles of interconnectedness spread through and across all their disciplines. In the natural sciences reductionism may be a highly effective intellectual style; in social science it is more often a pathway to banality, sterility and simple irrelevance.

That favourite question, is social science truly scientific, is many layers too simple. In a naive sense the social sciences are not as 'objective' as the natural sciences – but only, perhaps, because the questions they try to answer cannot be insulated from the environment which has given rise to these questions. Inevitably their answers are less categorical. But this does not make these answers intellectually primitive any more than the capacity of the natural sciences to detach problems from their environment in order to study them, and so produce more 'objective' solutions, makes scientific results intellec-tually naive. Yet, in Britain, social science has had to struggle hard to maintain its scientific credibility. This struggle came to a head in a controversy centred on the Social Science Research Council, now the Economic and Social Research Council. Unlike the other research councils established in the 1960s, which related to already established disciplines, the SSRC played an important leadership role in the academic development of the social sciences. Its influence was intellectual as well as managerial. The first stage of the controversy came in the early 1980s when, already under political pressure, the council decided to reorganise its committee structure. This was far from being an arid bureaucratic manoeuvre. Previously its committees had been organised by discipline – sociology, economics and so on. Instead, the SSRC decided to organise them by issues or areas of social concern. In one sense it was an admirable plan. The new arrangement conformed to Karl Popper's philosophy of science with its emphasis on problem-solving through falsification, that is, through the disproving of hypotheses. It also reflected a politically influential view of education that stressed the learning of skills rather than the acquisition of knowledge. But the message that was received most clearly in the social science community was that the SSRC was hostile to disciplines and suspicious of theory. Yet, many argued, the identity and so the utility of social science depended on strong disciplines. The SSRC's claim that its new committee structure encouraged multidisciplinary inquiry was undermined by the counterargument that collaborative inquiry depended on the prior existence of healthy disciplines.

The second stage in the controversy came when the then Secretary of State for Education and Science, Keith Joseph, insisted that the SSRC, as part of the price to be paid for its survival, should drop the word 'science' from its title. Hence the ESRC. It seemed a small price compared to others that might have been exacted. Yet the surrender of the label 'social science' was a real, not a token, loss. It came at a time when individual disciplines had begun to question their membership in a larger social science enterprise. Part of this questioning was simply a matter of expediency. Management science, business studies and economics may have felt that they suffered from being too closely associated with sociology, psychology and other out-of-political-favour disciplines. But part may have arisen from a growing lack of cohesion among the social sciences. In its best years, the former SSRC had been able to encourage an intellectual solidarity among the different social science disciplines. They came to be seen as part of a wider enterprise. The original title of the research council affirmed the existence of a unified social science. Its new title emphasises the diversity, even disparity, of the social sciences, an almost randomly associated series of disciplines anomalously strung out between the arts and the (real) sciences.

Of course, social science has penetrated and been penetrated by the arts on one frontier and by the natural sciences on the other. In the case of the arts, academic priorities have been strongly influenced by the agenda of the social sciences. This influence is most marked in history, arguably a hybrid arts–social science discipline anyway, and certainly one with highly eclectic intellectual traditions. But it can also be traced into literature and philosophy. Social science methods have been influenced just as strongly by the techniques of the natural science. Partly this has been because the natural sciences seem to offer (some) social sciences a superior model of intellectual discovery, and partly because they provide the security of their high prestige. But these many links with the arts and with natural science must not be allowed to detract from the distinctiveness of the social science tradition, which should be judged in terms of its own values and intentions and understood in terms of its own long history.

A brief sketch of that history suggests a division into four main periods. First came the heroic age of social science's founders – Smith, Ricardo, Marx. To this list perhaps should be added Bergson, Freud (a late start for psychology?) and pioneers of social investigation like the Webbs. The heroic age was succeeded by the age of the consolidators. One group secured the scholarly foundations of social science; prominent among them were Durkheim, Weber and Marshall. Another popularised social science perspectives, mainly through higher journalism; Veblen was a typical example here. The third period was social science's imperial age, beginning in the 1930s, reaching its climax in the postwar decades and dwindling away in the 1970s. It was imperial because during this half-century social science displaced the arts as the intellectual language of the West's ruling establishments, and even came close to challenging the natural sciences for leadership of the whole academic enterprise. Its Fabian reformism, its classless modernity, its end-of-ideology corporatism, its 'New Frontier' idealism exactly captured the mid-century spirit in the West. In the United States its representative figures were Talcott Parsons and Hughes and his disciple David Riesman, despite their very different intellectual styles. In Britain, A. H. Halsey has described how the London School of Economics' brightest and best sociologists went out in the 1950s and early 1960s to colonise Britain's expanding higher education system.[22] For a long time the influence of an older, more ideological, style of social science that continued to flourish in Paris and Frankfurt was kept at bay by a curious Atlanticist provincialism, despite Britain's flirtation with theory.

It was in this golden age that the respective claims of economic man and social man were argued out, although that argument has never been satisfactorily concluded. Before Weber, social science had been dominated by economics. Social relationships were generally regarded as subordinate to economic ones, while the affective world of families, groups and individuals was ignored. Political economy seemed to be a straightforward business. Two things changed this. First, the growth of the state in the late nineteenth and twentieth centuries, with its increasing involvement in areas like education, health, the relief of poverty and distress, which previously had been the province of private and voluntary action, and the development of professions to underpin the state's engagement undermined a narrowly economic view of social activity. Clearly there were many new and important relationships that could not be understood within the limited frameworks of either political economy or classical economics. New occupations demanded new forms of training which in turn required new intellectual structures. So there was considerable pressure from below to modify the old economic conception of social science.

Second, there was a growing intellectual conviction that the social order could not be reduced simply to its economic components. It was both too complicated and too mysterious. Weber, of course, was first to argue that modern society could not be interpreted solely by the utilitarian calculus of classical economics. Instead it had to be understood in terms of the spread of rationality and legality, what he had called 'the dis-enchantment of the modern world'. Hence the growth of bureaucracy to express and implement these rational and legal principles. Talcott Parsons developd Weber's arguments in the years before and after the Second World War.[23] Like Weber, he recognised that the social order could not be understood simply in terms of utilitarian economics, not least because of the irrationality of the market. But unlike Weber, he did not believe that the social order could be explained simply in terms of the spread of rational and legal principles underpinned by a developing bureaucracy. There were still too many unexplained institutions and networks which clearly played an important part in upholding the social order, like the professions (medicine was a particular concern of Parsons) and the family. More recent social scientists, influenced by the insights of psychology and anthropology, have gone beyond Parsons just as Parsons went beyond Weber. They have developed models of social action ever more distant from the presumptions of classical economics. In the end, even economics may have fallen into line, when under the influence of Keynes and his followers those presumptions were abandoned in favour of a much more liberal (and ambiguous) interpretation of economic behaviour. So there was also pressure from above, from the theoreticians, to broaden the scope of social science far beyond the territory occupied by old-fashioned Benthamite political economy.

With mixed results. In one sense the influence of this expanded social science was profound. These changes made possible postwar society – practically, in the case of the new professions linked to social science, and intellectually, in that the welfare state would not have been possible if it had not been accepted that society was much more than an aggregation of economic relationships. But in another sense the outcome was disappointing. The increasing emphasis on uncovering the mysteries of the social order, on discovering the mechanism of its equilibrium, rather than on constructing grander, all-embracing theories led instead to the ever-more-detailed investigation of smaller and smaller social systems. What Dahrendorf called 'the interest in total societies, as well as in their historical dimension'[24] declined among social scientists even when it was masked for a time in the 1960s and 1970s by the radical rhetoric of the New Left. Weber, Parsons, Keynes had many followers but no real successors able to carry their arguments forward on as grand a plane. An intellectual vacuum came to exist which in the 1980s had been filled by the resurgence of primitive Benthamite political economy.

After empire come the decline and fall. Such, it seems, has been the fate of social science. But it is important to clear away the trivia of intellectual fashion and the ephemera of political fortune. Social science, precisely because it had played such a prominent role in the postwar growth of higher education, was bound to be sharply criticised when the pattern of that growth was called into question and higher education itself placed on the defensive. Nor did it help that social science appeared to have been the intellectual inspiration for the uninspiring but successful corporatism that ruled postwar society and which the political generation of the 1980s seemed eager to shake off. But it is a mistake to conclude from either that social science is everywhere in retreat. 'Right-wing' free-market ideas may have begun to challenge (but hardly to supplant) 'left-wing' liberal or socialist ones. But all are contained within patterns of thought characteristic of social science. It was in the late eighteenth century that political economy established itself as the subject most worthy of serious study by men of public affairs. It became the leading preoccupation of those groups which in the next century were to be labelled an intelligentsia. This primitive social science developed its own eschatologies, Marxism or Freudianism, to supply the emotional engagement which may have been lacking in its original formulation. Two centuries later, despite many transformations and much sub-division, it has maintained its place.

Professions, occupations, communities, classes, groups – once defined in terms of traditional humanistic culture or of customary expertise all have been reinterpreted in the light of new insights derived from social science. 'Socio' has become a pervasive prefix – socio legal, socio-linguistic, socio-religious, socio-economic, socio-cultural and so on. In its crudest form the attempt to transform the social sciences into a common intellectual culture for the twentieth century, rather as classical humanism held sway in early modern Europe, has not succeeded – more perhaps because such an ambition is unrealisable in our centrifugal modern age than because the social sciences were particularly unsuited to attempt it. Postwar PPE (philosophy, politics and economics) at Oxford has never rivalled the influence once wielded over the minds of Britain's rulers by nineteenth-century 'Greats' (classical studies in all their Victorian splendour). But in more subtle ways social science has transformed our intellectual being. We may not like the idea, but we are all social scientists now.

SCIENCE AND TECHNOLOGY

The cramped definition of science common in English, as in the them-

and-us phrase 'arts and science' rather than as a more precise synonym for knowledge, is both anachronistic and accurate. It is anachronistic because it recalls the subordination of experimental (if not speculative) science to the humanism of the scholar-gentleman who once ruled Britain's intellectual life. It also recalls the disdain felt by gentlemen-scientists for the lower mechanical arts of engineering and technology. It is accurate because the natural sciences are at the heart of the modern knowledge business. They have a record of academic achievement that no other family of disciplines can match. Their advance seems to confirm that grand old nineteenth-century belief in a linear progress that is irreversible. Moreover, they provide analytical tools and techniques that have become a commanding model for all other disciplines – to such an extent that 'scientific' has become a substitute adjective for 'rational'. Finally, of course, the natural sciences create the knowledge that modern states transform into power: power that shapes society through the technologies of mass circulation and the habits of mass consumption; power that builds the economy by new inventions and processes; power that defends the nation or super-power *imperium* by military technology. Whether judged externally by their social, economic and political utility or internally by the intrinsic values of the academic system the natural sciences are truly imperial disciplines.

The superiority of the natural sciences seems so natural and inevitable today that it is difficult to imagine it was ever otherwise. But their hegemony was produced by the coming together of two quite separate currents. The first was abstract speculation about the natural world, a centuries-old tradition that reaches back beyond Plato and forward beyond Einstein. In earlier times such speculation was difficult to separate from a more purely metaphysical tradition – for two reasons. First, the absence of experimental tools, except perhaps in astronomy, made it almost impossible for these proto-scientists to turn their speculations into solutions. Nothing could be proved. So progressive science was hard to establish. Second, and more important, the intentions of intellectual inquiry were different from those which are familiar today. In a pre-technological world man had little command over the natural world except by the slow accretion of material civilisation. Progress was made by the more effective exploi-tation of existing techniques and their piecemeal improvement. The abstract speculations of science seemed to offer little practical help. Technology transfer was a slow and unspectacular process. Moreover, it was in the resignation of religion, or in the consolation of philosophy, that human worth was discovered and measured. So the role of proto-scientists, like that of all intellectuals in preindustrial society, was passive and moral rather than active and instrumental. The natural world had to be explored so that its meaning, over which human agency had limited influence, could be appreciated, not in order to push and pull it into shapes more useful to mankind. Knowledge was more sacred than useful. Proto-science shared in this general perspective.

The second current was entirely practical. Artillerymen wanted to know where their shells would fall; mariners to navigate safely; rulers to assess the wealth of their territories; landowners to increase the productivity of their estates. The development of some of today's most fundamental sciences was accelerated by such demands. Famous institutions like the Royal Society, and similar academies of science in the rest of Europe, were created as much for practical as for academic purposes. Indeed such a distinction would hardly have occurred to the Society's founding Fellows. Under the stimulating conditions of the industrial revolution, scientific advances of exceptional importance were made by amateur inventors and entrepreneurs preoccupied by feasible solutions to practical problems. They saw little need to relate their work to an existing body of established knowledge. If they did it was as a gentlemanly diversion, even a hobby to be indulged in literary and philosophical societies.

The mingling of these two currents has never been complete. The contrast between theory and practice, concept and experiment runs like a faultline through many of the natural sciences. The tension between proto-science and practical science can still be felt in the over-strict demarcation between pure and applied sciences that is characteristic of British intellectual life. But even this incomplete mingling has produced the modern scientific tradition with its extraordinary power and prestige. Indeed that tradition's inevitable ambivalence is a source of great creativity. Theoretical austerity is balanced by practical utility; methodological naivety is qualified by conceptual clarity. Both currents contribute intellectual qualities that seem opposed but in effect enhance each other powerfully. Even today the relationship between them is complicated. The simplest view, of course, is that the idealism of proto-science has been superseded by the materialism of practical science. This is perhaps the working hypothesis of most rank-and-file scientists. For them the lines of scientific advance have been selected by 'rules' developed within their discipline or sub-discipline. They see no need to ask awkward questions about the origin or validity of such 'rules'. One problem suggests another; one experiment leads to another. Speculative proto-science is dead – or the ethereal stuff of which Nobel prizes are made.

Philosophers of science, and maybe those Nobel prize winners too, have never been content with such a view. Some, most famously Karl Popper, have argued that science makes progress not by verification through experiments but by the falsification of hypotheses.[25] Laws or theories cannot emerge from the accumulation of detailed data acquired by experiment or observation as Bacon supposed, because of the logical frailty of empirical induction identified by Hume. Scientific theories are not bodies of objective facts about the natural world but creative products of the human mind. In that sense Newton's achievement may be compared to Shakespeare's. Of course scientific theories can then be tested which makes them logically superior to artistic creations. But their origins are not so very different. Such a view has revolutionary implications for the relationship between the proto-science and practical-science strands within the modern scientific tradition. Far from being redundant, the former has a superior status. Disciplined idealism is elevated above dull materialism. However, the Popperian account of the ultimate source of that creative speculation out of which scientific theories are shaped is less satisfactory. How are the problems defined for which hypothetical solutions are suggested? Where do they come from? One possible answer is that man is a problem-solving animal driven by Darwinian imperatives to be endlessly curious. Another is that these problems are simply suggested by the momentum of scientific advance, which in practice if not in theory begins to look suspiciously like the inductive empiricism the Popperians reject. For the sequence of Popperian science is still progressive. After each cycle of inquiry a better theory is produced. Copernicus is superior to Ptolemy, Einstein to Newton.

Other philosophers of science go further in their critique of common-sense empiricism. According to Thomas Kuhn the progress of science is marked by the rise and fall of successive 'paradigms', overarching theories about the natural world that dominate detailed research, or 'normal science', in his phrase. Paradigms decay partly because their authority is eroded by the accumulation of contradictory evidence, partly because they come into conflict with the development of a broader intellectual culture which in turn reflects social and economic change. This does not mean that creationism is equal in scientific status to Darwin's theory of evolution. His argument is that both are elaborate scientific and cultural systems of belief which must be judged in their own particular context if they are ever to be properly understood.

Of course epistemology bores most working scientists. They want to get back to the laboratory bench. They are less interested in debating the nature of science than in doing good science. The reductionism which so effectively produces the latter discourages the former. But these first-principles questions have to be considered in order to understand the blend of proto-science and practical science that has produced the modern scientific tradition. And, although the alignment is not exact, it may help to illuminate the densely-packed distinction between pure and applied sciences. For this is a distinction that suggests not only a contrast in intellectual styles but also different practical priorities within disciplines.

These questions also have to be asked if a clear demarcation is to be established between, not truth and falsehood, which is too difficult, but the knowable and the unknowable. Establishing this demarcation is not simply a technical operation, although improved experimental techniques can expand the territory of the knowable. It is also a philosophical question. Scientists can hardly neglect to explore the criteria by which they calculate success and failure. The philosophy and practice of science are inextricably linked. Epistemology and the laboratory bench are not as far apart as they seem. Finally, scientists must address these first-principles questions if they are ever to encourage a more sophisticated public understanding of science. Too often they concentrate so much on answering 'how' questions that it almost seems as if the 'why' questions have never occurred to them. Or else they offer answers that are naive and banal. Neither inspires much public confidence or leads to a clearer understanding.

But there is a more significant reason for allowing epistemological speculation: it allows us to assess the accuracy of the common assumption that the natural sciences, unlike arts and social science and unlike (in a different sense) technology, are value-free. The validity of scientific inquiry, it is supposed, can be judged without regard to its social context. In fact there is little in the history of the natural sciences to sustain this claim to intellectual, as opposed to technical, objectivity. Certainly there is nothing to suggest that proto-science was ever divorced from its wider intellectual culture, or practical science from the urgent problems that concerned its powerful patrons. Popperian problem-theories are reflections of the human imagination; Kuhnian paradigms are elaborate cultural constructions. Neither supports science's claim to possess a superior objectivity because neither is capable of self-contained explanation. Social scientists and scholars in the arts, angered perhaps by the insinuation that their disciplines are prescientific, have sometimes argued that the natural sciences are pre-social. But the best science is far from being the myopic experimental routine that this slur suggests. It transcends the reductionism that is its most effective technique. The contemporary brilliance of the natural sciences is built on a willingness to take intellectual risks of the highest order, not on a dull incremental objectivity.

Certainly the development of the natural sciences over the past two centuries suggests a complicated relationship, and a creative one, between their inner disciplinary momentum, shifts in the wider intellectual culture and the growth of urban society and of an industrial economy. For much of the nineteenth century chemistry in its many branches was the leading natural science, reflecting no doubt the primacy of chemical processes in many developing industries. Of course, chemistry could not match the intellectual excitement of the faith-or-reason controversy associated with the biological sciences in the age of Darwin, or, at the end of the century, the charisma of physics and mathematics. But it had the big battalions of teachers and researchers, a quantitative superiority that persisted well into the present century. It also offered a model of scientific utility and progressive inquiry that seemed more relevant than the speculative and abstract traditions of its rivals. In the present century, chemistry lost its place to physics. Scientists, subsidised by the state and organised into autonomous institutions and professions, felt less need to defer to industry. They enjoyed greater freedom to pursue their own intellectual inclinations. The preoccupations of proto-science were resurrected in the modern guise of fundamental research, the purer the better. The objective remained the same: a complete and penetrating account of the natural world in the cause of science. But as these fundamental inquiries into the nature of matter often produced startling new forms of energy and powerful new weapons industry and politicians were well pleased.

More recently, biology has taken over as the key discipline. A number of explanations can be offered – apart from the inventive brilliance of biology's leading postwar figures. One is simply that superior experimental techniques have opened up pathways of investigation that were previously closed. A second is that health care in its broadest sense is the most rapidly expanding industry in the modern economy (The National Health Service is the largest employer in Europe) and also the core public service around which the modern welfare state is organised. In addition, the life sciences, through biochemistry, have acquired the pervasive industrial relevance once possessed by unadorned chemistry. 'Bio' is now as ubiquitous a prefix as 'socio'. A third is that the life sciences have wide-open frontiers. They are interpenetrated not only by other natural sciences but also by much of social science. The study of organisms in their own environment, whether natural or social, is an intellectual preoccupation capable of almost infinite variation. A fourth may be that biology now offers the most satisfying synthesis between proto-science and practical science. It addresses questions as fundamental as physics but apparently in a more humane context. The mystery of life is more appealing than the music of distant spheres. Some, of course, may interpret this contrast in more negative terms, as a significant shift from the macro to the micro, from gazing at the far horizons of the natural world to contemplating its (and ours) navel. But the interconnectedness of all the natural sciences is now so dense, and disciplinary labels and boundaries count for so little, that such an interpretation may be regarded as naive.

In the knowledge industry that now dominates the modern world economy the natural sciences provide by far the most significant raw materials and most powerful techniques. But their influence is not confined to materials and techniques. It extends also to values and to goals. The patterns of thought, of non-scientists as decisively as of scientists, have been irreversibly shaped by the triumphant experience of the natural sciences. In the knowledge society they form its leading intellectual elements. Indeed their influence penetrates perhaps still more deeply. The natural sciences may be creating a modern culture in their own image. A common but profoundly mistaken view is that this knowledge society will be essentially a technological phenomenon, a land overflowing with satellite television and supercomputers. Those who fear that the values of humanist civilisation may be hard to sustain in such a technocratic society sometimes accuse scientists of a myopic, amoral and impoverishing positivism. Perhaps they mistake their target. The true knowledge society, not the high-technology consumer fantasy conjured up by the media, will be an intellectual and cultural phenomenon, a scientific civilisation. And the values that the natural sciences will bring to that civilisation will be far richer and more complicated than the humanist opposition imagines in moments of bleaker pessimism. Creativity, imagination, optimism, curiosity, logic, rigour, reason – these are science's values. They are values that sustain rather than undermine our civilisation.

Technology is both a hate-word and a buzz-word. As the first, it is used to stigmatise a mechanistic approach to both intellectual enterprise and social and economic progress, gadget-ridden and gimmick-crazy, in which human ends are subordinated to technical means and high science to low consumerism. As the second, it is used to describe the creative application of new knowledge to improve individual and social well-being, an attempt to integrate thinking and doing in ways that enlarge rather than trivialise understanding, an effort to recreate the wholeness of man, the celebration of a combined competence and intelligence. Technology, therefore, is seen as either the enemy of liberal and humane values or the cutting-edge of the knowledge revolution on which our future prosperity, and perhaps cultural vitality as well, are said to depend. Of course distinctions are often made. 'Social' technologists like town planners, social workers or lawyers are regarded as less threatening to liberal values (but also less useful) than old-fashioned and new-fangled engineers. But these distinctions should not be exaggerated. In the knowledge society there is growing emphasis on the integration of whole systems, software and hardware, human resources and technical capacity, theories and machines. So professional and disciplinary boundaries have been eroded. Today's total technology embraces ideas, images and values as well as processes and products.

Technology, it can be argued, reflects both an archaic and a futuristic vision of knowledge. It is archaic because technology relies on the blending together of character, experience, intelligence, training and knowledge to produce useful outcomes. Most of its forms are obliged to reject the minute divisions of intellectual labour and the imposed (and artificial?), demarcation between theory and practice on which more academic disciplines rely. Modern medicine may be specialist in its science but the doctor must remain a generalist, a synthesiser. So in this sense technology is a throwback to the days before our present distinctions between arts and science, practice and theory, pure and applied had set into their present solid forms.

It is futuristic because technology's preoccupation with useful outcomes rather than particular methods, with results rather than reflection, makes it a plausible vehicle for general education in a postindustrial world. Instead of defending academic orthodoxies, technology values flexible skills – practical, intellectual and human. Instead of protecting its special proprietary knowledge it encourages lateral thinking. It is an intellectual scavenger, cheerfully raiding other disciplines. Technology is all about problem solving – practical and comprehensible problems rather than abstract or arcane ones. In the capacious shape of vocationalism it is the common core of advanced education, the everyday language of our expert culture.

Not everyone finds the growing power of technology congenial. Some have argued that disciplines with an external non-academic focus cannot be regarded as scholarly or scientific. They do not allow for reflection, contemplation, detachment and those other cerebral qualities out of which true learning is said to grow. They cannot get far enough outside their own imposed preoccupations to gain fresh insights or to achieve a critical perspective. They simply do not create sufficient room for intellectual manoeuvre. They are constrained by the demands of government, industry, professions or lay customers. They cannot imagine what they cannot make. This argument against technology is often regarded as anachronistic today. It brings to mind grand Victorian battles between sweetness and light and fire and strength, between Arnold and Huxley. No one perhaps expressed it better than the poet A. E. Housman in his inaugural lecture at University College London in 1892:

> Let a man acquire knowledge not for this or that external or incidental good which may chance to result from it, but for itself; not because it is useful or ornamental, but because it is knowledge and good therefore for men to acquire. . . . For knowledge resembles virtue in this, and differs in this from other possessions, that it is not merely a means of procuring good, but is good in itself: it is not a coin we pay down to purchase happiness but has happiness indissolubly bound up in it.[26]

It sounds as if it were settled long ago. Misleadingly perhaps. The strength of the idealist (and aristocratic?) tradition should not be underestimated even today. Nor should the prejudice against practicality be ignored. Just a few years ago Roger Scruton, a Birkbeck College professor and ardent admirer of a modernising Conservative Party, wrote in a newspaper article:

> The more irrelevant a subject, the more lasting is the benefits it
> confers. Irrelevant subjects bring understanding of the human
> condition, by forcing the student to stand back from it. . . . This is
> the secret which civilization has guarded – that power and
> influence come through the acquisition of useless knowledge. . . .
> A person who knows only engineering or microbiology finds
> himself hampered by his knowledge which casts little light on his
> experience and leads to no communication with his fellow
> humans.

The solemn rhetoric of the nineteenth century may have been replaced
by the mischievous, perhaps cynical, rhetoric of the twentieth. But the
argument remains the same. The belief that learning must transcend
experience, that knowledge must transform not so much the world but
our perception of it, is deeply rooted. This belief is influential not only
in the traditional academic disciplines but also in those technological
and professional subjects which lean heavily on the arts and social
science. It is an important source of our bias against technology.

Yet there are terms, other than those of immediate utility, in which
technology can be judged a distinctive category of knowledge and
vocationalism a valid approach to learning. An intellectual, rather than
functional, justification of technology's claim is to argue that it is a
superior form of knowledge because it brings together thoughts and
deeds, theory and practice. 'Action' teaching and 'action' research
sound flaky or nouvelle-vaguish (in French sense and English sound!).
Nevertheless they are embedded in the traditions of most professional
and technological disciplines. How else can the practice of medical
schools or schools of architecture be described? But usually this first
argument is pursued rather gingerly. The emphasis on technology's
broader intellectual and educational benefits is distrusted by many
technologists who are wary of back-door attempts to academicise their
work. They fear that woolly thinking from other disciplines will drive
out good professional practice as the organising principle of effective
technology. Others are afraid technology will go soft under this
influence and lose its hard scientific edge. To some extent the
'Education for Capability' campaign launched a few years ago by the
Royal Society of Arts has suffered from this ambivalence. In sceptical
eyes its values seem to owe too much to an arts-and-crafts ethos and
too little to a high-technology vision.

But the same argument can be approached from another angle. The
utilitarian ethic in which technology is invitably bound up is not
necessarily philistine. A commitment to usefulness interpreted liberally
– if that does not sound a contradiction – can have a much more
positive aspect. In his inaugural lecture as Regius Professor of modern
history at Oxford thirty years ago Lord Dacre (Hugh Trevor-Roper)
argued: 'History, that is not useful, that has not some lay appeal, is

mere antiquarianism'. This is a familiar enough argument. To retain their vitality even the most academic disciplines must be associated in some sense with a wider culture; to maintain that association they must satisfy criteria of relevance, even utility, that transcend their private scholarly values. No subject is an island – or if it is no one wants to visit it. But to apply the same argument to rescue the intellectual reputation of technology rather than, as Lord Dacre did, to defend the open tradition of the arts against a narrowing scholasticism is unfamiliar. The usefulness of the arts is clearly different from the close-grained instrumentalism of technology. But the gap is narrower than the knowledge-for-knowledge's sake claims of Housman and Scruton imply.

The second defence of technology's academic validity is an extension of the first. It is that the interpenetration of theory and practice, reflection and experience, a feature of all professional and technological disciplines, leads to a more thorough understanding. The well-educated engineer, doctor or social worker has to be able to reflect on his or her practice with detachment. Maybe this reflective practitioner – Schön's phrase again – is even superior to the myopic expert and the scholarly analyst. In a famous passage in the preface to one of his novels, Henry James wrote: 'There are degrees of feeling – the muffled, the faint, the just sufficient, as we may say; and the acute, the intense, the complete, in a word – the power to be finely aware and richly responsible'.[27] As with feeling, perhaps with knowing and doing? Such intensity is commonly associated with the defence of high culture against the philistines with their shrunken consciousness. Technology is still felt to be on the wrong side of this argument. Yet those who *apply* the arts and the sciences, in technology and the professions, may aspire to a not dissimilar intensity of experience which our arts-bound culture is reluctant to recognise.

Technology's intellectual merits may not be readily recognised because perceptions of technology have lagged far behind its actual evolution. We are prisoners still of a Victorian iron-and-steel myth. Throughout the last century and during much of this the old industrial technologies were dominant. Manufacturing industry, the heavier the better, remained the keynote of the British economy even if its precise significance was never as great as grim memories sentimentally suggest. Technology was shaped and coloured by this industrial context. Dominated by heavy engineering, it acquired a deep-rooted anti-intellectual ethos. Book learning was minimised and workshop practice maximised. Industry was master and education servant. As industries at the forefront of contemporary technology – iron and steel, chemicals, textiles – were generally large and secure while science and engineering departments in universities and colleges were often small and precarious, this balance of advantage was inevitable. Also, links between technology and the professions remained weak. They seemed contradictory worlds, one entrepreneurial, the other customary, employing incompatible styles of knowledge, one technical, the other traditional. The human and social sciences penetrated only slowly into the apparently alien world of technology still dominated by heavy engineering.

The shape of today's technology is utterly different, although the old stereotype has persisted. Two developments of fundamental consequence have been undervalued. First, the industrial context has changed beyond reasonable recognition. Manufacturing industry has declined. The new industries which have displaced it have different and even opposite characteristics. Their company structure is unstable. New enterprises come and go at a hectic pace. Even the most established have to accept the need for constant change and endless re-organisation. These industries are also knowledge-intensive. Superior technology now confers such obvious and immediate commercial advantages that companies can no longer safely regard their relationship with the world of science and education as incidental. Second, the intellectual context has changed as radically as the industrial structure. New technologies today are as likely to be developed from scientific research as from industrial practice. Indeed, in many cases the relationship between the two is so close that they cannot easily be distinguished. The scope of technology has also been progressively enlarged. Economics, management, psychology and many other non-engineering disciplines have moved from the periphery closer to the centre of technology's mission. This in turn has stimulated the growth of closer links with the professions, old and new. The effect has been to strengthen the common intellectual threads that run through most technological and professional disciplines.

So technology has drifted far from its conventional image. It has become a more intellectual business less tied to the work bench. In many industries the follow-through from concept to product is rapid and direct. A more balanced partnership between industry and academy has been produced as the former has been fragmented into smaller and more flexible units while the latter has substantially upgraded its commitment to technology. The physical evidence of both trends can be seen in the science and technology parks spawned on many British campuses and the penumbra of high-technology industry that clings round many major higher education institutions.

Technology, of course, has also become highly interdisciplinary. It long since burst the narrow banks of engineering and spread out across the wide plains of the natural, social and even human sciences. Indeed there are few disciplines outside the high humanities that have remained unaffected by the advance of technology. But this move towards total technology has made it more difficult to maintain theoretical and practical coherence and to avoid a knowledge overload when so many disciplines have been so promiscuously exploited. Yet modern technology is also integrative as well as eclectic. In its intellectual style it is catholic, even opportunist. It has to resist the fragmentation of knowledge into academically convenient packages. Perhaps technology shares this common ground with the arts, so that both reach beyond knowledge to knowing, the arts with the ambition of improving man's moral condition and technology his material condition. Perhaps in a society that must live by expert knowledge the second is at least as important as the first. Indeed they may be inseparable. Perhaps the technologist must acquire 'the power to be finely aware and richly responsible' in as acute a sense as the humanist.

3

MODERN TIMES

Culture is one of the most difficult words in the English language, less precise than *knowledge* but more resonant. Outside academic circles it still has an overwhelmingly aesthetic meaning. It is what happens at Stratford, or in the Royal Festival Hall, or all over Edinburgh for three summer weeks. Inside the academic system, in contrast, culture is generally used in a quasi-anthropological sense to describe the tribal customs of those who live on Sunderland council estates or go to the races at Ascot. But culture does have an intermediate meaning, something less intense and elitist than the museum culture of the past and the high culture of the present yet more prescriptive and discriminating than simply a description of the life styles of modern tribes. From before Matthew Arnold to after T. S. Eliot, culture has been used in this more catholic sense, not aspiring always to be synonymous with grand civilisation but containing sufficient moral impulses to represent a society's essential continuity, its accumulated interpretations of what is valuable and virtuous.

Almost certainly this is the meaning that the Robbins committee, which inquired into higher education in the early 1960s, had in mind when it suggested that the fourth aim of a university education should be 'the transmission of a common culture and common standards of citizenship'.[1] Even a generation ago, in 1963, the committee had to half-apologise for using language which already sounded anachronistic. But its members nevertheless insisted: 'We believe that it is a proper function of higher education, as of education in schools, to provide in partnership with the family that background of culture and social habit upon which a healthy society depends'.[2] How much more difficult it would be to write those words on the brink of the twentieth century's last decade. If our grip on any sense of a common culture had already become slack in 1963, and if our confidence that higher education had a significant contribution to make to sustaining, as well as investigating, that culture had already been shaken, a generation later our grip has grown feeble, and our confidence almost gone. Yet for Robbins the transmission of a common culture was among the most important aims of higher education. And in an eloquent if incoherent sense many still have ultimate hopes of higher education that can be summed up in a

similar phrase. Beneath the layers of academic specialisation and
vocational ambition a simpler and perhaps more generous faith in
education lies hidden.

An attempt to explore the idea of a common culture in late twentieth-
century Britain therefore is still worthwhile. Nor does this attempt need
to be regarded as a reactionary project, denying the multinational,
multifaith, multiracial complexity of modern culture or seeking to
reassert prescientific values. Our common culture has never been more
than a branch of the civilisation first of Europe, then of the West and
today of the world. The diversity of modern Britain, ethnic and ethical,
has undermined any claims that could ever have been made for the
insular particularity of our culture. In any case, the aspect of culture
discussed in this chapter is not the British identity, our historical
memories, our social habits, our economic behaviour and so on – this
difficult task will be attempted in the last chapter – but the quality of
our intellectual civilisation. Its focus is those values and beliefs which
have grown equally out of scientific inquiry and social change, the big
ideas that have shaped and moved British, Western and world culture.
The chapter is divided into four sections. Each discusses a particular
theme, or stage in the evolution, of this common culture and is
illustrated by a brief sketch of the life and work of an emblematic rather
than comprehensive figure. The starting point, despite what has just
been written, is British exceptionalism.

IS BRITAIN EXCEPTIONAL?

At the end of *Homage to Catalonia* George Orwell describes his return
from the Spanish Civil War in terms that emphasise the particularity of
English culture and of the British experience.[3] He writes as if the bitter
fighting of communists, anarchists, syndicalists and fascists were
taking place in another world. The killing passion represented by the
dead bodies in the Barcelona streets did not seem to belong in the same
place and time as the gentle, even genteel, banality of the bank-holiday
crowds in Brighton or Blackpool. It is easy enough to accumulate
literary anecdotes like this to illustrate the apartness of the British. But
the rhetorical force of this accumulation of evidence about our peculiar
culture is not matched by a clear understanding of *how* it is apart or *why*
it is peculiar. The culture of France can be described in terms of
Descartes, Molière, Napoleon – and perhaps, in this century, de Gaulle
and Sartre. That of Germany in terms of Kant, Hegel, (and Hitler?).
Italy has its Garibaldis, Croces and Gramscis. And so it goes through
the nations of continental Europe. But who are the equivalent totems
for the culture of the British? Is the Tory traditionalism of Jane Austen
or the Brontës more representative than the progressive idealism of
George Eliot? Is not the socialist Clement Attlee in some important
senses a more English figure than the imperialist (and half-American)

Winston Churchill? William Cobbett or Walter Scott? The conclusion seems to be that however sharp the external boundary of Britishness its internal contours are difficult to detect. Our native culture seems to be at once eloquent and indeterminate.

One explanation is that because political and ideological contests have been so much milder in Britain than in the rest of Europe since the eighteenth century there has been less need to suppress dissident components of our national culture. The last decisively excluded group was probably the Jacobites (the Irish always excepted). Even they were partially rehabilitated with the growth of romanticism. Dissenters and rebels, although often persecuted, hung onto some shreds of legitimacy. So our culture, in contrast to that of many of our neighbours, tends to be inclusive rather than exclusive. In this the British may be exceptional. What place in the culture of modern Italy could be found for the (many) supporters of the Bourbons and the Hapsburgs? The incoherence of the French right may be explained in part by the way in which after 1789 the rules of the national game were tilted against its adherents. Even in the United States the Confederate defeat in 1865 left the American south excluded, at first by coercion and later, more subtly, by choice for almost a century. Only in our relations with Ireland have we faced the same poisonous issues of demarcation with which other national cultures have always had to grapple. A few may argue that Scotland and Wales too have been dishonestly incorporated into a British state dominated by the English which has suppressed their native traditions. But the failure of these nationalisms to attract majority support and their lack of rancour seem to demonstrate the opposite conclusion: that our national culture, whether English or British, is a broad church.

Our culture's quietism and breadth may explain other, more obvious characteristics. First, to adopt for a moment language more appropriate to 1960s California, its 'space'. Deviancy is not seen as a terrible threat, but rather as something to be deflected or incorporated. Looking back, it is not surprising that the counterculture – pop, punk and the rest – found a more comfortable home in Britain than almost anywhere else. In intellectual life too our culture has encouraged a similarly easy-going toleration of different opinions, a toleration which at times is difficult to distinguish from philistine indifference. This may suggest that British tolerance arises as much from a historical experience which suggests ideas are not worth fighting over as from a positive commitment to intellectual pluralism. Closely linked may be our sympathy for idiosyncrasy, which reflects the belief that ideas, like people, should have 'character'. More cynical observers, of course, argue that this impression of 'space' has to be set against the dominant background of an essentially conformist culture. The tolerance of (or should it be complacency?) its various establishments is explained by their unchallenged sense of superiority. Certainly the philistinism and conformism of British culture need to be balanced against its breadth and idiosyncrasy. This contrast may be a distorted reflection of that larger paradox in the British character which curiously blends individualism with fraternity.

A second characteristic of our culture is its retrospective quality. We never seem to be far away from our history – without necessarily knowing much about it. This history, too, is seen in terms of the continuity, the ordinariness, of everyday life rather than in terms *la gloire*. Ours is a civilian culture. Memories of the two world wars are etched more deeply in the numberless experiences of the people than in the bronzed achievements of prime ministers and generals. We have no grand and paralysing historical myths of *revanche*, *risorgimento* or revolution to bind our present. Nor are the British imprisoned by an ancient preindustrial culture. The industrial revolution was so long ago and so complete that our agrarian past has vanished for ever. It is the dark Satanic mills which provide the sentimental memories. Yet our sense of history – or of *place*, perhaps a better term to neatly balance space – has remained. This sense, personal and intimate, perhaps, rather than public and heroic, is still one of the most creative agents in British culture at the end of the twentieth century. Retrospection, a different quality entirely from the reactionary spirit familiar throughout Europe, has been a key characteristic of English art, thought and life over the past two centuries. Here, we might think of Jane Austen celebrating a traditional squirearchy menaced by metropolitan novelty and industrial change;[4] Water Scott recreating "'tis sixty years since' in *Waverley*;[5] George Eliot feeding her imagination on memories of a Midlands childhood in the 1820s and 1830s;[6] A. E. Housman's 'blue remembered hills';[7] Richard Hoggart recalling growing up in a working-class Leeds in *The Uses of Literacy*.[8] Admittedly, this habit of retrospection has sometimes degenerated into sentimentality and mawkishness.

A third characteristic, our distrust of theory and abstract thought and our liking for pragmatism, may be closely linked to this sense of place. The lived experience of history, especially on a private and intimate scale, does not encourage theorising and abstraction. The patterns of such history provide an alternative framework in which ideas and values can be organised. They offer as it were a concrete theory. R. A. B. Butler's perhaps banal *The Art of the Possible*[9] or Alec Douglas Home's amiable autobiography preoccupied with fishing on the Tweed may take us closer to the heart of British Conservatism than the doctrines of free-market economists or saloon-bar ideologues.[10] For Conservatism is as much a set of historically determined values as a collection of abstract ideas. This may still be true despite the radical changes in the Conservative Party since 1979. The story on the left is similar. The clichéd remark that the Labour Party and trade unions owe more to Methodism than to Marx is not strictly accurate. After its early years Methodism was a conspicuously conservative movement, while the roots of the British left were not substantially less ideological than those of socialism and trade unionism in the rest of Europe. But the myth this conventional account suggests would not be so powerful if it contained no grains of truth. The progress of the left has been measured as much in retrospective as in revolutionary terms – Levellers and Luddites, Tolpuddle martyrs and the General Strike. Of course, it can be argued that historical memories like these, whether of the right or left, are a particularly pernicious form of theory, disguised as unchallengeable pragmatism and fashioned by the winners (so that they can win again?). Perhaps, but it still has a lived-in and concrete quality that is denied to formal theory and our taste for it cannot be without significance.

A fourth characteristic is our preoccupation with the aesthetic, or at any rate affective, as much as with the rational. Fine feelings, especially if expressed in well-bred terms, are regarded as superior to rational inquiry. Or rather the reconciliation of art and life, feeling and intelligence, within an aesthetic framework which also serves as a moral code is regarded as civilisation's most important task. The central position occupied by the novel, and of essays and history with a strong literary flavour, is perhaps evidence of this aesthetic strain within British culture. From it flow two subsidiary characteristics, our idealism and our anti-practicality. Not idealism in a strictly philosophical sense, of course, but something too close at times to sentimentality. The anti-practical quality of the British tradition too can be exaggerated. In a highly urbanised and industrialised society the expression of aristo-cratic sentiments is as much an exercise in hypocrisy as a true reflection of deeply-held values. Both idealism and anti-practicality are stimulated by a culture which places a higher value on the quality of individual or community experience than on detached rational analysis of the situation of society or of the economy. The result is good and bad. This tendency helps to explain our weak sense of the state but strong sense of community (whether street, city, golf club or trade union), and so the British taste for fraternity. But it is also an ingredient in the anti-entrepreneurial tradition, real and pretended, from which Britain is assumed to have suffered.

This benign and tranquil account of our culture can readily be disputed. Some will regard it as not much more than a repolished Whig interpretation modified to explain our more recent, and relative, decline from national greatness. This criticism would be fair if any claim had been made to present a complete account, in however general terms, of British culture. But its inclusiveness makes a complete account impossible. (Almost) anything goes. Intellectual life in Britain has always been such a mess that there have been few clear winners.

On this side of the channel the great predatory ideologies have had to learn to live together, Marxism, for example, on its return to Britain was softened and smoothed. It went native. The peculiarity of British culture can be overestimated, of course. We have never been cut off from Europe and the world. Ours is simply a component of a broader intellectual culture. Yet our particular likes and dislikes, preoccupations and prejudices, may have distanced us from two of the most prominent dangers inherent in that broader culture, the imperialism of predatory ideologies and Max Weber's iron cage of narrowing rationality. Our sense of space and distaste for theorising (as opposed to generalising) may have served as an antidote to the former; our sense of place and aesthetic-moral preoccupations to the latter.

RICHARD HOGGART[11]

'For my part I am very sorry for him. It is an uneasy lot at best, to be what we call highly taught and yet not to enjoy it: to be present at this great spectacle of life and never to be liberated from a small hungry shivering self'. This quotation from George Eliot's *Middlemarch* is the superscription on the most famous, and maybe most personal, passage ever written by Richard Hoggart, 'Scholarship Boy' in *The Uses of Literacy*. Perhaps it comes dangerously, but creatively, close to autobiography. In some eyes Hoggart is his own scholarship boy, this personal insecurity the key to his life and work, to his compassion and his ambition, his public longing for his roots in working-class Leeds and his private hobnobbing with the powerful in London corridors.

This, then, is the first version of Richard Hoggart: inside the author of *The Uses of Literacy*, acknowledged even by severe academic critics as a modern classic; inside the star witness for the defence at *Lady Chatterley's Lover* trial, that key episode in the struggle for personal freedoms which became a hallmark of the 1960s; inside the founder of the Centre for Contemporary Cultural Studies at Birmingham and so a pioneer of that controversial modern discipline; inside the assistant director general of the United Nations Educational Scientific and Cultural Organization; inside the warden of Goldsmiths College and the first (and only) chairman of the Advisory Council for Adult and Continuing Education; inside the vice-chairman of the Arts Council is 'a small hungry shivering self'. If this version of Hoggart is accepted, it becomes easy to patronise or dismiss his work. *The Uses of Literacy*, the 1972 Reith lectures with the characteristically Hoggartian title *Only Connect*, the book about Unesco, the numerous essays– all can be dismissed as the shapeless projection onto the intellectual plane of his personal predicament. As such, they lose interest as intellectual productions and become cultural phenomena, important for what they are rather than what they say. Hoggart's work can be relegated to the status of raw material for an anthropology of mid-century Britain, the ambition and anxiety of the scholarship-boy generation.

This version of Hoggart, of course, is a cruel caricature. But there may be some truth from which this caricature has been twisted. There is a tentativeness, an incompleteness, maybe even a naivety about Hoggart's work. Some criticise his books because they regard them as being in an abiding sense non-academic, amateur, extramural – certainly not the product of detached scholarship. Others praise them for adjacent qualities: a personal engagement and a quasi-literary imagination that may be as respectable a set of intellectual tools as the citation-bound number-crunching or cliché-strewn theoretical structures that have become standard practice in so much social science. There is also a similar ambiguity about his public career and his private values. The enemy of 'Admass' became the culture bureaucrat in Unesco where language has been elevated to the highest vapidity, and then, at Goldsmiths and the adult education council, the spokesman for a quietist tradition of adult learning that seeks to evade political commitment. At the climax of his career, from the publication of *The Uses of Literacy* to his departure for Unesco, Hoggart was both an old-fashioned liberal, whose account of working-class culture emphasised its passivity and even conservatism, and an influential figure on the fringes of the New Left whose work helped form our dark view of mass communication as alienation rather than enlightenment. A revolutionary Reithian perhaps?

There is a second version of Richard Hoggart. This is the prophet spurned. The chronicler of working-class culture holding out against the false prosperity of the 'never had it so good' society and the credit-card economy; the advocate of public service broadcasting in its most austere and elevated form; the defender of *Lady Chatterley*, not because permissiveness liberates but because censorship imprisons (and out of a respect for D. H. Lawrence's high place in the Leavisite canon); the upholder of liberal education in a utilitarian and politicised world – yesterday's or yesteryear's man, always right but always on the losing side. Here too there is some truth behind this dismissal of a lifetime's energy and commitment. Hoggart has ranged himself against some of the most powerful (and least pleasant?) forces in contemporary Britain. In these unequal contests he was often a loser.

The fraternity of the working class in the face of a common austerity, celebrated in *The Uses of Literacy*, may in fact have been exaggerated by Hoggart. But it has been remorselessly eroded by thirty years or more of easy credit, package holidays and all the other tinsel of postwar prosperity. In broadcasting, Reithian ideals have been progressively submerged by the ratings-war between the BBC and independent television, pop radio, breakfast-time television, political interference, cable and satellite, and deregulation. The road from *Lady Chatterley* now

seems to lead not to a higher and freer sensibility but to exploitation
and pornography. The emphasis has switched from liberal adult
education to more utilitarian forms of continuing education. The arts
are under siege. Both versions of Hoggart, as 'a small hungry shivering
self' and as a kind of liberal luddite, are unfair and misleading. Both,
nevertheless, are illuminating, about Hoggart himself and more so
about his critics who are attached to these stereotyped caricatures. His
life and work, and the reactions both have provoked, offer remarkable
insights into the quality of social and intellectual change in Britain.

Richard Hoggart was born in 1918 and left Goldsmiths for an active
retirement in 1984. The sixty-six years in between can be divided into
five periods: his 'roots' in working-class Leeds; his experience as an
extramural tutor in Hull; his entry into the university mainstream first
at Leicester and then in Birmingham; his five years in Paris at Unesco;
and finally his return to England, to Goldsmiths. The first third of his
life was spent in Hunslet, the working-class community into which his
family had been sucked by Victorian urbanisation. These years had a
decisive influence on Hoggart, providing him with much of the raw
material for his later work and forming his personality and values with
an insistence which he freely acknowledged. Much of the rhetorical
force for which *The Uses of Literacy* is justly memorable derives from its
evocation, direct and indirect, of his Leeds childhood. For Hoggart
used his own childhood to evoke the culture of the prewar working
class – home, mother, father, neighbourhood, a landscape with figures
that he both experienced and observed. Even in his Surrey retirement
he returned to the Leeds of half a century ago as he wrote his memoirs.

His parents died while he was still a child and he was brought up by
his grandmother. This accident may help to explain Hoggart's most
distinctive qualities. His reach back into working-class history through
the extended oral tradition that only grandparents can provide may
explain his preoccupation with the long haul of culture. The central role
played by women in his sense of community may illuminate its passive,
domestic, even private character. His early Leeds experience may also
help to explain two decisive patterns of behaviour which moulded his
whole career. The first of these was the quest for security. Looking
back, Hoggart recalled that he had always wanted to be 'a writer more
than anything else' – not a detached academic analyst but a person able
to describe and make sense of his own experience with 'great patience,
great honesty and great courage'. Yet he sacrificed the freedom of the
writer for the security of a university post because the accumulated
wisdom of his family and class taught him to place security before
freedom.

The second was his urge to serve on any and every committee and
quango. When he left Birmingham he was serving on sixteen university
committees, while his quango count at the peak of his career was giddy

– Albermarle on the youth service, Pilkington on broadcasting, vice chairman of the Arts Council, chairman of the board of the *New Statesman*. As an academic bureaucrat and quango pluralist he moved ever further away from his literary ambitions, mainly out of a sense of civic responsibility but also perhaps from a desire to be wanted. After six years in the army Hoggart moved to Hull where he spent the next thirteen as an extramural tutor – although much of the time he was on the road in places like Redcar and Middlesbrough. Extramural teaching in Mr Attlee's new Britain was an exciting enterprise. The spirit of those years provided education, of adults in particular, with a cutting edge now lost. In this austere, intense and populist environment flourished not only Hoggart but others like Raymond Williams, Asa Briggs and Edward Thompson.

The Uses of Literacy was the product of this second period of Hoggart's life. Published in 1957 it did not create much of a stir until its paperback release a year later. Fourteen impressions and many thousands of copies later, the book remains the subject of controversy. For many it was a modern classic that shaped not only the detailed development of the New Left but also the much broader growth of social science in Britain during the succeeding decade. It was a cultural trigger as much as a work of great intellectual novelty. For others *The Uses of Literacy* was a genre work, a book firmly set in that tradition of working-class nostalgia which looked back to George Orwell and forward to Jeremy Seabrook. It was too sentimental, too loosely constructed, to bear the weight of its considerable reputation. Intellectuals, especially on the left, have always distrusted both the book's methods – Hoggart's distaste for theoretical speculation and love of the concrete and particular alarmed them – and its message that working-class culture was not all (or even largely) about political and industrial struggle.

In the light of this continuing controversy Hoggart's own account of the origins and intentions of his most famous book is of particular interest. According to Hoggart, the book grew out of his experience as an extramural tutor who had to 'get it (in his case, English literature) across without selling out'. For him the 1950s debate about high-brow and low-brow culture was not just an interesting speculation but a pressing day-to-day reality. *The Uses of Literacy* started as a book on aspects of popular culture, a sort of Leavisite handbook for low-brows. It was conceived in the firm belief that 'people could make something good out of something bad' and therefore that popular culture needed to be treated with respect. Only later did Hoggart decide that it was impossible to write about popular fiction and entertainment if no attempt was made to describe the people whom they addressed. So the more evocative and most enduring parts of the book – its first half, 'An "Older" Order', and the more personal chapters in the second half, like 'Scholarship Boy' – were almost an afterthought. Yet a powerful afterthought, for the eloquence of these descriptions will remain long after the succeeding analysis has been blunted. Maybe *The Uses of Literacy* should be judged in these quasi-literary rather than severely academic terms. Hoggart himself insisted that it was 'not a programmatic book but an attempt to capture something'. Thirty years after its first publication that something remains triumphantly captured.

The book's success marked the beginning of the third period in Hoggart's career, eleven years as a mainstream university teacher in from the extramural cold. For the first three he was senior lecturer in English at Leicester and then moved in 1962 to Birmingham as professor. Two years later he founded the Centre for Contemporary Cultural Studies. But even before this third period began a revealing incident took place. Shortly before *The Uses of Literacy* was published Hoggart showed the manuscript to a colleague at Hull, only to receive the fierce warning that the book would destroy his reputation and blight his prospects of an academic career. This warning was both wrong and right – spectacularly wrong because the book made Hoggart's name and launched his academic career, but subtly right because its unsteady reception in English faculties and enthusiastic reception by social scientists diverted Hoggart from literature to the more fragile discipline of cultural studies. Perhaps this turned out to be an intellectual *cul de sac*. A more sensitive view, one which was implicitly endorsed by Hoggart himself when he announced his ambition to be a writer, is that the uneven reception of *The Uses of Literacy* and the subsequent redirection of Hoggart's career showed that he had never been designed to become a conventional academic. He admitted, certainly with too much modesty, that he was 'not a powerful intellect'. Although a lover of English he had no regrets about deviating from academic conventionality. Nor did he see himself as an intellectual. 'I have no patience with the play of abstract ideas. I always want to return to the concrete.'

This lack of interest in theory led in the late 1960s to a gradual divergence between Hoggart and the new discipline of cultural studies which he had helped to found, rather as in the late 1950s the popular success of *The Uses of Literacy* had led to a parting of the ways with English. A new generation of teachers in cultural studies saw Hoggart as a bit soft. One former student called him 'a liberal, humanist, post-Arnold figure' – not intending it as a compliment. For his part Hoggart warned of 'a new higher illiteracy of hard-nosed sociologists of mass communication' for whom imagination, moral or otherwise, had no part to play in defining culture. He distrusted intellectuals and theoreticians who, he suspected, were afraid of their own emotions and tried to suppress them by hanging on grimly to intellect.

The final two periods in Hoggart's career, the five years at Unesco and the eight at Goldsmiths, were less creative. Although the book he wrote based on his Paris experience, *An Idea and Its Servants*, is very much underrated, his time at Unesco was not a happy or positive period. He had to endure the parochial incredulity of fellow Britons who failed to understand why he wanted to go to Unesco at all. Yet, for Hoggart, the idealism of Unesco's founders in the difficult years after the Second World War was still alive and closely related to his own idealism during the extramural years in north-east England. In Paris he was caught up in the increasing politicisation of Unesco, which was eventually to lead to the United States and Britain withdrawing from the organisation. Back in England, Hoggart went to Goldsmiths, half-in and half-out of London University, at a time when the end of the Robbins boom had blocked off the most desirable paths for the college's development. His ambition to recast Goldsmiths as a Birkbeck for south London could not be realised and he had to settle instead for fuller incorporation into the university, an outcome which foreclosed others more imaginative. A year later he became chairman of the adult and continuing education council established rather grudgingly by the Labour Government of 1974–79. But again it was too late. A new and more utilitarian climate in the 1980s destroyed what meagre hope there had been that the council might lead a revival of adult liberal education. Neither it nor he survived a first term.

For thirty years or more the tide seemed to run against Richard Hoggart. In recent years that illiberal tide has become a flood. Yet Hoggart remained resilient. He drew strength from his conviction that cultural change was very slow and that ordinary people were very successful in creating livable space however difficult their circumstances, a conviction that was at the root of the enduring optimism contained in *The Uses of Literacy*. Hoggart remained thankful for the freedom still enjoyed in Britain – what he called 'the sheer plushiness of a free society'. The privileged middle classes were now offered a far richer diversity of media, specialist journals and magazines and highbrow television, although this had been achieved by 'a greater massification' of the media for the bulk of the British people, an outcome bitterly regretted by Hoggart the cultural liberator.

What, finally, are the distinguishing marks of Hoggart's life and work, neither, of course, yet complete? Two things perhaps. The first is his preoccupation with culture and community, not in terms of the heroic myths preferred by activists and intellectuals who come from outside the working class, but in terms of a deep, rich, lived-in reality. He achieved this because, for him, inquiry was an engaged, subjective, even aesthetic process. It could never be detached observation. At a time when definitions of culture and community are more fiercely contested, in urban redevelopment or on pit picket lines, Hoggart's perspective has great moral value. Community is an experience, not a category, something to be understood fully only from the inside. The second is that in a postwar Britain which enjoyed high social mobility and so suffered from widespread cultural amnesia Hoggart's life and work affirmed an abiding loyalty to his roots. In a world of hard-nosed successful men with short memories he experienced the vulnerability that is the price of a rich personal memory. Not just a personal memory, of course, also the memory of a race. For his is a moral experience difficult to interpret outside its Englishness.

'MEN ARE GROWN MECHANICAL'

Ideology is a difficult and confusing word. It was first used at the beginning of the nineteenth century to mean the science of ideas. Later it acquired more powerful if less literal meanings: a grand intellectual scheme or, less formidably, an organic arrangement of ideas; a package of ideas and ideals, beliefs and customs, the familiar notion of *Weltanschauung*; or an interpretative code which can be used to make sense of the world. In simpler words, ideology as religion, ideology as culture and ideology as perception.

The concern in this part of the chapter is with ideology in the first two senses. In these forms ideology has provided the building blocks of modern culture. More particularly, the concern here is with the grand ideologies of the nineteenth and twentieth centuries which have shaped and reflected our understanding of that culture – nationalism, which systematised (some would add perverted) the older organic solidarity of family, community or estate; positivism, which in its primitive Comtian form tried to reduce the knowable to a rational classification and in its later, logical-positivist, form denied all metaphysical claims; liberalism/radicalism/socialism which first established the 'social question' as the most important issue in industrial society and in its later forms introduced a materialist (and reductionist?) conception of society; and the affective ideologies, ranging from romanticism to Freudianism, which began the exploration of the inner world of our fears and our feelings. Power and bureaucracy, rationality and secularism, materialism and equality, individuality and alienation – through these preoccupations the grand ideologies have come over the last two centuries to map out the modern condition.

They have also run in parallel with the great movements that have shaped modern society. Nationalism has been the ideology which represented and justified the centralised and bureaucratic nation state. The original model was cast in revolutionary France and then refined (and purged of all association with social radicalism?) in monarchist Prussia, which of course was also the home of Hegel, nationalism's most totemic philosopher. In the nineteenth century the nation state established itself as the most, perhaps the only, dynamic model for large-scale social organisation throughout western and southern Europe, in central and eastern Europe after the end of the First World

War and across the globe in the two decades after 1945. But there are interesting exceptions, most notably the two superpowers, the United States and the Soviet Union, neither of which is a classic nation state. The state was not only national but bureaucratic. The centralising and professionalising of politican authority were the instruments used to mould new national identities out of the chaos of regional and communal loyalties. Radicals too came to depend on centralised bureaucratic power to produce social reform. Nationalism acted as an ideological chorus for the growth of bureaucracy, royal or Jacobin, welfare-state or Soviet.

If nationalism celebrated the growth of the nation state, positivism marked the industrial revolution and the progress of science. Its early emphasis, however, was as much on organisation as on discovery. Its first message, carried over quickly into views of culture and society, was that existing knowledge could be organised more effectively to produce unparalleled progress. The idea that the discovery of new knowledge could transform the world was at first subordinate to this organising emphasis. Hence the obsession of nineteenth-century thinkers with machine metaphors for society. Comte's elaborate classifications of knowlege perhaps mirrored the pattern of the early industrial revolution, which depended as much on superior social organisation as on new technologies. A lesson first learned in Lancashire's nineteenth-century textile industry and now being re-applied in twentieth-century Korea and Taiwan. Later, of course, positivism was coloured by the dynamism of science and by the inevitable clash between reason and faith which foreshadowed the decline of organised religion. It became less a 'social' ideology which demonstrated a practical, even mechanistic, model for the reconstruction of society and more a 'philosophical' ideology, a secular religion that celebrated the superior claims of rationality. So it moved away from its early association with social engineering, the cruder utilitarianism of Bentham or Malthus, but tightened its grip on our thoughts and values. Max Weber's iron cage was where men came to live their public lives.

After the national and industrial/scientific revolutions the most significant movement in modern society has been the democratic revolution. This has been celebrated in a jumbo-ideology that embraces liberalism, radicalism and socialism. Whatever their differences they had this in common, that the organisation of society and the regulation of culture according to custom or tradition were indefensible and that a new society and a new culture must be established according to determined principles (whether those of economic efficiency, individual rights or social justice). As with positivism, this view has so thoroughly invaded the modern consciousness that other views have entirely lost their intellectual credibility, although not their actual relevance. The language of modern politics is made up of accumulated vocabularies that stretch from eighteenth-century Philosophes and Whigs to twentieth-century Marxists and neo-Conservatives, all of whom are accomplices in this rationalist tradition.

The fourth movement, the revolution of the senses, is mirrored in an even more diffuse ideology that ranges from the original revolt two centuries ago against the austerity of classicism to the confusion of modern art and postmodern literature. As the affective and irrational have been expelled from public thought along with custom and tradition these impulses have been concentrated in the world of private feeling. Literature and art have become the property of this latter world, inward, fearful, narcissistic. The novel has imploded. Painting has become non-committal. Interestingly, music, always the most personal of the arts, has changed its mature nineteenth-century forms least. The areas where private feeling and public thought meet, such as the family or sexuality, are among the most contested in modern society. The interpretations offered by the leaders of this fourth revolution, from Byron and Turner to Picasso and Freud, have only added to this disorder.

These, then, are the four revolutions that have shaped the modern world – the national, the industrial and scientific, the democratic and the affective revolutions. Their solidity is hard to deny. They form the substructure of our ideas, our values, our lives. Their cumulative achievement has been to sweep away the preindustrial world of custom and faith, which survived in Europe into the eighteenth and nineteenth centuries and in the rest of the world until very recently. Of course both aspects of this four-part revolution, its modernity and its comprehensiveness, need to be qualified. Many of the values regarded as exclusively modern, for example those of romantic marriage or the nuclear family, are in practice much more ancient, while in many countries, not all of them developing ones, modern values in any case are weakly rooted. These qualifications provide a valuable check to the imperialism of Western culture, but they do not damage reasonable claims for its global influence.

Yet the ideologies that celebrated these four revolutions have never achieved the same solidity. Nationalism, of course, has been undermined by the excesses of chauvinism and war and by the stubborn survival of other clusters of loyalty. Positivism has been undermined by a growing consciousness of the costs as well as the benefits of scientific progress and of the moral limitations of the rationalist tradition. Liberalism/radicalism/socialism have been undermined by an increasing disenchantment with government according to abstract principles. The claims of customary conservatism have revived, and radical utopianism, on both left and right, has flourished. The affective ideologies have been put on the defensive by a new puritanism – the so-called moral majority in the United States, for example. However, for all their fire and strength the check that such movements seek to impose on the revolution of the senses is feeble. Economic growth in free-market societies depends as much or more on the propensity to consume as to save. Deferred gratification is bad for business.

The reason for the decay of these grand ideologies, it is argued, was the growth of postwar pragmatism, that combination of internationalism, Keynesian economics, political corporatism and social welfare which will be discussed in the next section of this chapter. But this pragmatism, it must be remembered, only became possible with the decay of ideology. Further, this argument underestimates the extent to which that pragmatism was itself simply a restatement in less categorical terms of the old ideas and values. Why then did the grand ideologies decay? Three broad causes can be suggested. First, their influence was never uncontested even at their European climax in the century and a half after 1789. In *"Signs of the Times"*, published in the *Edinburgh Review* as early as 1829, Thomas Carlyle objected to the materialism which developed from positivist and liberal thought in terms echoed later in the century by Ruskin and Arnold:

> Not the external and physical alone is now managed by machinery, but the internal and spiritual also. . . . Men are grown mechanical in head and in heart as well as hand. . . . Nor for internal perfection, but for external combinations and arrangements, for institutions, constitutions – for mechanisms of one sort or another, do they hope and struggle. Their whole efforts, attachments, opinions turn on mechanisms, and are of a mechanical nature.[12]

From the start there was resistance to the modern project – not only from the kings, landowners and priests most directly threatened by it, but also from intellectuals like Carlyle who feared its demoralising crudity. Older values retained a submerged vitality which floated to the surface again, perhaps in unrecognisable forms like the counter-culture of the 1960s, when the authority of the grand ideologies came under renewed challenge.

A second cause was that these ideologies, however benign their practical consequences in the nineteenth century, seemed in the twentieth to condone and encourage practices which, far from being civilised, were among the most barbaric witnessed in human history. Nationalism seemed to lead to the Auschwitz gas ovens or the mutual massacres of Hindus, Muslims and Sikhs in India at the moment of her freedom. Positivism seemed to lead to the Moloch-like social engineering of Stalin's Russia, to nuclear weapons and to environmental pollution. Liberalism, radicalism and socialism produced a mass society which undermined community, despised intelligence, destroyed high culture and alienated the individual citizen. The affective ideologies seemed to lead not to personal liberation but to demoralisation and *anomie*.

A third cause was the growing belief that these grand ideologies were not only pernicious but also false – which, of course, redoubled their danger. In the 1930s John Maynard Keynes saw the dilemma but not its danger: 'The ideas of economists and political philosophers, both when they are right and when they are wrong, are more powerful than is commonly understood. Indeed, the world is ruled by little else. . . . I am sure that the power of vested interests is vastly exaggerated compared with the gradual encroachment of ideas'.[13] Keynes' throw-away remark – 'when they are right and when they are wrong' – raised a moral issue others took more seriously. The nineteenth century had looked with condescending horror on religious wars in which men and women had died for shades of unprovable faith. Was there not a danger that the ideologies of the modern world would demand the same loyalty, and require the same sacrifices, as the religious sects of the world that had passed? Karl Popper, for one, turned away from his early enthusiasm for Marxism on these grounds. In his biography he recalled: 'I realized the dogmatic character of the creed, and its incredible intellectual arrogance. It was a terrible thing to arrogate to oneself a kind of knowledge that made it a duty to risk the lives of other people for an uncritically accepted dogma and for a dream which might turn out not to be realizable.'[14]

So the grand ideologies came to be questioned on grounds similar to those used to assault religious faith and customary tradition a century earlier. They were unprovable – and therefore unscientific, however elaborate their intellectual claims. They commanded uncritical loyalty and were therefore dangerous, a judgement which seemed to be amply confirmed by the dark experiences of the twentieth century. In the spirit of this reaction against ideology Lionel Trilling in *The Liberal Imagination*, published in 1950, wrote about 'the habit or the ritual of showing respect for certain formulas to which, for various reasons to do with emotional safety, we have very strong ties of whose meaning and consequences in actuality we have no clear understanding'.[15] In the first section of this chapter it was argued that the particular likes and dislikes, preoccupations and prejudices, of the British distanced us from two of the dangers inherent in modern culture, the imperialism of the grand ideologies and Weber's iron cage of rationality. Ideas were not taken as seriously as in the rest of Europe, it seemed, while trained intelligence was generally qualified by the British taste for clubbability. This argument now seems a difficult one to sustain. Britain has been prominent in developing the key elements in modern culture and is compromised by their accompanying ideologies. Our sense of national-ism may be less intense, perhaps because it has never been tested. Patriotism, on the other hand, has always been a powerful force in British society. Our commitment to positivism, at any rate in its earlier nineteenth-century form, was notable for its enthusiasm. Our contribution to the rationalist tradition of government was decisive. J. S. Mill was among the most influential political thinkers throughout Europe a century ago. As for the loosely-grouped affective ideologies, British culture offers some of the most effective examples, from the high culture of the nineteenth-century novel to the low culture of twentieth-century pop music. So in what sense can Britain be said to have stood apart from the grand ideologies?

Yet a case may still be made for the exceptionalism of British society. Even a century ago when Britain seemed to be in the forefront of efforts to establish a modern society and develop a modern culture, it retained powerful remnants of older values. The form of state which gradually replaced Cobbett's 'Old Corruption' between 1830 and 1860 was never on the root-and-branch Napoleonic model. The influence of Gradgrind-style positivism has to be set against Martin Wiener's evidence of the decline of the entrepreneurial spirit in Victorian England: its enthusiasm for the chivalric and antique. Romanticism, after the briefest of flirtations with radicalism in the 1790s, was always an aesthetic rather than an intellectual movement. But the real break may only have come in the present century. The drifting-apart that began to be discernible in Edwardian–Elgarian England was accelerated by the First World War. German culture, for so many nineteenth-century Britons the most powerful point of reference, was abased. Later, in the 1920s and 1930s, the collapse of European civilisation intensified the feeling that Britain stood apart. Exiles from that collapsing civilisation, such as the historian Lewis Namier, the philosopher Karl Popper and the economist Friedrich von Hayek, enriched intellectual life in Britain. In one sense they brought us closer to the mainstream of modern culture but in another they confirmed our separateness. They found in Britain a refuge, a corner of the old Europe. Their more radical peers generally travelled westwards to the United States. But perhaps another way to put it is that the decay of grand ideology and the triumph of pragmatism, which the rest of western Europe and the United States experienced after 1945, arrived a little early in Britain.

GEORGE STEINER[16]

George Steiner's essay, 'A Kind of Survivor', is an attempt to describe why he, a post-Holocaust Jew, does not want to live in Israel. But the title of the essay and the themes it explores can also be used as a metaphorical description of Steiner's life and work that transcends its Jewish context. Not that Steiner is literally a survivor of the death camps of Nazi Europe. His family left France for the United States in 1940. But intellectually and psychologically his safe teenage exile in New York may have made him a more immediate survivor of the central European civilisation consumed by Hitler, the inheritance of Marx, Freud and Einstein. A literal survivor would perhaps have found it difficult to retain the same sympathetic identification with Kafka's Prague, Wittgenstein's Vienna, Adorno's Frankfurt – the cities which Steiner has called, almost affectionately, 'the inner capitals of the twentieth century'.

He is also a survivor in a more recent and literal, but less awful, sense. His unconventional method of entry into the academic profession, through Geoffrey Crowther's *Economist* and Robert Oppenheimer's Princeton Institute for Advanced Study, and his commitment as a scholar to broad philosophical speculation derived from the study of culture and comparative literature made him a difficult man for fellow academics to digest. Many distrusted his pungent intellectuality – part-American, part-French, part-British. His determination to excavate language and explore its hidden contours and his iconoclastic attitude to traditional literary scholarship has offended the guardians of literature. But he has never signed up with the deconstructionists and semiologists despite the strong French undertow in his intellectual preoccupations.

His academic progress has been pitted with difficulty. As a young research student his first attempt at an Oxford D.Phil. ended in controversial failure. In the 1960s, as a fellow of the newly-founded Churchill College, he was ostracised by Cambridge's English faculty with a ferocity surpassed only by its earlier exclusion of F. R. Leavis. His most substantial book, *After Babel*, was written in a period of deep and unhappy isolation. Yet all this time his intellectual and public influence grew, dragging his academic reputation bumping along behind. Oxford, to its credit, finally relented, allowing Steiner to rewrite and resubmit his thesis, so launching him on his academic odyssey. At Cambridge, only his own college has always been loyal; it was not until the 1980s that the university finally invited him to deliver the Leslie Stephen lecture, a symbolic reconciliation, although the faculty itself never relented. Fortunately the University of Geneva rescued Steiner from his isolated predicament by appointing him to the double chair of English and comparative literature.

But if Steiner has been a survivor, more recently a successful and even triumphant one, he has also been an outsider: a schoolboy in an American school in prewar Paris; a teenager in a French school in New York; a student at Chicago, rather than Yale as his father had wished; an American and French citizen who commutes between Cambridge and Geneva; a man who speaks and writes fluently in three languages to the eternal unease of the monolingual majority; a Jew nostalgic for the destroyed 'central European humanism', suspicious of Israeli nationalism and author of the novel *The Portage to San Cristobal of A. H.* with its ironic apologia for Hitler.

These two identities, the survivor and the outsider, may be the keys to understanding Steiner's academic preoccupations and intellectual styles. In the same essay he admits: 'I have never been sure about houses', and a few sentences later he refers to 'the edge of strangeness and temporary habitation' that has been the experience of many Jews – and which may be generalised to illuminate Steiner's own choices as a postwar intellectual. Part was involuntary: his inheritance as a member of a family transplanted from Vienna to Paris in the 1920s and from Paris to New York in the 1940s and the consequent denial of a settled intellectual identity. Discussing Jews and language in the essay – again the feelings can be generalised – Steiner wrote in a characteristic phrase: 'But a final "at homeness" may elude us, that unconscious, immemorial intimacy which a man has with his native idiom as he does with the rock, earth and ash of his acre'. Part, however, is chosen, a deliberate adoption of distance, movement, and perhaps isolation, and a deep-grained fear of the intellectual claustrophobia that is their opposite. Steiner is a free-trade intellectual, not a mercantilist scholar. Trying to explain why he could not accept Israel as the culmination of Jewishness he wrote: 'A few may want to stay in the cold, outside the sanctuary of nationalism – even though it is, at last, their own. A man need not be buried in Israel. Highgate or Golders Green or the wind will do'. Freed from their immediate context these words describe George Steiner as well as any can. He has chosen to live at the edge, in the cold, in the wind.

Steiner was born in Paris in 1929 but his family came from Vienna. His father was a successful lawyer and scholar; his mother was, in his own phrase, 'immensely finely educated'. There never needed to be any discussion of what career the young Steiner should follow. Although his parents were emancipated Jews with the purest Voltairean convictions, a millennium of Talmudic tradition could not be shrugged off: Steiner was predestined to be a teacher, a learned man. His father was a man who believed in 'setting up tensions' and disliked equilibrium, characteristics he passed on to his son. Sending him to an American school in Paris and a French lycée in New York, the deliberate confusion of linguistic milieux was part of that. Another influential figure in his childhood was his informal godfather, the historian Sir Lewis Namier. Many years later Steiner still fondly recalled the family story that his father and Namier when young and poor shared the cost of Monypenny and Buckle's six-volume biography of Disraeli, a book that acted as a symbol of hope to emancipated European Jews with an intensity unimagined by its Victorian authors.

As a schoolboy in wartime New York Steiner found himself in an intoxicating environment enriched by the enforced presence of many European intellectuals often struggling in humble jobs. Levi-Strauss, Arendt, Maritain and Gilson were among them. As Steiner was still young claims of intellectual inheritance can hardly be justified; the only thing he remembered about de Beauvoir on a lecture visit to New York was her great Mexican skirt. But perhaps some intellectual excitement rubbed off on Steiner as did a curious sense of displacement in wartime America with the war so far and yet so near, normality and enormity in such a narrow proximity. After gaining his baccalaureate – still an austerely classical degree, of course – he went to Chicago. This was his first rebellion against his father who had wanted him to go to Yale – 'I suspect that my father did not believe the mid west really existed'. There he discovered unknown subjects like sociology and also encountered the natural sciences. It would have been difficult for an intelligent young man in Chicago in the late 1940s not to, with Fermi lecturing on physics and Urey on chemistry.

Science became a secret thread that has continued to run through the mature Steiner's career. His lack of genuine creativity defeated his own ambition to become a scientist. Since in the 1940s science had been dominated by physics, his mathematical weakness was a decisive handicap; the biological revolution still lay in the future. But Steiner's Chicago science was far from being a *cul de sac*. In two senses it shaped his future. First, he was introduced to a network that led via *The Economist* and Oppenheimer's institute to J. D. Cockcroft's Churchill College. Secondly, his empathy with science, maybe his sense of its inexorable offensive against traditional literary culture, continued to influence his scholarly work.

More immediately, however, Steiner faced a difficult choice. Clearly he could no longer hope to become a scientist but his rebellion against his father had not extended to rejecting the family expectation that he must become a learned man. But learned in what? His immediate dilemma as a graduate student, for a year at Chicago and then at Harvard, was the choice between literature and philosophy. His apparent choice of the former is misleading. Steiner's academic career has been spent in the borderland between the two disciplines, developing a philosophy of language and studying the relationship between words and ethics, between language and the arts.

After Harvard, Steiner went to Oxford as a Rhodes scholar, an unusual honour for a recently naturalised American. At this point his father's old friend Namier intervened, to fatal effect. As Steiner's field was literature a college like Merton might have been a better place for the young graduate student, but for Namier Balliol was the only college. So to Balliol Steiner went. His Oxford experience was not happy. No one had told him how to set about writing a thesis and he was quite unprepared for the cynicism of some Oxford dons. Although his thesis was later to be remodelled as an important part of his second book, *The Death of Tragedy*, his viva verged on a show trial in Steiner's memory. His use of references from 'paper-backed books' was ridiculed; he was savagely criticised for not knowing the difference between *belles-lettres* and literary criticism; to Steiner it seemed as if he were being run out of town.

But the story had a happy ending. Steiner spent the next four years working at *The Economist* writing on European politics, America and science – 'incomparable years in a place I still remember as very donnish'. The donnishness was clearly important because it was in these years that Steiner began work on his first book, *Tolstoy or Dostoevsky*. It was also while still at *The Economist* that he made his peace with Oxford. An unexpected opportunity to rewrite his thesis led eventually to a congratulatory viva. The stigma of the belletrist was cast off. A second controversy, however, was not far away. After leaving *The Economist* he spent four years in Princeton, having been head-hunted by Oppenheimer in a chilly interview in which he was told his efforts to write *Tolstoy or Dostoevsky* while working as a journalist were 'nineteenth century British amateurism'. It was Oppenheimer who recommended him to Cockcroft in 1961 when the latter was searching for a scientifically sensitive humanist for his new college.

Steiner recalled his early years at Churchill with great affection as 'a kibbutz adventure'. But these were years of biting controversy. He was rejected by the English faculty and never appointed to a university lectureship. Despite – or maybe because of – the popularity of his lectures with undergraduates and his eager desire to move beyond the core of English into comparative literature the breach was complete. Oxford may have given Steiner the benefit of the doubt by deciding that after all he was not a belletrist; powerful people at Cambridge have never been convinced, although their doubts have been expressed with mounting discretion. The temptation is strong to pass quickly over Steiner's troubles at Cambridge. Such conflicts of academic personality are generally bitter – and rather too common in the Cambridge English faculty, with outbreaks stretching back to I. A. Richards and forward to Frank Kermode. In any case, Steiner moved to Geneva in 1974 and his remaining link with Cambridge has been only as an extraordinary Fellow at Churchill. His academic career, far from being blighted, boomed.

Both sides could be blamed. Steiner admitted that he had made miscalculations. Quite wrongly he believed that comparative literature would find an easy opening in 1960s Cambridge. He incautiously used the Eliot lecture to develop the polemical argument later elaborated in *In Bluebeard's Castle*. In his 1965 essay 'To Civilize Our Gentlemen' he provocatively wrote of the malaise in literary scholarship. On the other side, the faculty's establishment, obsessed by the breach with F. R. Leavis, made no concessions to accommodate this combative representative of a strange new intellectual species, half-scholar and half-polemicist, half-critic and half-philosopher. As a matter of personal biography, this episode is best regarded as closed long ago. Yet the incompatibility of intellectual styles it revealed has to be considered in any examination of the life and work of Steiner. On the one hand was his desire to take part in the sharp contest of ideas – 'eating cactuses' in a memorable phrase, on the other, the opposing English tradition of academic gentility with its puzzling taboos about 'talking shop'. On the one hand, Steiner's unease about the inwardness and rootedness of English literature's guardians, their 'unconscious, immemorial intimacy' with their native idiom, maybe associated however faintly in his mind with the chilly atavisms of *Blut und Boden*; on the other, their view of Steiner as an essayist rather than a scholar, not the complete academic gentleman.

In an important sense Steiner's life and work has been an attempt to prove that it is not only possible but essential to be both a (public) essayist and a (private) scholar. For him the two are the twisting strands of the rope of a responsible humanism. The amoral detachment of much scholarship has always disturbed him. The contrast between the fineness of Anthony Blunt's aesthetic judgement and the depth of his treason, the early collaboration of Martin Heidegger with the Nazis, the tension between George Lukacs's high intellect and the coarseness of the Communist régime he served in Hungary – all have fascinated and dismayed Steiner. But he has a deeper fear that professional scholarship is not only too often amoral in its intentions but also on occasion may be immoral in its outcome. A central question to which he has returned again and again is, why do the humanities not civilise those who study them? His image of the concentration-camp guard relaxing by listening to Schubert or reading Rilke has a recurring power, despite its becoming a cliché. His phrase about the cry in the poem possibly seeming more real than the cry in the street sustains a chilling echo. His *In Bluebeard's Castle* argued that high culture and abstract speculation might infect human consciousness with an ennui out of which, in the wrong conditions, could grow a fascination with savagery. The highly educated might become fellow travellers with barbarism.

The same preoccupation infused his more scholarly books, such as *After Babel*, *On Difficulty* and *Antigones*. His unease about the attempts of deconstructionists to dethrone the authority of the author and to deny the moral context of the work; his sense of the decay of literary culture based on the classics, of learning by heart and of received tradition; his fear of pornography and defence of reticence, the 'dictions of silence'; his insights into translation as a universal ingredient in all acts of comprehension – all this detailed work has been informed by a controlled effort to define the conditions of humanism.

Those who teach literature, in Steiner's derogatory phrase, as 'some kind of urbane trade, or professional routine' have never admired his work. They have grudgingly valued some specific work on translation only to dismiss the rest. The more generous and thoughtful have offered more measured criticism. One reviewer of *After Babel* accused Steiner of attempting what 'only a team of scholars and specialists should undertake'. Another called it 'this bad book which is also, alas, a classic'. Some have said that Steiner has spread his knowledge too thinly – Aeschylus one moment, Einstein the next; others, that his books have been too long, their rhetorical prose stalking round and round a few simple themes. Yet over the years Steiner's reputation has slowly accumulated. The danger now is not that he is ignored but that he is absorbed. For in a crucial sense criticism and even conflict, 'eating cactuses', have always been an important ingredient in the Steiner phenomenon. For a man thinking and writing at the edge, in the cold, in the wind, the approval of the academic establishment at the warm, still centre might prove fatal. Steiner could never come in from the cold.

It is still too early to offer a settled account of George Steiner. When Penguin decided to publish a collection of essays and extracts, he rejected the title 'The Essential George Steiner' because he considered it equivalent to an intellectual death sentence. So 'George Steiner: A Reader', a more provisional title, was chosen instead. Yet his latest book, *Real Presences*, does have something of the quality of a culmination, a summation of all his most pressing preoccupations. It has two themes, one familiar, the divorce of the word and the world, and the second less so, life-after-the-death-of-God.

The first theme is that language has been separated from meaning, understanding swamped by learning. The culprit is the elaborate apparatus of academic scholarship with its unreal and amoral theorising and its desensitising divisions of intellectual labour. Instead of reading literature aloud or reciting it from memory, we 'read' it with the unnecessary and baleful assistance of secondary works, explaining, commenting, deconstructing. Instead of being engaged by art, we analyse it – and evade its moral intentions. So Steiner imagines a republic of letters in which only primary texts are tolerated and all secondary literature is forbidden. Like so many of Steiner's accounts it achieves its rhetorical effect by exaggeration that stops just short of caricature. Such a republic could never exist. Even if it could it would be a chilly and philistine place where an authoritative canon might easily degenerate into an authoritarian art and literature. For Steiner, of course, the divorce between word and world is not simply an academic or aesthetic concern. It leads, potentially and inevitably, to that moral displacement that made possible the Holocaust.

The second less familiar theme in *Real Presences* is the theological reassurance which he believes lies hidden at the root of all worthwhile knowledge and art. For more than two centuries we have been drawing, unwittingly, on the capital accumulated by the world's great religions, without replenishing the stock. God may have become impossible, in terms of rational inquiry, but the death of God is equally impossible, in terms of all that is best in Western culture. We think and act *as if* God were still alive. And it is this *as if* that is the source of our intellectual integrity and artistic creativity. But *as if*, of course, can be read in two senses. The first is a conscious determination to imagine the presence of God even when it can no longer be rationalised. This is not a new position. It is close to that taken by Kant. The second is a recognition that our whole culture – conscious thoughts and implicit routines, radical beginnings and slowly modulated traditions – is suffused by a history that is Christian (although with important classical and Jewish influences). This second *as if*, although incontrovertible, says very little. Unless sustained by active faith the Judaeo-Christian tradition is like a dying note on a piano, reverberating into silence. And even in *Real Presences* Steiner is not prepared to make that personal leap into transcendence. He, and we, are the victims of a refusal to accept, in his words, 'the ultimately theological re-insurance of the very concept of meaningfulness without offering in return the collateral of an avowed faith'.

But that is too negative a note on which to end an account of Steiner. A thousand years of Talmudic tradition are represented in his preoccupations – but so too are the fragile prospects for our civilisation, postindustrial and post-Auschwitz. Whatever the ultimate scholarly fate of his books – and they appear in twelve languages – George Steiner will be remembered for simple things: a principled affirmation of a humanist agenda in a time of great human difficulty; a determination to confront rather than evade the moral ambiguities of western civilisation; and, most important of all, the courage not to conceal his own anxiety and vanity, not to be afraid 'to see through a glass darkly' rather than not to look at all.

THE TRIUMPH OF PRAGMATISM

'Yesterday all my troubles seemed so far away' ran the refrain of a rather mawkish popular song by the Beatles in the 1960s. A fair comment, perhaps, on the culture of yesterday, that remarkable mid-century flourishing of common-sense pragmatism that succeeded the decay of grand ideology. As this culture provided the version of modernity to which so many remain attached, it is difficult to be objective about its character. For it is *our* culture, the ideas, attitudes and habits of our youth or middle years – in any case, of our best years. Difficult to admit that it may now be yesterday; impossible to go further. Yet from the start a great dislocation, like a silent earthquake fault, ran through this postwar culture. It can be simply described: in no age was utopianism, in an intellectual sense, more out of fashion, but in no age was more hopeful progress made towards the goals that utopians of the past valued most highly. Nowhere was this dislocation more obvious than in intellectual life. Our claims were modest compared with those made by the ideological giants of the nineteenth and early twentieth centuries; at the same time, our scientific achievements were immensely more impressive than theirs. The more we shrank from offering grand explanations, the more effective became our technology. Postwar pragmatic man stood on the moon; prewar ideological men had stumbled through the aftermath of Auschwitz and the ruins of Dresden.

But it was not simply in intellectual life that this contrast could be observed. The ethics of nation, family, religion, work, which previous generations had believed to be the essential cement of a civilised society, were disregarded and despised – but the world did not fall apart. On the contrary, it advanced to new levels of material civilisation, social relaxation, political harmony and individual freedom. Unmemorable politicians with passionless programmes presided over great advances in the human condition, which their memorable predecessors, filled with great passion and guided by grand programmes, had failed to achieve.

So postwar culture is a puzzle. Why did such a deliberately undistinguished age have achievements of such distinction? One explanation is that the rise of postwar pragmatism in the political, social and economic spheres and the parallel decay of grand ideology in the postwar intellectual world, although sharing some common origins and offering each other mutual reinforcement, were two quite distinct phenomena. The former grew out of the ashes of ideological exhaustion. Therefore it was always streaked with pessimism, a dark memory of just how barbaric the world could become if enthusiasm was not restrained by common sense, and passion by dullness. Because such a memory played a decisive part in forming postwar pragmatism, this pragmatism could never be entirely innocent and carefree. It was a retreat to sanity – and retreat never feels the same as advance. Even at its most hopeful climax around 1960 it never lost this recessional quality. Kipling at an earlier imperial climax had wondered when its magnificence would be 'one with Nineveh and Tyre'. The postwar world did not have to wonder; it had experienced the destruction of too many modern Ninevehs and Tyres.

The latter was very different. The intellectual assault on the grand ideologies was not a retreat but an advance. New knowledge and better ideas were inexorably condemning them to the fate of the dinosaurs. The trouble with these ideologies was not their past horror but their present naivety. In the postwar world theories ceased to be admired for the splendid symmetry of their organisation of ideas; instead they were regarded as common-sense tools which could be used to clear a few more square miles of the forest of ignorance. When they became worn out they were sharpened or replaced by better ones. For twenty years or more after 1945 the advance of knowledge according to these mundane principles seemed unstoppable.

This forward march was most keenly felt in the natural sciences and technology. But other disciplines were also deeply affected in the 1950s and 1960s. Economics in the high noon of Keynesianism developed into a benign form of social engineering the morality of which was rarely questioned and the success of which seemed assured. Under the influence of scholars like Talcott Parsons, David Riesman and Daniel Bell[17] the social sciences adopted a perspective similar to that which guided the development of science and technology, although Riesman's and Bell's analysis also emphasised the powerful currents of irrationality which continued to flow through postwar society. Even the arts, although touched more tenderly by the recessional spirit of the postwar years, did not remain unaffected by such pragmatic optimism.

But the forward march of knowledge after 1945 was very different in ethos and spirit from that which had animated the Victorians a century earlier. It was not accompanied by a similar growth in optimism about the perfectibility of human society. Faith in the latter could only be regarded as naive in the light of European history between 1914 and 1945. So the intellectual optimism of the postwar years was not rooted in a deeper social optimism. It was an autonomous phenomenon that depended on its own internal intellectual self-confidence, sustained by a diet of scientific 'successes'. This self-sufficiency, in 1950 so admirable, had come by the 1970s to be interpreted much more negatively as indifference to the key preoccupations of modern society. The thinking classes, often referred to pejoratively as the 'chattering classes', seemed to be out of step, and touch. Yet for almost thirty years after 1945 the new pragmatism that had emerged from the confusion of war sustained an environment in which a new intellectual pragmatism – perhaps pluralism is a better word – was able to flourish. In return, that pluralism sustained the legitimacy of the new postwar order. These two phenomena, pluralism and order, must be considered independently from one another in order to be fully understood. Yet their incestuous relationship also has to be recognised, especially in any discussion of that slippery idea of culture.

The most important question to be asked in this context is really very simple. Did postwar culture represent a clean break from the ideological agenda established in the one-and-a-half centuries between 1789 and 1939, or did it simply amount to a restatement of the same ideas and values in more moderate terms, a cleaning-up of the modern project after the painful excesses of the first half of the twentieth century? The answer seems obvious enough. The exuberance of grand ideology may have been discarded along with its excess but the modern project itself remained intact. The national, industrial/scientific, democratic revolutions and the revolution of the senses continued to dominate the cultural agenda. Of course it can be argued that the first of these, the national, was substantially recast after 1945 and that a new age of internationalism was inaugurated. In Europe maybe – but in the rest of the world? Certainly in western Europe aggressive nationalism seemed to be a spent force. But even here not only did the nation state remain the effective political unit but nationalist feelings were channeled into new movements of great significance – racism, regionalism, great-power rivalry. Even in the anodyne states of western Europe no sensible person could dare pronounce nationalism dead. The crab-wise progress of the European Community towards unity is evidence of the enduring sensitivity of national feelings. In eastern Europe, where prewar nationalism had been repressed by Soviet power, the outcome has been a volatile alliance between the national and democratic revolutions.

In the world beyond Europe the years after 1945 saw the apotheosis of nationalism. More new nation states were created in the succeeding quarter-century than at any previous time in history. Most of these new nations were unrestrained by historical fears about the absolute exercise of national power which had become almost pathologically endemic in Europe. Just as in the nineteenth century the nation state, in its democratic form, was regarded as the best instrument to curb internal privilege, the customary power of courts, nobles and churches, so in the later twentieth century the nation state, sadly not always in a democratic form, came to be regarded as the best defence against external privilege, the old and new imperialisms of the developed world. The rise of nationalism in the third world was such a remarkable phenomenon that it could not be ignored by even the most confirmed pragmatist. In *The End of Ideology*, a book that, published in 1960, provided a title for the whole postwar age, Daniel Bell argued that welfare state politics and Keynesian economics had established a benign corporatism in the advanced West, and that virulent ideological conflict had been relegated to East-West superpower rivalry and to the decolonising third world. This analysis may have been generally true, at any rate until the playful explosion of a counter-culture in the heart of the West in the later 1960s and the end of the long postwar prosperity in the 1970s. But the reaction of intellectuals to the excesses of nationalism after 1945 was especially strong, and the most spectacular advances, in science and technology, transcended national frontiers. However, rather than offering proof of a weakening of nationalism after 1945 this may simply emphasise a growing gap between intellectual and political cultures in the postwar years, a dislocation as significant as the contrast between intellectual optimism and social pessimism discussed earlier in this section.

Even if the memories of 1914–45 and the rise of a new internationalist spirit took some of the shine off the national revolution, the postwar years saw an immense reinforcement of the industrial/scientific revolution and its supporting ideology positivism. Not only did the spectacular progress of science shore up the wider faith in the inevitability of human progress which had been shaken by the experience of wars, revolutions and depression; it also offered an effective metaphor to describe the better organisation of human society. This metaphor was seized upon by social science, which adopted an increasingly technocratic perspective. The evolution of economics offers an illuminating example. The triumph of Keynesianism, which was so thorough and complete that it surprised even Keynes himself, switched the focus from micro-economic fine-tuning to macro-economic planning. Anything seemed to be possible. In Daniel Bell's *The Coming of Post-Industrial Society* the progress of science and a technocratic vision of society were brought together in an impressive display of positivist futurology.

Nor has the third item on the agenda of modernity, the democratic revolution and its ideologies ranging from liberalism to socialism, been ignored in the postwar years. All the newly-founded states adopted its rhetoric if not its substance. None attempted to reassert precolonial customary values as a basis for organising their independent government. Perhaps the expansion of Communist rule into eastern Europe in the 1940s and parts of Asia a few years later may be regarded as an exception to that rule. But it is difficult not to include Communism as bound up in this third revolution, despite the tyranny it has often come to represent in practice. It too is committed to the organisation of society according to materialist principles rather than idealist tradition. In the West the rise of welfare-state politics marked an intensification of the democratic revolution. Its footprints were everywhere – in the reform programme of Labour Britain between 1945 and 1951, in West Germany's 'social market', in the successive new-this and new-that that have littered American politics since 1933. The benign consensus which Bell described and which in Britain came to be called (retrospectively) 'Butskellism' was based on widespread agreement that the agenda of the democratic revolution had to be extended to include large areas of social life. The popularity of Anthony Crosland's *The Future of Socialism*, published in 1956, reflected not so much the originality of its interpretation of altruistic collectivism but how routine such values had become in the postwar years.[18]

The revolution of the senses, the final item on the modern project's agenda, also accelerated after 1945. In the north Atlantic world, at any rate, external focuses of authority and loyalty became weaker. Organised religion declined further, its place filled by fundamentalist cults or secular *anomie*. The power of community and tradition was eroded. Yet the result was not a golden age of rationalist sensibility. Instead, at the highest levels of culture modernism seemed to lead to a disjunction between meaning and form, language and words, which had profound moral consequences. At lower levels, popular taste and personal life style became tradable commodities, the raw material of modern society's most important industry, the media/leisure/life-style complex as powerful in its own way as the much more noticed military/industrial complex which so concerned American radicals. The revolt of Romanticism in the late eighteenth century had been to a considerable extent a protest against the inhibition of individuality within pre-modern society, by immemorial custom, by inherited hierarchy, by the chilly canons of classicism. Yet it led, although by tortuous routes, to a late twentieth-century society in which personal responsibility had been diluted by linguistic and aesthetic indeterminacy and popular choices were intensively exploited in the market of mass culture. Dust to dust in less than two centuries.

Postwar culture, therefore, did not really represent a clean break with the ideological past. Rather, it reaffirmed, moderately but decisively, the agenda of modernity that had been drawn up since 1789. That was the trouble, the source of the unease that bubbled away under the surface of postwar success. Postwar pragmatism was undermined by that success. It met its objectives – and then had nowhere else to go. Ralf Dahrendorf wrote in his essay *The End of the Social-Democratic Consensus?*: 'The classical social-democratic position has lost its fire. A grand programme has been realised; it is no longer a force for change'.[19] Many who remember disappointed hopes of twenty or thirty years ago will instinctively recoil from this assessment: it cannot be true; their work is only just begun. But the inadequacy of postwar culture, rather than being the result of flaws within the new pragmatism that grew up after 1945, reflected deeper fissures in the modern project itself. Its very successes exposed the intellectual, moral and even personal limits of modernity. To adapt a sentence from Matthew Arnold, postwar culture failed to relate its undoubted success to our sense of private and public conduct and our sense of beauty – and it fell victim to the weariness and dissatisfaction bred by that failure.

DAVID RIESMAN[20]

The passage from innocence to maturity marks the life of David Riesman, not just as it does for any man but as it must for a leading sociologist of his generation and an American who has experienced the turbulent twentieth-century power of his nation. For Riesman has a long reach – back across half a century of sociology from its age of innocence before and after the Second World War to its age of disillusion in the 1980s, and back across even more years of the history of the United States, almost exactly those years which marked the translation of Jefferson's and Lincoln's republic into a world power.

When Riesman was born in Philadelphia in 1909 the nineteenth century was not properly over in America. The Civil War was as near as the Second World War. His father, the director of the city hospital, had to tread carefully between the corrupt Tammany Hall-style political machines and the progressive 'mugwumps' who challenged their power. For his mother, an early Bryn Mawr graduate, Europe was the centre of the world. The flow of American writers eastwards across the Atlantic was still a familiar phenomenon. The reverse flow of Europeans seeking cultural asylum in the United States lay in the unimagined future. The departure of Henry James was as close as the arrival of W. H. Auden. These were Riesman's beginnings – in an almost nineteenth-century world of corrupt political machines, of *fin de siècle* aestheticism, of America as Europe's outpost, of a grandmother who kept a horse and carriage until the late 1920s when coachmen could no longer be found. He was born into a rich and cultured German Jewish family long established in the United States, before the easy incorporation of such families into America's protestant elite had been compromised by the influx of the 'Russians', the poor Jews of eastern Europe, and before their cultural confidence had been undermined by the anti-German feeling of the First World War. Yet this child of innocent early twentieth-century America became successively a New-Dealerish lawyer; one of America's leading postwar sociologists (and, through his authorship of *The Lonely Crowd*, the surprised prophet of the affluent life-style of Eisenhower's America and even of the first stirring of youth culture); the ethnographer of higher education, that most distinctive and dynamic of transatlantic industries, and a member of the university great-and-good called to serve on the Carnegie and other commissions; and a committed opponent of the Vietnam War, the first faltering of imperial America.

Riesman's personal and intellectual biography offers a fascinating descent through the layers both of twentieth-century America and of sociology, that most distinctive of postwar disciplines which helped shape the public culture of that happy age. Riesman is much more than a postwar figure, *The Lonely Crowd* more than a 1950s publishing success. The decades fall away – the radical but brittle 1960s, the affluence and cold-war politics of the 1950s, the wartime solidarities of the 1940s, the progressive New Deal of the 1930s, the F. Scott Fitzgerald hedonism of the 1920s. Riesman's childhood and upbringing were in an even earlier decade, at a time when the confidence of the nineteenth century was only beginning to curdle, when Victorian values of probity and progress had only just begun to be eroded by a weary Spenglerian pessimism and had yet to be confronted by the stark counter-evidence of world war and holocaust.

The young Riesman grew up in a privileged, but unsettling, world. He had a German governess as a child and was sent to private schools, including the William Penn Charter School, a seventeenth-century foundation which he remembered as 'decayed classical'. His family was part of Philadelphia society; among the visitors to their home was John

Dewey. But Riesman had to overcome a strong sense of inferiority in relation to his parents, both formidable people in different ways. His father was highly successful – a doctor, hospital director, professor at the University of Pennsylvania and appointee to national commissions by President Hoover, he had an international reputation that extended to Soviet Russia (as Riesman was to discover, recovering from a twisted knee in a Moscow hospital in 1931). His mother, he later recalled, was 'an aesthete who had the misfortune to regard herself as uncreative'. She read the novels of D. H. Lawrence and Virginia Woolf in their first editions. She worshipped art but dismissed the practical world, partly out of aristocratic disdain and partly out of cultural pessimism. Both parents were secular rationalists who made nothing of their Jewishness. They were also committed to a high moral seriousness. The Riesmans' wine cellar was locked up during Prohibition. Riesman's inheritance was confused. It included, perhaps, a slow sense of guilt about his privileged upbringing that showed itself first in his adolescent solitariness and later in his curiosity about Russia and about depression-hit Detroit, where briefly in the summer of 1934 Riesman put himself like George Orwell in the bleak position of the jobless. An oppressive expectation of professional success perhaps derived from his father's dominant example but perhaps, too, from an unconscious desire to discover gentler patterns of moral guidance than an overpowering parental authority. A reaction against his mother's weary high culture showed itself in a passion for sport, especially baseball, and a fascination with detective stories.

Riesman went not to Princeton, so fashionable in the 1920s, but to Harvard. Both he and his parents preferred the more solid charms of America's oldest university. Princeton seemed 'too near, too athletic, too thespian, too socially self-assured, too anti-intellectual and too clubby', Riesman later recalled. Outwardly his Harvard career was a success. He did well enough as an undergraduate to stay on at the law school, and he wrote for the Harvard *Crimson*. But inwardly things were different. Riesman felt he was not popular. He was attracted to history but believed himself too slow a reader to plough through archival material. His decision to go to law school was not the result of any clear ambition. Riesman was an awkward and even aimless student in his early years at Harvard. Yet in his last year there he formed a crucial personal and intellectual friendship with a young German political scientist, Carl Friedrich, who had moved from Heidelberg in the 1920s. Perhaps Friedrich exorcised the stifling ghost of parental authority. He certainly introduced Riesman to the social sciences and became a close personal friend. Together they bought a Vermont farm and spent many weekends during the 1930s clearing the brush wood from the surrounding land. Riesman also helped Friedrich with his book *Constitutional Government and Democracy*, which offered an oblique

apprenticeship in political science and an unconventional introduction
to the social sciences.

Despite the influence of Friedrich, Riesman's passage from law to
sociology took more than a decade. He went first to Buffalo to help
found the law school there and even spent a year in the New York
district attorney's office. Buffalo he found exciting, a western city
compared to Philadelphia and Boston. Law he found less exciting,
although at that time it was an important route into social science.
Riesman never lost the impression of lawyers as 'crisp, bright but non-
intellectual' which he had formed at Harvard. He rejected Friedrich's
advice to do a Ph.D in political science because it was too close to law,
abstract and lifeless. At Buffalo he began to meet social scientists who
were more open intellectually. Already his interests were moving away
from mainstream law. While many lawyers, under the impact of the
New Deal, were now interested in labour and administrative law,
Riesman chose instead to study the tension between democracy and
defamation. Already he had become fascinated by the power of
language, in both a literary and an anthropological sense. Many years
later he admitted: 'If I had known where I was going I would have liked
most of all to be an anthropologist'. He went to New York, got himself
psychoanalysed, and met the Trillings.

Riesman spent the war years in industry working for the Sperry
gyroscope company, an experience which provided him with an insight
into industrial man not immediately available to a well-bred Phila-
delphian or academic lawyer. In 1945 came an extraordinary piece of
luck. He was invited by Edward Shils to teach social science courses in
the (undergraduate) college of the University of Chicago, then the
powerhouse of American sociology. He recalled: 'Sociology had a very
low threshold of entry but a very high ceiling. I would never have been
accepted into anthropology'. (Or perhaps into sociology itself a decade
later.) Although it took more than ten years for Riesman to switch from
law to sociology, his rapid ascent from novice to superstar (marked by
the publication of *The Lonely Crowd* in 1950) took fewer than five. He
learned sociology on the job, sitting in on survey methods courses
given by Shil's colleague (and rival) and Riesman's mentor and later
friend, Everett Hughes. He learnt fast, at a time when sociology was
rapidly developing into the independent empirical science familiar
today. By such serendipity Riesman joined that small group which so
decisively moulded modern sociology in America in the years following
the end of the War. But he never was and never became, a mainstream
sociologist. His interests were opposed to the functionalism of Talcott
Parsons and others which became the postwar orthodoxy. For Riesman
the illicit attraction of anthropology continued. *The Lonely Crowd*
seemed to many a work of intuitive ethnography rather than of

empirical sociology. Riesman himself, of course, eventually retreated from wrangling Chicago, back east to Harvard.

Riesman's reputation rests on, but is also the victim of, the spectacular success of *The Lonely Crowd*, and of its more academically conventional follow-up, *Faces in the Crowd*. The former was not an instant success. It received a harsh review in the *New York Herald-Tribune* and no review at all in *The New York Times*. Not surprisingly for a book that Riesman and his co-authors Nathan Glazer and Reuel Denney had conceived as a speculative essay on the American character, its initial academic reputation was ambiguous. Daniel Bell and Parsons were among its early critics. Even Freidrich found it a book of great subtlety but one that might give rise to misleading simplification. But these doubts were soon swept away. Lionel Trilling praised *The Lonely Crowd* in a book club essay. Anchor, America's pioneering paperback publishers in the Penguin mould, brought it out as one of their first two titles along with Edmund Wilson's *To the Finland Station*. Its description of a fundamental shift in the American character from an 'inner-directed' type governed by internalised parental authority to an 'other-directed' type less repressed, more social, more playful, was greeted with a shock of popular recognition. It seemed to explain so much – the decline of traditional authority, the erosion of inherited morality, the culture of postwar affluence. It seemed to speak with an eloquence and a directness which could not be matched by the abstraction of Parson's functionalism or the generalisation of Bell's postindustrial futurology.

The Lonely Crowd was a book of great contrasts. It was, as Riesman himself admitted, 'a book of innocence'. Nineteen-fifty was probably the last date when it could have been written. Later its tentative speculation would have been overwhelmed by the accumulation of sociological research. But it was also a book of great complexity. It had grand ambitions. One was to re-do de Tocqueville, to illuminate the quality of the American character in the postwar age with the same imaginative insight applied by de Tocqueville to the early years of the republic. It was intellectually eclectic. Psychoanalysis, anthropology, popular culture and public opinion surveys were all important ingredients. Maybe it was obliquely autobiographical. Riesman had certainly been brought up in an 'inner-directed' culture but he had witnessed, and perhaps participated in, a shift towards an 'other-directed' culture. Certainly he was concerned that the book should not be misinterpreted. He always resisted the identification of 'inner-direction' with autonomy and 'other-direction' with conformity. He saw his famous contrast in different terms. In a later preface to *The Lonely Crowd* he wrote: 'He [the other-directed person] lives in a glass house not behind lace or velvet curtains', and later: 'The problem for people in

America today is other people. The social and psychological landscape has become enlarged because other people are more in number and, possibly, in heterogeneity than ever before. But other figures in the landscape – nature itself, the cosmos, the Deity – have retreated to the background or disappeared.'

On the prompting of McGeorge Bundy Riesman moved back to Harvard in 1957 as professor of social science, a chair he held into the 1980s. Much of his later work has been in the study of higher education, an invisible field in Britain but a more central academic concern in America. One reason for his choice, a strange one for such a well-known sociologist, was his preoccupation with civil liberties. This interest went back to his early work on defamation but had been reawakened by the threat of McCarthyism. Another was simply a sense of being at home – 'Here was an ethnographic territory where I did not feel alien.' Riesman's interest within higher education was always its social psychology, not its political and administrative structures. But through his service on the Carnegie and other commissions and inquiries he was co-opted into that public-spirited fraternity of university and college presidents which struggled through the 1960s and 1970s to articulate the changing meaning of American higher education. As the growth of college experience was perhaps the most decisive social phenomenon in postwar America, Riesman's interest in it was inevitable and logical. The campus also seemed to be a place that bred 'other-direction'. Riesman's speculation of the 1950s seemed to many to prefigure the student troubles of the 1960s and 1970s, when playfulness too often turned into viciousness. More conservative critics in the 1980s have even blamed Riesman for this revolt of youth against authority. He was the victim of sneering references and sniping footnotes in Allan Bloom's *The Closing of the American Mind*, which denounced higher education's leaders for acquiescing in the denial of reason and the dethroning of authority.

Two aspects of Riesman's character mark him off from his peers and contemporaries. In an American intelligentsia attuned to over-confident rhetoric, (whether Michael Harrington's or Allan Bloom's), he has displayed a tentativeness, even a lack of confidence, and also a stubbornly counter-factual streak which has been mistaken for perversity. Both characteristics, tentativeness and stubbornness, may have roots in his 'inner-directed' childhood in early twentieth-century Philadelphia. Both have been apparent in the political positions he has taken up – sympathy for rather than allegiance to the New Deal; an instinctive pacifism but an equal determination to see the defeat of Germany and Japan in the war; a Kennedy liberalism and Peace Corps enthusiasm, opposed to the Vietnam adventure and ever-sceptical of anti-Soviet hysteria; a distrust for Zionist patriotism. Just as his father manoeuvred between the machines and the 'mug-wumps' for the good of his hospital, so Riesman has found being a zealot difficult. He has had many friends but few disciples. Riesman seemed untouched by the drift to the right so strong among many of his academic peers. To characterise David Riesman in the terminology he made famous, he seems to have been an honourable example of 'other-direction'; but, in his case, the 'other' by which he was governed was not a conformist and superficial peer group but the rich twentieth-century experience of his nation. And, deep inside, perhaps there has always remained traces of another, 'inner-directed', person, of a small boy playing in Rittenhouse Square in Philadelphia under the watchful eye of his German governess before the First World War, a world ago.

BACK TO THE FUTURE?

Late twentieth-century society is contested ground in the West. Political passions which a generation ago seemed to have been stilled for ever are reviving. The corporatist structures built in the years after 1945 to moderate conflict are being dismantled. Commitments which were once common ground – to full employment, to the welfare state, to the defence of the north Atlantic basin – are being repudiated. In intellectual life similar phenomena can be observed. Pragmatism is out of fashion. Those systems of ideas, values and beliefs which emphasise the progressive organisation of the state, society and the economy, such as Keynesian economics, Parsonian functionalism or Tawney–Titmussite welfarism, have come under critical intellectual interrogation. Theories which emphasise instead dissonance and alienation have become influential. Others which celebrate political and cultural reaction or justify an unadorned utilitarianism with regard to social and economic questions are now popular. There has been a revival of interest in substantive issues of value and meaning, issues which had often been ignored in the postwar years. Then, the emphasis in many disciplines was on procedural and technical questions, presumably because it was believed that the substantive questions had been resolved satisfactorily or else that such questions could never be resolved.

The commonest view of this shift from a consensual mid-century society to a contested late-century one is that it reflects a justifiable revolt against the political complacency and the intellectual sterility of the postwar years. In the 1970s the radical left led the attack on pragmatism and in the 1980s the radical right has taken over. Athough rivals, leftists and neo-conservatives had a common target, the social democracy of thought and deed that dominated postwar society. It was young people, especially the more privileged congregated in higher education, who first articulated the objections to this orthodoxy. This may have been doubly significant. First, the location of the anti-pragmatic revolt, in its original and most virulent form, within the academic system may suggest a close relationship between political and intellectual change. It may not just have been, as is commonly alleged, that students, and some of their teachers, had both the time and the opportunity to revolt. They may also have been in a better position to observe the decay of pragmatism as a set of intellectual values and so its weakness as a justification for the postwar political order. If the ideas were wrong how could policies based on them be expected to work? Second, young people in the late 1960s were the first genuinely postwar generation. They had been born after Hitler and Hiroshima. The dominance of pragmatism in both intellectual and political culture after 1945 was partly the result of ideological exhaustion. The unheroic ambitions of postwar politicians and the procedural rather than substantive preoccupations of postwar intellectuals reflected that recessional quality which was a consequence of this exhaustion. In the 1960s Western society recovered from ideological exhaustion and the recessional spirit lifted. It once more became possible to have grand ambitions and to think big thoughts. Dreaming no longer seemed dangerous. Not surprisingly, this renewed optimism was first felt among the young who had no personal memories of war or holocaust. From the middle 1960s intellectual risk-taking came back into fashion.

The romantic left took the first risks. But it was handicapped in two senses. First, it derived its intellectual resources from the grand ideologies, particularly Marxism of the nineteenth and early twentieth centuries. Of course the new left attempted to distance itself from the old Marxism by 'rediscovering' an earlier, more idealistic, more Hegelian Marxist tradition (Gramsci was seen as a significant figure in this respect). But the new left was never able to shake off a damaging association with old ideas which seemed to have been responsible for a future that did not work. Second, the radical left in the 1960s and 1970s was never able to distinguish itself sharply enough from the postwar order it so fiercely criticised. Of course it rejected the apolitical pragmatism characteristic of postwar society. But in practice the programme of the new left was difficult to distinguish from that of social democracy. Both were collectivist, corporatist, welfarist. The new leftists, under protest and in disgust, ended up looking like advanced social democrats. Their revolt against postwar pragmatism, however absolute intellectually, was a politically limited affair.

In the 1980s the new right mounted a much more serious challenge to postwar orthodoxy. Both in Britain and the United States it seems to have successfully fostered a shift in political culture, if not a full-blown cultural revolution, on a scale never achieved by the new left. Of course the significance of that shift can be exaggerated. One reason for the new right's success and the new left's failure is simply the accident of timing. The right was active in the late 1970s and 1980s when the economic security of the postwar world had been shaken by inflation and recession and its political security threatened by domestic conflict and international uncertainty. Its liberal and social democratic rivals were certainly tired and probably disillusioned when the new right mounted its challenge. The new left, in contrast, was active in the late 1960s and early 1970s when the postwar order still appeared to be triumphantly intact. The left's challenge came too early to be effective. Another very obvious reason is that the new right is in power while the new left has always been out of power. The right's resource is the authority of the state rather than that of its own ideas.

This has been a source of both strength and weakness. The influence of the new right has been strengthened because it has been able to put its prescriptions into effect. It has been able to start dismantling the corporatist welfare state established in the postwar years. Of course this is an anomalous procedure, to use the power of the state to reduce state power. But this argument mistakes the nature of the new right's project. Its enemy is not the state but civil society. The latter is the true heart of collectivism. Arguably, the ideological and institutional momentum behind what can conveniently but crudely be called collectivism is so strong that the new right is bound to fail. Public services may be transformed into private monopolies, or even oligopolies, but they remain collective enterprises. But whatever qualifications are accepted, the new right's political power has enabled it to create facts difficult to ignore. In its attempted remoulding of society it has also been able to rely on the grudging consent of the silent pragmatical majority which today swims as easily with the radical-right tide as it did with the liberal-left tide a generation ago.

However, the influence of the new right has been weakened because it has had little need to argue for its ideas. The result is an enduring intellectual naivety, which, when political fortune turns against the new right, is likely to prove a fatal weakness. In Britain this naivety is particularly prominent. For example, the free-market ideas developed by the right-wing Institute of Economic Affairs, which was founded in 1965, are regarded as influential in shaping the social and economic policies of Margaret Thatcher's Conservative Government which came to power in 1979. The standard interpretation is that the lonely revisionism of the IEA in the fat years of social democracy, reinforced in the 1970s by other right-wing 'think-tanks' like the Conservative Party's own Institute for Policy Studies, helped to make possible the 'Thatcherism' of the 1980s. It gave intellectual coherence to the untidy collection of instincts and prejudices that had always mistrusted postwar reformism but had been denied a respectable language in which to express that distrust. Yesterday's prejudices were restyled as tomorrow's ideas. In these new clothes they were able to penetrate deep into the world of high policy and challenge the weakened social democratic programme which had been high policy's ruling orthodoxy.

The IEA and its allies, according to this interpretation, invented an intellectual language able to sustain an alternative to collectivism. But there are a number of objections to this standard interpretation. The first is that the influence of such ideas can easily be exaggerated even within the Conservative Government. The management of the economy has continued along semi-Keynesian lines, although the substitution of incentive for equity as the keynote of the taxation system may be attributed to the influence of the new right. Across social policy its rhetoric is promiscuously distributed but its detailed impact has been less substantial. The second objection is that the IEA and its new right allies have been unable to overcome the stigma of pamphleteering journalism. They have never been able to match the intellectual fire-power of their enemies on the liberal left entrenched in powerful higher education institutions and prestigious publishing houses. The third is that they have remained preoccupied with administrative and economic reform, the very areas in which the silent undertow of collectivism is most powerful. They have shown little interest in trying to influence personal and social values or to reshape Britain's public culture, perhaps because these cannot be reduced to market categories. The fourth is that, perhaps because of this neglect, the new right has failed to promote a cultural revolution to sustain its ideological counter-revolution. Social surveys suggest that the British continue to support the fraternal values on which collectivism and reformism depend.

But the fifth and most powerful objection to the claim that the new right possesses both political power and intellectual influence is that its message is confused. Alongside the ahistorical (and amoral?) free-market ideas promoted by the IEA and its allies is an openly reactionary school of thought which is passionately historicist, hierarchical, moralistic, organicist. Among its leading figures are Edward Norman, the dean of Peterhouse and scourge of liberation theologists and Whiggish bishops; Maurice Cowling, author of the magisterial but whimsical two-volume *Religion and Public Doctrine in Modern England*, which can be regarded as an attempt to excavate (or invent?) a reactionary intellectual tradition in response to the challenges of modernism and secularism; Jonathan Clark, whose revisionist *English Society 1688–1832* portrayed eighteenth-century England as an *ancien régime* by no means predestined for liberal reform and whose more recent book *Revolution and Rebellion* has reaffirmed this anti-Whig thesis; Roger Scruton, the author of much gadfly journalism in *The Times* and elsewhere and also of *The Meaning of Conservatism* in which he argues for an instinctive personal conservatism remote from free-market preoccupations.[21]

To argue that such people form a coherent group would be misleading. It would also be wrong to exaggerate their political motivation. For most, their politics are incidental to their scholarship. Their target is not so much the collectivism ingrained in Britain's political culture but the progressive orthodoxies which have become entrenched in our intellectual life. They seem themselves, perhaps ingenuously, as keeping the politics *out* of scholarship. Up to a point their efforts can be applauded. Many disciplines are cluttered with their own particular 'Whig interpretations', many less obvious and so more pernicious than history's celebrated version. Further left, similar complaints are also made about these entrenched liberal orthodoxies. The nerve of the Cowlings and Scrutons can also be admired. They are prepared to champion *ancien régime* values in opposition to the Enlightenment values of the modern project. They are not afraid of being labelled anti-liberal or anti-populist or even anti-democratic. Theirs is a battle for the soul of our nation's culture, not a scramble to invent more efficient administrative mechanisms. Their goal is to recreate an organic society of conservative tradition, a society as alien to the free-market ideas of the new right as to the liberal ideals of the old left. This attempt to re-run the grand intellectual battles of the nineteenth, or even eighteenth or seventeenth, centuries in the hope that this time the *ultras* rather than the Whigs will win seems an implausible enterprise. But its claim that conservatism is above all a moral project adds to the intellectual incoherence of the new right. In Britain, this movement is a curious, and unconvincing, amalgamation of postliberalism and preliberalism.

Perhaps Britain is too narrow a stage on which to display the talents, political and intellectual, of the new right. Here the American experience is central. Neo-conservatism (a better phrase to describe the movement's intellectual potential) in the United States is regarded as an epiphenomenon of American foreign policy, a kind of Rambomania for eggheads. Or else it is seen as the driving force behind the efforts of recent administrations to deconstruct the chaotic welfare state inherited from the Democratic presidents of the 1960s. Or it is dismissed as rightist chic, New York-style. But all these characterisations are incomplete. Although the accelerating cold war pushed many New Deal radicals across from the left to the centre, general disillusionment with the disappointing results of Lyndon Johnson's 'Great Society' (and the escalation of social welfare under Presidents Nixon, Ford and Carter), also pushed many from the centre to the right. It is also misleading to regard neo-conservatism as a *chic* east-coast ideology. The academy has remained largely liberal in the Kennedy–Johnson sense, while the literary and intellectual establishments of New York have retained their leftish colouring.

Neo-conservatism in America is an inchoate but catholic movement. By a reasonable definition it embraces both William Bennett, the smooth-tongued but tough-talking Secretary of Education in President

Reagan's cabinet and anti-drugs 'czar' in President Bush's, and Daniel Patrick Moynihan, New York's senior senator and a leading Irish American politician with deep roots in the urban coalition that is the Democratic Party. Many different groups inhabit this neo-conservative territory – disenchanted radicals, amoral technocrats, revisionist liberals. They are (still) almost as likely to vote Democrat as Republican. Many continue to draw a significant distinction between New Deal liberalism (OK) and Great Society welfarism (not OK). Not all neo-conservatives are hawkish on foreign policy, enthusiasts for the Contra rebels in Nicaragua, or battlers against the 'evil empire' of the Soviet Union (pre-Gorbachev, at any rate).

But the frontiers of true conservatism and of unrevised liberalism are well marked. Neo-conservatives are unlike old conservatives because they are utilitarians rather than moralists. Their goal is the prosperity of postindustrial society, not a recovered golden age. Their objection to abortion, for example, is not that it is wrong, which they regard as a judgement that only private consciences can make, but that liberals have politicised an issue incapable of rational resolution. They admire Mormons not because they respect their beliefs but because Utah is a well-ordered state. As Nathan Glazer, a collaborator with David Riesman in the writing of *The Lonely Crowd* and now a leading Harvard neo-conservative, put it with platonic assurance: 'The people should believe the myths but the philosophers need not.' Neo-conservatives are also clearly distinguished from liberals. They believe that the intellectual apparatus of liberalism, the many-layered social sciences, has tended to undermine its claims for social reform. Neo-conservatives rest their case against liberals on the empirical evidence. Irving Kristol, editor of the leading neo-conservative journal, *The Public Interest*, has pointed out that while social science is not very good at inventing social policy it is a highly effective critic of such policy.

But there is another dimension to the difference between neo-conservatives and liberals. The former may be intellectuals (both Bennett and Moynihan were professors before entering politics, Glazer still is, and Kristol is an editor in a very New York sense), but they are also populists. They may have taught at Harvard but, typically, they were students at City College in New York. They are divided from many old-style liberals by a social fissure which outside the United States would be described in terms of class. Neo-conservatives are not Ivy League liberals, patrons of the Roxbury or Harlem poor from the safe distance of Long Island, Cape Cod or the harbours of Maine. Nor were they ever the gilded youth co-opted into the politically sterile establishments of multinational corporations, Wall Street banks or metropolitan law firms. They are very different from the mandarinate of Achesons, Harrimans, and Kennans that indirectly ruled postwar America. Theirs is not the world of Harvard Law School, Rhodes

Scholarships and State Department postings, even if prominent neo-conservatives have enjoyed all three. Many are first- or second-generation Americans. They have not forgotten the ghetto or the immigrant ship. Despite this, or maybe because of it, they are true Americans, instinctive patriots. They suspect the sophisticated ambivalence of the heirs of Anglo-Saxon colonists who still look longingly from the New World to the Old.

But that is to run ahead of the story. However simplistic a pocket history of neo-conservatism may be, to ignore that history altogether is to mislead. The intellectual roots of neo-conservatism may now be hidden but they still nourish a luxuriant superstructure of right-wing 'think-tanks' and conservative newspaper columns. It is a two-stage history. First, those young radicals at City College forty years ago were deradicalised. In this, the escalating cold war and the McCarthy episode played a part. Many of today's neo-conservatives were on the left in the 1940s, potential quarry for political witch hunts. But more significant were the waning of populist enthusiasm for the New Deal and the retreat of Marxism before more sophisticated social theories. The title of Daniel Bell's *The End of Ideology* (1960), summed up the trajectory from left to centre followed by many fledgling neo-conservatives. Bell, professor of social sciences at Harvard, is an archetypical neo-conservative, albeit an ambivalent one. In the mid-1960s he played a key role in founding *The Public Interest*. Much later he recalled: 'The orientation was to look at American domestic policy in non-ideological terms. I still think I keep to that kind of orientation. Some of my friends have not.' Today the magazine is the house journal of serious neo-conservatism and has parted company with Bell. In a recent book, Michael Harrington, the closest America has to a respectable socialist, and coiner of the word *neo-conservative*, called it 'the theoretical journal of all those who develop sophisticated arguments for turning the nation's back on the poor'.[22]

The second shift, from non-ideological centre to ideological right, is more difficult to explain. Why did revisionist liberals become neo-conservatives? Some, of course, did not. Bell has become increasingly detached from the group, still insisting 'I am a socialist in economics, a liberal in politics and a conservative in culture.' Moynihan, too, although a prominent early member of *The Public Interest* circle and despite a rumbustious period as United States representative at the United Nations during which he earned a reputation as a baiter of the Third World, is difficult to characterise as a neo-conservative. But, whether dragged or dragging, most moved right. One reason for this was that the end-of-ideology group quickly came under attack from the old left of Wright Mills and the new left of student activism. The latter attack, which became an uncomfortable and anarchic presence on many American campuses in the late 1960s and early 1970s, was felt with particular intensity by would-be neo-conservative professors. But the real agent of change seems to have been foreign policy. Some neo-conservatives, such as Norman Podhoretz, editor of *Commentary* magazine, moved to increasingly hawkish positions on nuclear arms control, relations with the Soviet Union, the Third World, and the Middle East. Several crossed the rubicon to Republicanism, and their altered political allegiance encouraged their incipient conservatism with regard to domestic issues.

The revival of morality in foreign policy, whether Jimmy Carter's preoccupations with civil rights or Ronald Reagan's enthusiasm for an anti-communist crusade, stimulated a similar revival of morality in social policy. Did social welfare demoralise its beneficiaries? A question which already interested neo-conservatives on empirical grounds began to agitate them on moral grounds too – and not only in order to express their solidarity with the values of the moral majority. In the 1985 twentieth anniversary issue of *The Public Interest*, James Wilson in a provocative but significant article demanded renewed emphasis on virtue and character in social policy.[23] Here was a more closely-argued version of the call familiar in Britain for a return to 'Victorian values'. Serious neo-conservatism in the United States has remained preoccupied by domestic issues, but its preoccupations have been curiously refracted through the patriotism of American foreign policy. One response has been Wilson's: the injection of patriotic values into social policy to produce a responsible rather than a welfare state. Another is Bell's: he blames liberals for politicising and nationalising non-negotiable moral issues like abortion and school prayer, provoking a conservative backlash and producing an ideological impasse. Sensitivity to community, family, and individual values has always been emphasised by neo-conservative thinkers. Their objection to 'Great Society' welfarism is that it has attempted to manipulate social policy *in vitro*. Structures, such as church and family, that traditionally mediated between the citizen and the state have been deliberately by-passed. So these institutions have either atrophied or grown hostile to welfare values. Neo-conservatives are less comfortable with the liberal counter-argument that the need for social welfare has only arisen because of the collapse of such institutions, especially in the inner city and among disadvantaged ethnic groups. Liberal critics accuse neo-conservatives of naivety, of knowing what they do not like but not what they like. Certainly the family is more comforting than a welfare bureaucracy, but what if there is no effective family structure, as Moynihan himself has demonstrated in his work on Black families in American cities? The real difference between neo-conservatives and liberals is the contrast between the ideological perspective of the intellectual, who explains why policies cannot work, and the practical perspective of the administrator who must make them work as best they can.

Neo-conservatism offers a subtle if largely negative analysis of postwar American domestic policies and re-expresses a mentality of great historical significance, one that is resonant of the American experience, but is dressed in the crudest programmatic clothes, many of which are borrowed from the moral majority with its fundamentalist religion beliefs. Affirmative action – positive discrimination in favour of Blacks and other disadvantaged ethnic groups – is a good example. Neo-conservatives reflect the unease felt not only by the American majority but also by 'successful' minorities like postwar Jewish Americans and, more recently, Oriental Americans. Positive discrimination seems to sit uneasily alongside traditional values, substituting racial classification for individual effort. And, neo-conservatives say, it does not work. The question of race, as important, perhaps, as foreign policy, is a central concern around which a distinctively neo-conservative consciousness has coalesced. It marks an important difference between Britain and the United States. In America, social engineering has a sharp racial focus which offers neo-conservatism a clear target. In Britain it is a messy amalgamation of social paternalism and class resentment, which makes it a more difficult target for the new right.

In the United States there are almost as many interpretations of neo-conservatism as there are prominent neo-conservatives. Bell, for example, sees it in terms of the oscillation of American culture, perhaps the culture of the whole West. A century ago there was almost no regulation of the economy and yet a rigid monitoring of society. Later those conditions were reversed. The economy was tightly regulated, while in society almost anything was allowed. Now a reaction has set in, of which neo-conservatism is part. The economy has been abandoned to the free market once again, while moral restraints on social and individual behaviour are being reimposed. A more limited and relaxed interpretation is offered by Moynihan. He emphasises the significance of America's comparative economic underperformance, its demography with that middle-aged bulge, and its discovery of 'capitalism' as an active ideology rather than a passive description of the way the world must work, all of which have raised neo-conservative consciousness. But his view of neo-conservatism, despite his many contributions to *The Public Interest* over the years, is that of the pragmatic and sceptical liberal. A lot of bad social policy grew up in the 1960s and 1970s and is being critically reviewed in the 1980s; likely result, he argues, will be sounder social policy in the 1990s.

The same scepticism neo-conservatives applied to liberalism can be applied to their own ideas. Do they represent a sea-change in the character of America's culture? A move away from the paternalism of the east coast elite and its allies, the ethnically-determined big city political machines, towards the tougher, self-reliant individualism of the west and new south? Has populism, arguably the most dynamic force in American politics and society since the days of Andrew Jackson, changed sides? Once the life-force of the great coalitions of urban deprivation and agrarian poverty that powered the 'New Deal' and the 'Great Society', does populism today work through a very different coalition of wealthy suburbs, high-technology industry and the moral majority? Even if the answers to the speculative questions are affirmative, the significance of neo-conservatism remains obscure. Certainly its validity outside the United States looks doubtful, grounded as it is in social policies that reflect American exceptionalism. Maybe only the accident of America's military, economic and cultural hegemony has provided neo-conservatism with its global reach.

Generally, neo-conservatism in the United States has remained within the intellectual boundaries of pragmatism. Liberalism is not wrong; it just does not work. This characteristic makes it difficult to cast neo-conservatism as a backlash against postwar pragmatism. Rather, it sees itself as the continuation of that pragmatism by other, more effective, means. In America it is almost impossible to be a reactionary in the Cowling–Scruton mould. After all, the nation was founded by a revolution. So there have been fewer examples there than in Britain of any serious intellectual revolt against modernity. One such, perhaps, is Allan Bloom's *The Closing of the American Mind*, a sustained polemic against moral and intellectual relativism published in 1987. Bloom describes American culture as 'nihilism with a happy ending'. The ideal of many American intellectuals is a Weimar in which the good guys win. The flaw in his view is the powerful but unrecognised influence of German thought. 'All our (intellectual) stars are singing a song they do not understand translated from a German original and having a huge popular success with unknown and wide-ranging consequences, as something of the original message touches something in the American soul. But behind it all, the master lyricists are Nietzsche and Heidegger.' The good, the true and the beautiful have been displaced by the amoral, the relative and the banal; Socrates by Heidegger. The result is that 'the foundations of the university have become extremely doubtful to the highest intelligences.'[24]

Higher education is ruled by false or external values, or by none at all, Bloom suggests. It has become a desert of specialisation. Natural science may be 'doing just fine' (although Kuhnian concepts of scientific revolution show that it too is vulnerable to relativism), but other disciplines are in poor shape. Social science is doubly damned, for preferring 'German' intellectuals to Locke and for selling out to the philistinism of business education. The arts have only managed to survive by abandoning their claim to assert moral truth, by agreeing to be 'mummified' as the price of being allowed to stay within higher education. As a result, for students 'the differences and indifferences are too great'.[25] The university can no longer help to constitute the idea of an educated human being or of a liberal education.

Why such views should have become associated with neo-conservatism is puzzling. In Bloom's book there are many echoes of John Dewey, Robert Hutchins and the 1945 Harvard report, *General Education in a Free Society*.[26] This aim to establish a higher education which both reinforces the values of a liberal society and offers academic coherence is attractive. It was a frequent concern of those liberal corporatists who oversaw the development of the American multiversity during the 1950s, 1960s and 1970s, who sat on the Carnegie and other commissions and who, in Bloom's eyes, are the guilty men. In the United States this project has been especially influential, as a kind of intellectual agrarianism perhaps, but the idea of a common culture is a powerful longing in all modern societies. It is difficult to describe as a right-wing programme.

Yet *The Closing of the American Mind* was judged to be a neo-conservative coup. One reason was its polemical tone. It put leading liberal thinkers in the rhetorical dock. David Riesman was portrayed as a naive worshipper of Nietzsche, and John Rawls as the advocate of an equal distribution of hedonistic self-esteem. Unjust verdicts, of course, but designed to impress neo-conservatives. A second is that Bloom's argument was misunderstood. He has argued that 'contemplation of Socrates is our most urgent task' and specifically denied that the crisis of the American university could be solved 'if we professors just pull up our socks'.[27] Yet *The Closing of the American Mind* has been generally interpreted as an attack on the leaders of American higher education and of the nation's intellectual life. The most important reason for this was that the ideal of an open-minded and inclusive liberal education, as understood by Hutchins, has now been succeeded by the 'cultural literacy' programme of people like Fred Hirsch and Diane Ravitch, an exclusive and restrictive attempt to define the irreducible elements within a common culture. Playing around with a common curriculum is an innocent enough business in a still relatively homogeneous country like Britain, although even here there are dangers. In a nation as diverse as modern America it is a highly political affair. Conservatives like William Bennett have conscripted 'cultural literacy' in the ideological war against bilingual education in American schools or women's studies in American colleges. Liberal education no longer belongs to the liberals.

The claim of the new right in Britain, and even of the much more significant neo-conservatives in America, to have captured the leadership of Western culture from the faltering hands of the postwar pragmatists is no more substantial than the failed claim of the new left in the late 1960s. Their intellectual authority does not match their political influence. One or two adverse elections could so easily turn the neo-conservative tide. But if neither the new left nor the new right is the successor of postwar pragmatism, who is? In 1984, BBC Radio 3 broadcast a series of talks, later published in *The Listener* and in book form, under the heading 'The return to Grand Theory',[28] which discussed the work of Jürgen Habermas, Thomas Kuhn, John Rawls and Louis Althusser. The connecting theme of the series was that Grand Theory was making a comeback. But can the work of Habermas, Kuhn, Rawls, Althusser et al. reasonably be regarded as providing the intellectual scaffolding within which an alternative to mid-century pragmatism may be constructed? Up to a point, perhaps. Theory has certainly become grander again, in the serious sense that there is now a willingness to ask substantive rather than procedural questions, and in the trivial sense that some disciplines seem to be drowning in a flood of ideologese for which both the new left and the new right are responsible.

But, away from these ideological margins, there is little sign of a serious revival of the ambition to reconstruct grand overarching ideologies on the nineteenth- and early twentieth-century pattern which aspire to offer comprehensive accounts of the human and social sciences. Rather the reverse. In the last two decades the fragmentation of knowledge has continued. Intellectual synthesis has become an increasingly treacherous business. Certainly none of today's grand theorists, although they all operate on a broad front, makes the kind of quasi-metaphysical claims common a century or even half a century ago. Kuhn, for example, has resisted the extension of his interpretation of the nature of scientific revolutions into a general theory of knowledge. Rawls has remained within the established territory of philosophy, although he has returned to substantive issues of value neglected by postwar philosophers in their enthusiasm for procedural questions of meaning. Even the intellectual reach of Habermas and Althusser has been limited. Their work has undermined the pretensions of positivism, but only by arguing that the latter is an incomplete account of rationality. The genuine metaphysicians are to be found on the fringe, with Foucault, McLuhan and, now, their successors. But they are best seen as a froth of playful ideas blown across the surface of postwar pragmatism rather than as authentic examples of a post-pragmatic mentality.

And so Grand Theory, no; grander theories, perhaps yes. Just as it is a mistake to exaggerate the discontinuity between prewar ideology and postwar pragmatism it is equally misleading to attach too much importance to this revival of a taste for theory. The intellectual agenda has remained remarkably stable. It is still rooted in the four revolutions of the modern world – the national, the industrial and scientific, the democratic, and the affective. But does the revival of theory within the intellectual system re-echo wider secular changes, which together might amount to a significant modification of our culture, or is it simply evidence that academic and public cultures are increasingly disconnected? Both the new left and the new right are committed to believing the former. Certainly intellectual life has become embroiled in the brawling of right and left. But the relationship between ideas and politics is more complicated. In the postwar years intellectual pragmatism was a separate phenomenon from the political corporatism with which it was often associated. The former reflected the triumphs of empiricism and reductionism, especially in the natural sciences; the latter an ideological exhaustion that was the result of too much war and terror. Today the revival of theory in intellectual life and the return of ideology to the political field are equally distinct phenomena. The first is a modest attempt to counteract the theoretical (and moral?) blindness which often accompanies the successes of empiricism and reductionism; the second reflects an irritation with unheroic corporatism and a resentment of egalitarianism. Any relationship between the two is, at best, oblique.

Late twentieth-century culture is still constructed out of the great and simple ideas of modernism: nation, science, democracy, justice. There is no alternative vocabulary. But a century ago, even a generation ago, those ideas were able to inform the ultimate ends of society and of knowledge. Today they seem to have collapsed into a dull formalism, heavy expressionless words that no longer stimulate social change or excite intellectual inquiry. One reason for this, no doubt, is that too much harm has been done in their names. Another is that the 'highest intelligences', to borrow Bloom's phrase, have abdicated their moral and cultural responsibilities. Many scholars and most scientists believe their job is to refine the expert *means* rather than to define the ideal *ends*. A third reason is that the modern project left too little room for ethical manoeuvre. Did not the national revolution produce the centralised bureaucratic state and remove any possibility of appeals against its authority to older social associations? Did not the scientific and industrial revolutions, and the positivist ideologies which sustained them, suggest that the pursuit of truth through the application of reason represented an unchallengeable virtue? Did not the democratic revolution undermine the legitimacy of all claims that did not rest on the (necessarily imperfect) representation of the people's will? Custom, tradition, culture, even conscience were discounted. Did not the affective revolution lead to the expulsion or degradation of all noncognitive values, whether aesthetic or spiritual, from the territory of knowledge?

Yet if the modern project had an overriding aim it was to harness together the worlds of men and of ideas, to try to reconcile public duty, private feeling and organised intelligence. The grand ideologies of the nineteenth century attempted to achieve this reconciliation. Their aim was to link the political and intellectual worlds within a grander cultural scheme, a secular city in place of the heavenly city which they denied. Even postwar pragmatism had a similar object. Politics and ideas were still regarded as different aspects of a larger whole, even if this belief had become an implicit rather than an explicit one. Today we seem to have retreated even from implicit acknowledgement of this wholeness. Ideas seem to have been disconnected from culture. There is only silence. The possibility of transcendence is denied to knowledge.

THOMAS KUHN[29]

Perhaps no living philosopher, including the much older Karl Popper, is more often quoted and more frequently (and wilfully?) misunderstood than Thomas Kuhn of the Massachusetts Institute of Technology, author of *The Structure of Scientific Revolutions*. Kuhn's own five books and forty-odd articles appear a modest production beside the mountain of comment, criticism and interpretation of his work. A 1980 collection of essays on his work lists in its bibliography 254 items under eleven headings – philosophy, history and sociology of science, sociology, political science, economics, history, psychology, theology, art, and education. Among these scrutineers of Kuhn are many intellectual heavy-weights – Putnam, Merton, Bottomore, Lakatos. Of course these books and articles are only the visible tip of the Kuhnian iceberg. His ideas have been used and misused by hundreds, probably thousands, of scholars and scientists across the world. References and footnotes that evoke his work are everywhere. On some global computerised citation index Kuhn would probably register off the top of the scale. The Kuhn phenomenon, the accumulation of Kuhniana, seem to have a dynamic momentum of its own detached from the real Thomas Kuhn in his modest wooden World War II building at MIT.

But Kuhn's fame is not all a glorious accident. Maybe because he originally approached philosophy from an oblique angle he has always been, to adopt Kuhnian terminology, a 'paradigm' builder and breaker rather than a 'normal' scholar working within the intellectual examples devised by more creative minds. He has taken grand intellectual risks, and so has won grand rewards. Trained in physics he moved quickly into the history of science, prompted by the liberal preoccupations of Harvard general education after the Second World War. But the experience of writing history, in particular the close identification it established between the structure of science and the shape of intellectual culture, encouraged a second shift, this time into the philosophy of science. *The Structure of Scientific Revolutions*, published in 1962 and still his most famous book, was quickly recognised as a 'paradigm' (in the correct Kuhnian sense of being an example of successful 'puzzle-solving'), and thus a practical demonstration of its central thesis. The book's successful momentum carried the forty-year-old Kuhn far beyond the restricted frontiers of the philosophy of science.

Indeed Kuhn's influence has been felt most intensely outside his three home disciplines of physics and the history and philosophy of science. The real build-up of Kuhniana has been in social science. His argument that science is validated not by 'objective' positivist norms but by the collective judgments, necessarily subjective, of scientific communities has appealed particularly to social scientists. Not only does this description of how knowledge is validated fit social science well, but it also appears to undermine the superior authority of the natural sciences. The arts have been attracted by Kuhn's dichotomy between the revolutionary breaks of 'paradigm' shift and the continuity of 'normal' science as a metaphor to describe phenomena as diverse as the rise and fall of empires and the development of musical taste. Kuhn himself has always insisted that his work is 'species specific' and so can only be applied to the validation of knowledge in the physical sciences. He has even been reluctant to apply his conclusions to the rest of natural science. Their wholesale and apparently indiscriminate application to the social and human sciences has alarmed (and flattered?) him. But in his very first book, *The Copernican Revolution*, he wrote: 'It (the book) repeatedly violates the institutionalized boundaries which separate the audience for "science" from the audience for "history" or "philosophy".' The expansive intellectual ambition has always been there.

Kuhn was born in Cincinnati, Ohio, in 1922 into a German Jewish family that had emigrated to America in the middle of the nineteenth century. His father was a banker, but had trained as an engineer. His mother came from a family of New York lawyers. The conventional interpretation suggested by such a background, the temptation to emphasise the centuries-old Jewish tradition of learning, does not really work with Kuhn. Any Talmudic inheritance has always sat lightly on him. Neither parent made much of their Jewishness and Kuhn himself has been true to their secular instincts. Yet the examples set by his parents were still important in his intellectual development. From his would-be engineer father he inherited an interest in science and from his mother a taste for the arts. So Kuhn has shown piety to both in his own preoccupation with the history and philosophy of science.

Kuhn went to Harvard in 1940 and chose to major in physics, then approaching the peak of its intellectual prestige, rather than mathematics, which had been his other strong subject back in New York where his family had moved when he was a child. But in a foreshadowing of his later development he also decided to attend a freshman class in philosophy, a quick-fire survey of the field that

disposed of Plato and Aristotle before Christmas and moved on to
Descartes and Spinoza in the spring. But in 1941 war came to America.
Harvard's physics department moved over to military work and Kuhn
found himself involved in a practical problem, how to produce foil that
would confuse radar. It is an irony of time and place that Kuhn, thirty
years later, came to work in the very building in MIT two miles down
the road where other wartime researchers were trying to produce a
better radar that would not be deceived by Harvard's foil.

Kuhn resumed his interrupted education in the autumn of 1945 and
completed his degree in physics. But, to anticipate his own later
terminology, Kuhn had decided that life as a 'normal' physicist was not
for him. His interest in the context, philosophical and historical, in
which science developed had been awakened by his first formal contact
with philosophy five years before. That interest was decisively
stimulated by postwar developments at Harvard. Under James Conant,
Harvard in the later 1940s was approaching the climax of the most
creative of its periodic experiments in general education. Under this
programme Kuhn was asked by Conant to teach a 'science' course for
non-scientists, a request which a graduate student at the beginning of
an academic career could hardly refuse. In fact, what might have been a
chore for many of his physics colleagues was a challenge to Kuhn, and
his reputation has been fashioned largely from his response to it. His
starting point was physics, his own subject, and its ancestor, mechanics.
But the inaccessibility of post-Newtonian physics and of the Newtonian
revolution forced him back in history to find examples of scientific
progress that could be understood by non-science students at Harvard.
He chose the period of Copernicus and Galileo, when ancient and
mediaeval conceptions of the universe were overturned. To have
moved still further back in history would have been to run into another
form of incomprehensibility, as Kuhn himself had discovered some
years earlier when he had tried to read Aristotle's *Physics*. He later
recalled: 'I couldn't understand any of it. But then I realized I was
judging it by today's paradigm. By the standards of its history it was
very good physics.' This form of incomprehensibility was later to
surface in Kuhn's mature work as 'incommensurability'.

Already Kuhn was assembling many of the key elements out of
which he would construct his own theories about scientific development – the idea that scientific ideas are produced, and therefore
constrained, by the communities in and through which they are
expressed; the insight that for long periods scientific progress is quietly
cumulative, punctuated by brief periods of revolutionary change; a
scepticism about claims that the development of science is linear and
instead of a growing belief that there are no valid terms in which
successive paradigms – Aristotelian, Newtonian, Einsteinian – can be
compared and ranked into a great chain of progress. All these elements

can be traced back to Kuhn's Harvard years, which culminated in his first book, *The Copernican Revolution* (although it was only published after he had moved to the University of California at Berkeley). This book, as its subtitle 'Planetary Astronomy in the Development of Western Thought' suggests, was far more than a straightforward historical account of how the theories of Copernicus, Kepler, Brahe and Galileo overturned the Aristotelian worldview that had dominated perceptions of the physical universe for almost two thousand years. It was an excavation of the intellectual culture in which these scientific theories were nurtured. Implicit in its argument were many of the ideas which, when more theoretically presented in *The Structure of Scientific Revolutions* five years later, were to enthrall and annoy philosophers of science.

This second book, upon which Kuhn's worldwide reputation depends, has acquired a life of its own that had tended to push the particular intention of its author into the background. It has become a meta-text. But the text and pre-text remain deeply significant in any attempt to understand Kuhn's ideas. *The Structure of Scientific Revolutions* was published when Kuhn was at Berkeley, after he had spent an important year at the Center for Advanced Studies in nearby Palo Alto. It was the product of his Californian years. But the book had deeper roots stretching back to the east. Indeed, the ideas which the book later made famous were given their first public airing as eight lectures on 'The Quest for Physical Theory', given at the Lowell Institute in Boston in 1951. Among their sources were Piaget on child development, Whorf on language, Quine on analytical philosophy and, most directly, a 1935 monograph by Ludwick Fleck which foreshadowed much of Kuhn's later scheme of scientific development. It was out of these eclectic sources that the book was created.

The Structure of Scientific Revolutions contained an unsettling message for scientists. It suggested that their traditional view of the development of science, as a heroic and linear process, was a myth. It also challenged the analytical preoccupations of contemporary philosophy, and confronted the most cherished beliefs of the Popperians who still dominated the philosophy of science. Kuhn's alternative was simple – perhaps too simple, because it could so easily be only half-understood. He argued that scientific development was divided into two phases – long periods of what he called 'normal science', step-by-step advances within a reigning 'paradigm', and much shorter periods of revolutionary change when that 'paradigm' had decayed and rivals were fighting to take its place. In physics, Newton and Einstein were the obvious examples. Kuhn suggested that the legitimacy of a particular 'paradigm' was decided not by objective scientific norms but by its acceptability to the prevailing scientific community. He suggested therefore that 'paradigms' were largely self-justifying and so 'incommensurable', in plainer language, irreconcilable, one to the other.

The debate that followed the publication of *The Structure of Scientific Revolutions* concentrated on three elements in Kuhn's scheme. The first was the elusiveness of the term 'paradigm'. One critic, Margaret Masterman, claimed to count twenty-one different uses. In a 1969 postscript Kuhn recognised some of the force of this criticism. He admitted that he used 'paradigm' in two main senses: as a collection of the ideas, beliefs and assumptions of a scientific community – its worldview perhaps; and as 'puzzle-solutions', outstanding models of intellectual success that could substitute for explicit rules. It is 'paradigm' in this second sense that is crucial to Kuhn's philosophy of science, but the first interpretation has enjoyed greater popular currency. The second element was the definition of the scientific community that validated the 'paradigm'. The popular Kuhn, the man for all citations, stressed the breadth of this community. The precise Kuhn, the man himself, has always interpreted this community as a small, tightly-knit group of specialists. The third element was Kuhn's concept of 'incommensurability', which led to the charge of relativism being levelled against him. Kuhn has always denied this relativism, but in his postscript he still insisted: 'Debates about theory-choice cannot be cast in a form that fully resembles logical or mathematical proof.' Kuhn's intention was to break the naive teleological belief in a great chain of progress to which many scientists remained committed.

The fiercest critics of Kuhn have been the followers of Popper. Many saw Imre Lakatos, the Hungarian philosopher who fled after the 1956 rising and died in London in 1974, as a formidable rival. Lakatos used Kuhnian material to come up with Popperian answers. At first sight, the argument between Kuhn and Popper is hard to appreciate. Both were inspired by scientific revolutions of similar intensity, Copernicus's and Einstein's, to conclude that rival theories compete for supremacy in an almost Darwinian struggle. But the differences ran very deep. Popper's was a permanent revolution compatible with progressive science. Kuhn's was an occasional revolution separated by long periods of tradition-bound continuity. Moreover, his idea of 'incommensurability' made it difficult to conclude, as Popper did, that one theory is superior to another. But the greatest difference was more fundamental still. The Popperians suspected that Kuhn with his 'puzzle-solutions' was sneaking induction in through the back door and so challenging falsification as the Holy Grail of progressive science. He seemed to be asking 'What is right?' about a theory. For Popper the only legitimate question was 'What is wrong?'.

Kuhn's most uncritical admirers have been in social science and the arts. This popularity puzzled him. *The Structure of Scientific Revolutions* was intended to introduce into the physical sciences, still committed to the heroic myth of progressive science, the concept of periodisation, continuity interrupted by radical breaks that was routine in non-science subjects and also familiar to the biological sciences. He came to believe that the thoughtless translation of his ideas back into social science had been disastrous. But the worldwide Kuhn phenomenon depends heavily on the investment social scientists have made in his ideas, although many of the problems which Kuhn's philosophical scheme has encountered – the elusiveness of 'paradigms', the indeterminacy of scientific communities and the meaning of 'incommensurability' – have been exacerbated by their wholesale incorporation into the language of social science.

Kuhn had moved back east to Princeton in the 1960s and later to MIT. In the 1970s he put philosophy on one side, to the extent that the worldwide fallout of praise and criticism following the publication of *The Structure of Scientific Revolutions* allowed. He went back to the history of science and wrote two books on the development of quantum physics and published a collection of essays on scientific tradition and change. The reason for this retreat to history was simple. 'Writing philosophy is like walking around a stage set opening a series of blank doors, in the hope of finding something interesting behind them. It's not like history where reading the original sources suggests a shape and structure', he explained. But after a decade of opening blank doors and finding nothing interesting, and occupying himself with history instead, Kuhn returned to philosophy. He went back to the loose ends left dangling in *The Structure of Scientific Revolutions* and began to untie and retie them, in particular puzzle-solving and puzzle-solutions, which are so central to his scheme and the importance of which was so often underlined in the book's critical reception.

Kuhn's ideas have spread out across all disciplines and seeped into the broader culture of our age. Within his own and adjacent disciplines his philosophy has been established as a powerful paradigm. But the popularisation of his ideas is equally significant. They and he have matched our times. Popper, born in 1902, became the philosopher of science's last heroic age, before its progressive beneficence had been called into serious doubt. Kuhn, a generation younger, grew to maturity in the shadow of the atomic age. Maybe he has become science's court philosopher in its late twentieth-century ambivalence.

4
LINKS AND LIMITS

In the last two chapters knowledge and culture respectively have been discussed. In the present chapter an attempt will be made to link them both to education, and in particular to the modern university. This has always been a complicated and problematic relationship, one difficult to describe in precise terms but immensely evocative in the context of both nation building and the growth of western civilisation. So it is a link that is central to the theme of this book. 'Knowledge', of course, is a broad and diffuse category, even if the philosophical and procedural arguments about its proper definition are left on one side. It ranges from the so-called exact sciences and associated technologies to those branches of knowledge rooted in particular social and human environments. 'Culture', too, is difficult to define. It ranges from the aesthetic, the 'high culture' of Rembrandt and Mozart, to the quasi-anthropological, the values and routines of individuals, families, communities, social classes, nations and even entire civilisations. Culture in a middle sense, somewhere between aesthetics and anthropology, has been explored in the last chapter.

Despite these difficulties it is at the intersection between knowledge and culture that our modern consciousness has been formed. Our civilisation is the product of the tension, and balance, between reason and tradition, logic and belief – what must be argued and what is assumed. And this intersection is most powerfully felt in education. The university in particular has been a crucial intermediary between knowledge and culture and therefore a key institution in the making of the modern world. But it is hardly a simple institution with fixed goals, constant over the centuries. Modern universities with their spreading campuses, their great libraries, their sophisticated laboratories, their tens of thousands of students, their diverse (even centrifugal) missions are very different from the universities of the preindustrial world.[1] Also the university has always been an ambivalent institution. On the one hand it is a radical agent, the disturber of settled patterns of thought, the channel through which new ideas and techniques flow into the economy, society and culture. On the other, it is the upholder of hierarchy, partly because it is designed to reproduce as well as to modernise the established social order and partly because it embodies in its own intellectual and professional structures prevailing academic orthodoxies.

In the twentieth century an important shift seems to have taken place in the role of the university. It has become a much more powerful scientific institution but a less significant cultural agent. As modern society races towards a postindustrial future, when knowledge itself will be a primary resource, the first change naturally has received more attention than the second. In many fields the modern university is a near-monopoly producer of new knowledge. It is now the source of most scientific discoveries and plays an increasingly important part in technology transfer. Nor is its power purely a technocratic phenomenon. Ideologies are coined and intellectual fashions set within higher education which deeply influence the languages of democratic politics and popular culture. Former rivals have ceased to be important. Self-taught engineers, independent scientists, free-lance intellectuals, literary coteries, so influential in the eighteenth, nineteenth and early twentieth centuries have now become anachronistic. Under modern conditions, very little serious and sustained intellectual work can be done outside higher education.

However, despite these remarkable gains in scientific power, the modern university has lost cultural influence. It may provide the modern world with nearly all its science and much of its technology. It may coin the ideologies and set the intellectuals fashions that provide the patois of political debate. But the university no longer seems able to influence the cultural agenda in a wider sense. It now has to accept a context, or contexts, set by other forces, principally those of politics and the marketplace. One reason for the university's loss of cultural grip is its peculiar social situation. As semi-aristocratic institution, which it still is even in its most extended post-1960s form, or at any rate an institution imbued by notions of authority and discrimination, the university must operate within a mass society uneasy with such notions. In modern democracies there is an inevitable tension between the most and the best. Another reason is that the university's own traditions have been undermined by the postwar expansion of higher education. Today it is an open rather than closed institution. It has become too familiar to be treated with old-fashioned deference.

A third reason is that the university itself has evaded wide-ranging cultural questions. The rise of academic specialisation has made it difficult to confront fundamental issues of identity, meaning and purpose. The reductionist techniques of modern science, so effective within particular disciplines, are a barrier to such general inquiries. The university has become a prisoner of its own strict notions of expertise. A fourth reason is the cultural incoherence of modern society. Social standardisation and economic integration have been accompanied by a process of cultural disintegration, the decay of 'civil society'. Individualism, secularism, materialism, technology – despite their benefits such forces have made it more difficult to sustain a common culture, except at the mean level of mass consumption.

The university is both an ancient and a modern institution – ancient in the sense that today's universities can trace their first beginnings back to the universities of the high middle ages; modern in the sense that it was only in the twentieth, and perhaps late nineteenth, century that the university took on a recognizable form. But it is the modernity, not the antiquity, of the university that will be emphasised here. Four out of five universities in Europe, their ancient heartland, and an even higher proportion elsewhere were founded in the present century. Many of these were established after 1945. Most universities therefore are very recent institutions. They belong to a future-oriented present not a tradition-encrusted past. Even those universities which were founded in the preindustrial age have been transformed in our present times. The history of the modern university only began about a hundred years ago. The long centuries before, from Abelard's Paris to Humboldt's Berlin, were simply its prehistory.

But that prehistory must be briefly examined in discussing the relationship between knowledge, culture and the university. All three were simpler then, knowledge less complicated in its arrangement, culture more stable in its pattern and the university more coherent in its purpose and, of course, much smaller in scale. So their relationship may be less difficult to grasp. Just as by examining a primitive organism or a simple system it may be possible to derive principles that can be applied to the description of sophisticated organisms and complex systems, so it may be possible to discover something about the present relationships between knowledge, culture and the university by examining how they were connected in an earlier and simpler age.

In the long history of the university there have been three peaks of achievement, three periods when development was especially dynamic. The first, of course, was the high middle ages when the university first took on a recognisable institutional form distinct from the court and monastic schools that flourished in earlier centuries. This was when our oldest universities were founded – Bologna, Paris, Oxford.[2] The second period was the sixteenth and seventeenth centuries, the age of the Renaissance and Reformation when the intellectual, religious and political geography of Europe was transformed and when Europe first reached out to grasp a wider world beyond the oceans. During this period very many universities were established. The third period was that of the industrial revolution when the characteristic phenomena of the modern world – an urban society, a global economy, a mass culture, a secular civilisation – were first felt. This third period of university development has continued until the present.[3]

Of course, these peaks should not be overemphasised. Many

universities were established between 1400 and 1550, in the trough between the first two peaks. Awakening dynastic ambition was often the motive for their creation. Similarly, the period from 1660 to 1800 cannot be dismissed as a time of university stagnation, even though there were few new foundations except on the fringes of Europe and, in some institutions, the number of students declined. To take the example of Britain, it is hard to dismiss the Cambridge of Isaac Newton, the Edinburgh of David Hume or the Glasgow of Adam Smith as slumbering or moribund institutions.[4] It was at this time, and by such people, that the scientific and philosophical foundations of nineteenth-century industrial civilisation were laid. So the periodisation of university history is a speculative game.

At each of these peaks three ingredients seem to have come together to stimulate university development. The first was the discovery of new knowledge. In the high middle ages it was Aristotelian thought, transmitted through the Muslim world; in the sixteenth and seventeenth centuries, the revival of classical learning and the turmoil of religious controversy; in the nineteenth and twentieth, the irresistible force of modern science. The second ingredient was a cultural uncertainty that undermined old patterns of custom and belief. In the high middle ages heresy, urbanism, mercantilism and nationalism first stirred. In early modern Europe, mediaeval mentalities were destroyed. New ideas subverted the established order. The European world exploded outwards. The result was an age of anxiety, as well as of achievement. In the nineteenth and twentieth centuries the decay of religion, the spread of radical theories of society, the rise of individualism and similar movements destroyed the mental universe of the *ancien régime*.

The third ingredient was rapid socio-economic change. In the high middle ages the feudal state with its virtually cashless economy was being replaced by the nation state in which royal authority was exercised through bureaucratic government, and new patterns of trading and taxation reflected the growing sophistication of the economy. During the Renaissance and Reformation land and wealth, and so authority, changed hands on an immense scale. New elites were established. The state and the economy became increasingly elaborate. In industrial Europe, of course, social and economic relations were transformed.

And so on each occasion new knowledge, cultural disarray and socio-economic change were the forces that powered university development. But their relative influence was not constant. At the first peak in the middle ages new knowledge, or rather, intellectual techniques in the form of Aristotelianism, were perhaps the most significant, although the growing demand for clerical bureaucrats cannot be discounted. In the sixteenth and seventeenth centuries, particularly in Protestant Europe, cultural change was the most powerful influence. Universities were key institutions in socialising, perhaps synthesising, the new elites. But they also expanded to meet the demand for ministers, lawyers and other pre-industrial 'experts'. And the impact of new, or rediscovered, knowledge upon the university cannot be ignored.[5] At the third peak, socio-economic change was probably the decisive force. Despite the spectacular progress of science and the deep cultural anxiety of the modern world, the most powerful influences on the university were, in the nineteenth century, the demand for administrative, professional and scientific manpower and, in our present century, the democratic drive to expand educational opportunities.[6]

So no clear conclusions can be drawn about the respective weight attached to intellectual, cultural and socio-economic influences in shaping the university. No consistent pattern can be discerned in its long history. But it does seem clear that, unless backed by powerful cultural and socio-economic forces, intellectual change is not enough to transform the university. The potential for scientific advance is always there. It is change in our culture, society and economy that releases this imprisoned energy. The physics of Isaac Newton, the philosophy of David Hume and the political economy of Adam Smith were only fully realised when social and industrial change towards the end of the eighteenth century created a new cultural environment, a new way of imagining the world. If this is true, the retreat of the modern university from the cultural arena may weaken it as an institution; scientific power, however impressive, has never been enough to allow the university to fulfill its historical mission. The university's past peaks were times when it was a formidable cultural instrument as well as a powerful scientific institution.

Contemporary society, in which the modern university is firmly embedded, is marked by a series of confusing contrasts. It is defiantly secular, but prey to an emotionalism that verges at times on primitive credulity. It is highly structured and intensively interdependent, but hostile to the idea of organised hierarchies. It is rationalist, even positivist, in its formal ethos, but informally embraces an affective individualism that sometimes strays close to an anarchic spirit. It is deeply dependent on theoretical knowledge and expert skills, but regards both with suspicion. Also, this knowledge and these skills are increasingly technical rather than normative. All these contrasts, in their different ways, affect the position of the modern university.[7]

Late twentieth-century society is secular in two senses. First, religious observance and belief have sharply declined and, second, churches and other moral institutions have little influence over public policy. Liberal laws on matters such as divorce and abortion have been the result. Yet many people resist secular values. 'Born again' revivalist movements within regular churches and fringe religions are growing, while the popularity of horoscopes, astrology and other sub-religious phenomena suggest that credulity is still widespread. Magic is not dead in modern society. The university, as a secular and sceptical institution, is not able to respond well to such feelings, except as a scientific observer analysing them from the outside. Ideology does not fill the gap. It is far too abstract and cerebral, a poor substitute for religion outside the ranks of the intelligentsia. Philosophy has retreated from moral questions on the grounds that they are unscientific. Science has long ago abandoned its theological roots. Metaphysics are out of fashion.

Modern society, of course, is highly organised. Its structures are elaborate; its systems sophisticated. The democratic state is much more powerful than its apparently more authoritarian predecessors. Its potential for social control is much greater. But democratic society rests on the assumption that all citizens have equal rights. And equal rights lead to a demand for equal opportunities, which in turn lead to a desire for equal outcomes. Egalitarianism, whether pursued through politics or the market, is a deeply-rooted idea in modern society. So its hierarchies must be unobtrusive and provisional. Deep within its elaborate structures there lurks a levelling principle. Again the modern university finds it difficult to take a balanced view. It is an elaborately-structured organisation, now more managerial than collegial in its ethos.[8] It is committed to hierarchy, inevitably so in the academic sphere and probably so in the political sphere. So the university is badly placed to appreciate the levelling impulses in modern society.

That society is also organised according to apparently rational principles. This is what distinguishes it from the *ancien régime*. Although the naive vision of a positivist society, of a self-adjusting utilitarianism, popular in the nineteenth century, has faded, it is still assumed that social arrangements must be designed, or redesigned, to serve the best interests of the people. They have no pre-existing authority. The prevailing view of society, therefore, is mechanistic and pragmatic rather than organic and moral. But the rationality of modern society is not complete. The objective determination of the public interest according to logical principles is impossible because opinion in a democratic society is subjective, diverse and volatile. In a similar way the organised structures of the free-market economy, large enterprises committed to strategic planning, are apparently undermined by the chaos of short-term consumer choice. These tensions cannot be dismissed as accidental and therefore avoidable mismatches. They are inherent in both democratic politics and free-market economics. We are expected to be both sober citizens and impulsive voters, disciplined producers and frivolous consumers.[9] The university, as an institution dedicated to reason, finds it difficult to come to terms with the irrationality of modern society.

But the fourth tension, between society's growing dependence on technical knowledge and its distrust of normative knowledge, is perhaps the most significant in the context of links between knowledge, culture and the university. One aspect of this tension is that technology has mystified everyday objects. Televisions and videotape recorders are sternly labelled 'no user serviceable parts'. Prepared foods are bought in supermarkets, rather than fresh food in markets. This alienation has contributed to the powerful 'green' movements so prominent in most advanced nations. In modern society, science and technology are admired and wondered at, but also feared and even resented. The second aspect concerns the nature of postindustrial society. This is assumed also to be a knowledge society, and so one which will place increased value on higher education. But much of this 'knowledge' will be information not ideas, data not *logos*. In postindustrial society the key activity will be the technical manipulation of mass data. Although the discovery of new knowledge and the reinterpretation of old ideas will also become more important, the main thrust towards the creation of a knowledge society may take place in business, industry and public administration as much in the university.

This so-called fourth industrial revolution is powered by information technology, just as the third in the mid-twentieth century was by mass consumer production, the second in the later nineteenth century by iron, steel and coal, and the first, before 1850 by the mechanisation of traditional industries such as textiles. It will present as great a challenge to higher education as any, or all, of these. Although postindustrial society will encourage standardisation, and so social and economic integration, it will also encourage decentralisation, the formation of small enterprises with the technical resources once available only to large ones. The modern university, in contrast, has increasingly taken the form of the large-scale national or international corporation, a form that may now be obsolescent. In the postindustrial society, knowledge will also become highly volatile. Data will be discarded, processes made redundant and machines rendered obsolete at an accelerating rate. But the university is a stable structure that cannot easily write off decades of investment in people and plant or abandon the elaborate arrangement of disciplines in teaching and research. Third, postindustrial society will inevitably be eclectic and pragmatic. Its ideas and concepts will be tools, like computer programs, not moral statements. Old demarcations between theory and practice, pure and applied research, education and training will seem less valid. Although the reductionist techniques of many disciplines will be reinforced, the synoptic and summative ambitions of the university may be further discouraged. The idea of a canon, cultural or scientific, will become an anachronism.

The university has evolved a complexity to match that of modern society. In the 1950s and 1960s higher education expanded rapidly to meet the growing demand for student places generated by the expansion of secondary schools. In the process it became closely associated with the spirit of this postwar age – liberal, reformist, pragmatic, egalitarian. This was a time when social action, collective solutions and state provision were much favoured, a period that saw the culmination of the reforms in education, health and social security begun in the nineteenth century. The welfare state was more than a set of institutional arrangements. It was a moral model, a social ideal. And the postwar university was intimately linked to the welfare state. In the 1970s and 1980s universities continued to expand. But the ethos changed. The emphasis switched from satisfying social aspirations to contributing to economic efficiency. As that strong postwar sense of economic well-being wore off, the welfare state was succeeded by the enterprise state. The focus of public policy shifted from the distribution of wealth to wealth creation. Within higher education the new priorities were to meet skill shortages, to offer industrially-relevant courses, to promote technology transfer and to foster entrepreneurial attitudes among students. Business administration and information technology became the growth areas overshadowing the traditional arts and sciences.

The pattern of the 1990s may be different again. First, the gathering force of the fourth industrial revolution will help to restore the influence and prestige lost by higher education in the last two decades. Then, the university was stigmatized as an ivory tower, disdainful of wealth creation. This critique was unfair, of course, but it was widely believed. So there was pressure on the university to move closer to the world of industry. In the next decade it may be the other way round. Industry may have to move closer to the world of the university if it is to keep pace with the knowledge revolution. Under postindustrial conditions the latter will possess key resources, theoretical and practical, that are needed for economic success. Second, the link between the university and the advance of democracy, so strong in the 1950s and 1960s but less emphasised since, may again become prominent. Modern society has never ceased to be social-democratic in ethos. But the move towards a decentralised high-technology economy will underline the need for participatory rather than hierarchical management styles. As the big corporations crumble, democracy will invade the workplace.

The modern university has four main roles – as a finishing school, the last stage of general education; as a professional school that trains elite workers; as a knowledge factory that produces science, technology and ideology; and as a cultural institution that through its critical awareness expresses our sense of being, as individuals, nations or entire civilisations. Each of these roles will change as higher education moves through the 1990s.

The university's first role, as a finishing school, will become much more complicated. On the one hand, higher education will enroll an ever-increasing proportion of young people. Social ambition, academic sophistication and economic necessity will mean that, for a growing minority in the 1990s and for a majority in the next century, a secondary education will no longer be sufficient. So the massification of the university, already well advanced, will intensify. Of course, it can be argued that the university will only be reclaiming the more popular role it had before the elaboration of secondary education in the late nineteenth and early twentieth centuries. Then students were much younger, recruited directly from local schools and arguably less privileged. It was the growth of separate secondary schools that made the university, initially at any rate, a more remote institution. In the long run, of course, universal secondary education has led back to mass higher education.

On the other hand, the links between universities and secondary schools will loosen. There will be more mature students and more part-time courses; up-dating and retraining will become more prominent in higher education. It will no longer be possible to regard the university simply as a final stage of education. Instead it will have to be seen as part of the wider world of continuing education, *éducation permanente*. In a postindustrial society, as skills constantly change and knowledge becomes highly volatile, education will need to be a lifelong process. It will no longer be able to be concentrated into the years of adolescence and early adulthood. But these trends, towards mass enrolment of secondary school leavers and towards continuing lifelong education, are not in conflict. The former is an essential precondition of the latter.

The modern university's second role, as a professional school, will change in similar ways. Two influences will be important here. The first is the inexorable spread of credentialisation. Like mass enrolment, this is the continuation of an already well-established trend. The demand for bigger and better credentials, backed by the university's prestige, has many sources. The drive for higher social esteem, the elaboration of professions, the advance of technology, the equality of opportunities (particularly significant areas like teaching and nursing) – these are among the more important. Lawyers, doctors and priests, the university's original professional groups, have been joined by engineers, teachers, social workers, nurses and many others. Through business schools, managers too are being semi-credentialised. Who will be next? For the spread of credentialisation will not cease.

The second influence is the changing character of professional society.[10] Once the focus of the university's effort was on pre-industrial professions – the lawyers, doctors and clergy. Then it gradually shifted towards technical professions, principally engineering. In the postwar university the emphasis was on professions that grew up around the welfare state, so teachers and social workers became important. More recently it moved again to meet the needs of corporate business. In one sense this is an incremental process. Legal education is still as significant today as it was in the university's earliest days. New layers of professional training have simply been added to the old. So the changing character of professional society can be explained partly in terms of the spread of credentialisation. But not entirely. Today the tone is set by the 'enterprise' professions, not the 'welfare' ones. These are more individual than social, more entrepreneurial than bureaucratic, more practical than intellectual. This is reflected in the university's own priorities. In contrast, the professions that will dominate the 1990s are likely to be different again – postindustrial professions as different from today's 'enterprise' professions as the latter are from the mid-century 'welfare' professions.

The third role of the university is as a science factory, a producer of new knowledge. In the recent past its prestige has flowed from its scientific achievements. Research, particularly in the natural sciences, has become a key element in the modern university, almost its axial principle. Its institutional organisation and disciplinary structure reflect this hegemony of the natural sciences. The social and human sciences have been forced to mimic these habits or risk losing academic (and political) prestige. However, the university's science-factory role has been undermined in the 1980s and may be further compromised in the 1990s. In the past decade heavy emphasis has been placed on the applicability of science and on technology transfer. As a result pure science has been starved of resources. The university has been bullied into adopting semi-industrial priorities that may have weakened its scientific base. Although this shift from pure to applied science has been enthusiastically encouraged by governments, major industrial companies have viewed it with scepticism. They look to universities for primary research, not secondary development. But, because of budget cuts, many universities have been forced to overemphasise the latter because it brings in profitable income.

In the 1990s higher education may face a different problem. The elaborate, and expensive, infrastructure of scientific research makes it difficult for disciplines to change course quickly. The positivist ethos of modern science discourages those leaps of intellectual imagination, often made sideways, that lead to exciting new discoveries. 'Normal science', to adopt the language of Kuhn, is a linear and incremental business. Yet the fourth industrial revolution is likely to demand much greater academic flexibility. The university as science factory may need to be reorganised, even decentralised. The orthodoxy of the natural science tradition may have to be broken up. Other, more oblique and tentative, intellectual traditions may be better able to stimulate the lateral thinking that will be so badly needed in the knowledge society.

The modern university's final role is as a cultural institution. In this regard, the university has tended to atrophy for reasons briefly discussed earlier in this chapter. But the university's deficiency here is in the sum, not in its parts. Modern higher education is full of impulses, academic and aesthetic, that contribute powerfully to our sense of cultural being. What is missing is any sense of their connectedness. The failure may be more of imagination than of intellect. There are three levels at which the university is a significant cultural institution. First, through its critical standards, it celebrates, defines and refines 'high culture'. Of course the magnificence and meaning of that culture may be undermined by myopic academic specialisation or by destructive, or deconstructive, theory. But in modern society universities are almost alone in having sufficent intellectual room to reflect systematically on that 'high culture'. Second, as has already been suggested, the university is the source of the ideologies and intellectual fashions that provide the language of public affairs. The university is where the books get written which shape our political culture, and even our private lives. Universities are the source of the 'experts' that appear on television and write in newspapers. Yet the university as an institution often seems to stand outside these debates. It does not 'place' itself in the context of our wider society and culture. Third, higher education is an intensely human experience. For many young, and older, people, especially cadet members of national elites, their time at university is a formative period of often poignant influence. It is where they grow up, intellectually, socially and personally. It is remembered with a vivid intensity. But the connection between these three levels – 'high culture', the language of public affairs, and personal experience – is loose and unexpressed.

Two main strategies have been adopted by modern nations to cope with the complexity of today's higher education. The first, and less popular, is to establish comprehensive institutions that attempt to fulfill all four main roles. The second, more often chosen, is to encourage the stratification of higher education so that different institutions concentrate on particular roles. Sometimes this stratification has been determined by history. In France, the *grandes écoles* were established as higher professional schools in the nineteenth century when the universities had fallen apart into their constituent faculties. At other times this stratification has been the outcome of deliberate policy, as in the case of the Californian master-plan of 1960 which divided the state's higher education into three segments, the University of California, California State University and the community colleges. At other times again, stratification has been produced partly by history and partly by policy. The British 'binary policy' for example, perhaps gave added force to the distinction between the two traditions in British higher education, one based on the universities and the other rooted in technical education. Of course particular strategies or combinations cannot be prescribed.

There is no right way to manage the complexity of modern higher education systems. But two points deserve to be emphasised. First, despite their stratification, most systems contain within the profound urges to unity, to commonality. Second, the choice of strategies cannot be regarded solely as a political question, a matter of administrative convenience. Bound up in it are important cultural responsibilities, and possibilities.

The view can be taken that human history is a contest between transcendence, imagining things as they could be, and givenness, accepting things as they are. Perhaps this contest can be described in Kuhnian terms as a tension between paradigm shifts and the progress of 'normal' science. Past civilisations waxed as the potential for transcendence gained strength, the act of conceiving other and better futures making possible the reconstruction of social institutions. They waned as the giveness of things reasserted its grip, the re-emphasised routines of everyday life imposing a renewed immobility upon society. But our present civilisation may be an exception. For part of the givenness of the modern world is its urge to imagine others – in science, culture, politics. In the twentieth century, transcendence has become an essential component of the givenness of things, however paradoxical that sounds. The two are no longer opposed. Our contemporary civilisation thrives on change, not out of a restless ennui but because imagining a better future is at the root of modern consciousness.

It is tempting to align 'knowledge' with transcendence and 'culture' with givenness. But these alignments are not exact. Many branches of knowledge are rooted in things as they are; their capacity to transcend is purely technical. Engineering and business studies are examples. Some forms of culture, on the other hand, are organised attempts to imagine things as they could be; they deliberately reject the givenness of the world. Even in a broad quasi-anthropological sense, culture is not a prisoner of the present. There are many examples of secular routines and popular habits that consciously aspired to transcend things as they are, to dematerialise reality in the cause of its larger meaning, to see what seems given in the sum of the things that seem possible.

The modern university is inevitably caught up in these crosscurrents of transcendence and givenness. Indeed, it is a crucial intermediary between them, as it is between knowledge and culture. As a social and economic institution, the university is rooted in everyday life, meeting demands for new knowledge, improved techniques and professional skills, and satisfying the desires of individuals for enlightenment and self-improvement. But as an intellectual and cultural institution the university is future-oriented and other-directed. It looks beyond the horizon of what is presently known and believed. Its role is to imagine other worlds, whether material in the case of nuclear physics or moral in that of English literature. The university has to operate at the edge of givenness.

The university's capacity for transcendence is expressed in four ways. First, higher education transforms the lives of individual students. It offers, or should offer, not only professional training to secure higher socio-economic status but new ways of thinking and feeling about the world, and themselves. A university education, at its best, is more an enfranchising than an enabling process. Perhaps there can be no enabling without enfranchisement. The university draws students out of the givenness of their families, their classes, even their nations. It opens doors to new worlds. It excites their imagination of better futures.

Second, mass access has transformed the social situation of the university. Higher education is no longer an exclusive and inward operation, designed gently to modernise elites and produce high-grade experts. In advanced countries higher education is now a common, even routine, experience. It has ceased to be a privilege and is verging on becoming a right. But mass access is not the result principally of a 'pull' from above, of an official desire to widen old elites and keep pace with the demand for experts. If that is all it had amounted to, the expansion of higher education would have been little more than a liberal extension of its given role. But in modern democracies elites have become diffuse, and in postindustrial society expertise has become volatile. The primary cause of expansion has been the 'push' from below, from ordinary people seeking an enfranchisement only loosely coupled with socio-economic advantage. It is this that has led to the rewriting of higher education's social situation.

Third, the university transcends the givenness of things through its science. It has transformed our understanding of the material world, exposing old beliefs as baseless and explaining phenomena that once seemed beyond our mental reach. In the nineteenth century, advances in biology and zoology undermined the certainties of received religion. In the present century, Einsteinian physics have qualified apparently solid and commonplace notions of time and space. Nor have these changes been confined to the intellectual world. Through technology they have invaded the social world. New products and processes have revolutionised the structure of the economy. Telecommunications have transformed business and leisure. Relations between the sexes, and maybe the whole pattern of family life, have been changed by consumer goods and contraception. The old balance (and respect?) between generations has been upset by medical advances. The secrets of human reproduction are close to being unlocked by genetic engineering.

Indeed, such is the place of technological change that it has become an anachronism to talk of the givenness of things. The capacity to transcend is inherent in modern science, and so in the modern university. But the restless search for new and better technical explanations is not the same as the fundamental questioning of the intellectual structures within which these explanations are pursued. These paradigms are more durable phenomena. Aristotelian and Newtonian physics were, and modern physics are, more than coherent summaries of the current state of scientific knowledge. They were, and are, delicate combinations of belief and proof, metaphors of culture as well as science. It is not clear that the modern university can bring the same sceptical force to bear on these grand theories as it can on particular technical problems. The reductionist techniques and positivist values to which it is attached discourage the adventurism and iconoclasm that are needed to imagine new worlds.

Yet this is the fourth and most fundamental expression of the university's ability to transcend the givenness of things. It is the only institution that now has the capacity, if not always the courage, to invent and reinvent these powerful paradigms, these metatheories. And it is these paradigms – in history and economics as much as, or more than, in physics – that embody the representations of reality by which we have to live. It is not enough to provide the setting in which individual students can imagine a better future for themselves, in which they can experience enfranchisement from a personal givenness. It is not enough to break the social limits of the old higher education bound up in the narrow need of elites and experts, however extended or diffuse. It is not enough to transform through science and technology the socio-economic order. Unless the university is also able to express wider cultural transcendences, to possess the right to remake the moral as well as the material worlds, these subsidiary projects will falter. Individual students will be discouraged by the gap between things that are and the better things they have glimpsed. Mass access will be frustrated by arguments that society and the economy need fixed numbers of relevantly trained graduates, not undetermined numbers of critically educated citizens. Even scientific advance will be slowed if pragmatical experts whose intellectual horizons are governed by present limits curb future visions of what could be.

Only a university that is free and philosophical can fulfill its modern mission. It must be free in the sense that it is not too tightly constrained by the givenness of the present – and many universities are too tightly constrained today. It must be philosophical in the sense that it has the intellectual (and moral) resources to reorder things as they are so that experience is not as given but as willing, and so open to change. To many this will seem a naïve, even reactionary, claim – a reversion to elitism, a retreat from social and economic responsibilities, an attempt by the university to reinsulate itself from the practical world. To others it will seem a presumptuous, even aristocratic claim, an attempt to subvert democratic choices and to second-guess the market. In fact it is a simple endorsement of the university's central place in the world. That world, our world, tries ceaselessly to extend the frontiers of the knowable and the valuable, to transcend the givenness of things, to imagine a new and better world – whether as a scientific civilisation or a New Jerusalem. The university is simply its voice – but a voice that cannot be stilled without hazarding the whole modern project.

5

HIGHER HOPES

Plus ça change, plus c'est la même chose – Alphonse Karr's cynical aphorism of 1849 can well be applied to the experience of higher education in Britain since 1960. In one perspective, perhaps the dominant one, there has been a revolution. The old order has been overthrown. In another, little has changed. The values and hierarchies of the academic system remain not only unshaken but unchallenged. On the one hand, a three-fold increase in student numbers; on the other, an instinctive but stubborn and peculiarly British determination to maintain a proper distinction between 'higher' and other forms of postsecondary education. The development of a diverse array of institutions, the proliferation of new universities, polytechnics, colleges and institutes of higher education *and* the elaboration of a national system of higher education under the stricter supervision of the state. The growth of a powerful rival force led by the polytechnics and based on further education's 'open door' tradition, which challenges the inherited predominance of the universities, *and* the rigid maintenance of a divisive binary policy which sustains that predominance by discriminatory patterns of funding and administrative procedures.

This list of apparent paradoxes can be extended. The prosperity of the 1960s was succeeded by the austerity of the 1970s and 1980s. Global inflation, which rapidly eroded the purchasing power of higher education budgets, was the main culprit during the years of Labour rule. But after 1979 across-the-board cuts in public expenditure ordered by the new Conservative Government were the principal (but not sole) cause of the difficulties faced by the academic system. Yet there remains much argument about how these difficulties have been resolved. The dominant view within the system, especially in universities, is that these budget cuts have led to diseconomy and even chaos.[1] Financial insecurity has discouraged coherent planning. Academic priorities have been disrupted by short-term expediency. Valuable teachers and researchers have left, either because they have found non-academic professions or transatlantic posts more attractive or because they have been encouraged by their institutions to leave in order to balance the books. Yet a contrary view is that these budget cuts have benefitted higher education, at any rate in the long term. The system has been shaken out of its old autonomist ivory-tower ways which discouraged it from playing a fuller part in the social and economic life of the nation. It has been forced to act in a more entrepreneurial fashion, which has made it less of an elite dependency of an arms-length state. Universities have become leaner and tougher, with clearer priorities and crisper management. Polytechnics and colleges have become more cost-effective and also more self-confident. According to this second view, the budget cuts of the 1980s have been the leading edge of a higher education revolution that has not only overturned out-of-date practices but also assaulted the anachronistic aristocratic mentality that, despite the postwar expansion of the system, still endured.[2]

No satisfactory answer is available to the most important question of all. Is British higher education in the last years of the twentieth century a shrunken academic enterprise, its great scientific and scholarly achievements behind it? Or has its potential for intellectual excellence been enhanced by the redirection of its priorities and the reordering of its institutions? The arguments are tossed to and fro. Because of budget cuts universities have been unable to recruit able young teachers and researchers – but these same cuts have enabled them to dispose of ineffective teachers and inactive researchers. Also, in many cases the universities' loss has been the polytechnics' gain. If university posts had not been in short supply the latter would not have been able to build up such an impressive cadre of academic talent. There certainly has been crude discrimination against the arts and social sciences (and brutal political threats to sociology in particular) – but this must be set against the encouragement of science and technology, for example the Alvey programme in information technology.[3] The budgetary and political pressures on institutions to establish clearer priorities have led to the closure of departments and research units, thus, arguably, undermining their academic comprehensiveness – but not all rationalisation has had ill effects. In many cases more viable units, economically and intellectually, have been established. Similarly, the increasing expense and sophistication of scientific equipment have encouraged academic concentration, which, it can also be argued, has produced a more stimulating environment for research.

EXPANSION AND REFORM

Higher education has been the beneficiary and the victim of a long revolution which began in 1963 with the Robbins report[4] and ended, for the present, with the Education Reform Act of 1988. The report and the Act had far more in common with each other than was generally supposed. The seeds of the second were planted by the first, even if the crop grew slowly during the intervening quarter of a century. Certainly it is misleading to imagine that the Act represented a blueprint for reform and the Robbins report the 'blue remembered hills' of liberal nostalgia. Robbins assuredly was a liberal document, but one that, in a sense, has been badly understood in the 1980s. As assuredly, the report wrote the constitution for Britain's postwar higher education, and was affirmed rather than amended by the 1988 Act and the White Paper, *Higher Education: Meeting the Challenge*, which preceded it.[5]

The liberalism of the Robbins report had five main qualities. First, its prescriptions were rooted in an aristocratic rather than utilitarian view of higher education. The individual citizen, not economic man or the mass consumer, was at the centre of the Robbins inquiry. Secondly, Robbins grew out of a firmly statist tradition of public policy, a liberal corporatism which cherished a progressive state as the principal instrument both for improving the individual and for reforming society. Thirdly, Robbins belonged in a moral tradition which regarded social reform as far more than material improvement. The religion had not long gone out of this tradition. The good life was still imagined as the godly life, lightly disguised in the secular clothes of postwar prosperity; the good society was seen as much more than an expanding economy. Fourthly, the Robbins report was part of an organic tradition of public affairs. It took its place in an almost apostolic succession of social reform and educational improvement. The inevitable expansion of university education was prefigured in the growth of elementary schools in Victorian Britain and the development of secondary education after 1944. Finally, Robbins reflected the spirit of its age. A quarter of a century ago 'Butskellite' politics seemed to have been drained of all ideological passion; building a modern society at once more equal and more efficient seemed a feasible enterprise; and institutions (such as the universities) tried and tested by world war enjoyed an unchallenged prestige.

These old-fashioned liberal qualities exhibited in the Robbins report explain how that committee came to endorse, even to encourage, enlarged state sponsorship of higher education. For the liberal values which informed its members were not those of the market (the individual-against-society) or of the opposition (the individual-against-the-state). The committee's preoccupation with citizenship and a common culture echoed its instinctive loyalty to ancient Whig rhythms of public thought and to an assured civil religion. In the early 1960s the elaboration of a state system of higher education and the continuing autonomy of the institutions that made up that system did not appear to be incompatible goals. At the time of Robbins it did not yet seem incongruous to seek to extend private freedom by expanding public power. The state and the individual were still not at war. So a committee committed to a dignified liberalism was able with equanimity to advocate greatly increased state intervention in higher education.

By endorsing the demand for the expansion of higher education, a task which could only be undertaken by the state, Robbins made it impossible ever again to imagine universities and other advanced colleges as a loose collection of small, exclusive, isolated and semi-private institutions. After 1963 such a view ceased to be tenable, which explained the anger and betrayal felt by the upholders of the university *ancien régime* when the report was published.[6] With Robbins' help the decisive frontier which separated the private from the public had been crossed. Higher education was brought within the irresistible orbit of state power. The Robbins committee, of course, did more than acquiesce in this irreversible change; it approved it. Before the early 1960s few people talked of 'higher education'; still fewer thought in terms of a 'system' of higher education. The former was still essentially an administrative category, rather as 'tertiary education' is today, while the latter implied a degree of integration which few regarded as either necessary or desirable. Robbins removed both inhibitions. It wrenched the advanced colleges, both direct-grant and local authority, away from their traditional home in 'further education' and associated them with the universities in a new category, 'higher education'. It also transformed teacher training into teacher education. And it explicitly endorsed the need for a 'system' of higher education under national direction. In the process, the Robbins committee wrote the constitution of modern higher education in Britain. Anthony Crosland's binary policy two years later (which led to the creation of the polytechnics) and the 1988 Act were merely drafting amendments.[7]

In the past quarter of a century these two themes – the nationalisation of higher education, which recently has degenerated into an unfortunate politicisation, and its systemisation – have become dominant. Universities, polytechnics and colleges have come under the ever more detailed and peremptory supervision of the state and been regarded increasingly as a common system that must be managed as a whole. The 1988 Act endorsed both these themes. It abolished the University Grants Committee, that powerful symbol of the separation of universities from politics, and established instead a Universities Funding Council as a direct instrument of state power. And it removed polytechnics and colleges from the control of local education authorities and placed them under a parallel funding council. These measures greatly increased the power of the Department of Education and Science over higher education and its capacity to plan for a national system. In this respect the 1988 Act was the culmination of the Robbins process.

But, if the administrative context established by the Robbins committee had simply been elaborated by the actions of subsequent governments, up to and including the 1988 Act, the educational values esteemed by its members passed into the wind. The spirit of aristocratic liberalism, of social optimism, which animated higher education reformers a generation ago, died. Or, at any rate, it was turned out of power. So although the outcome of the 1980s reform of higher education engineered by the Conservative Party was entirely consistent with the proposals made by the Robbins committee a quarter of a century before, its intentions were utterly dissimilar. First, higher education had come to be justified in instrumental rather than liberal terms. Moreover, emphasis was placed on collective rather than individual benefit. The interests of the nation or of the economy were regarded as enjoying precedence over those of the individual student. When the interests of the latter were discussed the extrinsic and material rather than intrinsic and moral benefits of higher education were emphasised. The Green (or consultative) Paper, *The Development of Higher Education into the 1990s,* published in 1985, was widely criticised for justifying state control of and public expenditure on higher education in utilitarian terms.[8] But the White Paper which preceded the 1988 Act, although more skilfully drafted, used similar language. A high level of scholarship in the arts, humanities and social sciences was acknowledged to be 'an essential feature of a civilised and cultured country'. But even this brief nod in the direction of culture was not allowed to pass without a utilitarian gloss – 'Clearly too, undergraduate education of quality in these disciplines is valued by employers, both as a basis for professional training and in its own right.' There could be no possible doubt about the Government's overriding preoccupation. The White Paper continued:

> Above all there is an urgent need, in the interests of the nation as a whole, and therefore of universities, polytechnics and colleges themselves, for higher education to take increasing account of the economic requirement of the country. Meeting the needs of the economy is not the sole purpose of higher education; nor can higher education alone achieve what is needed. But this aim, with its implications for the scale and quality of higher education, must be vigorously pursued.[9]

A quarter of a century earlier the Robbins committee, although it always had in mind the contribution of higher education made to the economy, would never have based the case for reform on such philistine foundations. A generation ago higher education still seemed capable of speaking to the ultimate ends of human existence and identity, of enriching the culture of our nation and the civilisation of mankind.

The second difference between the current climate and that of a generation ago is that the public interest has shrunk. In the 1990s, public interest no longer embodies a consensus about national priorities much wider than the policies of a particular Government or the programme of a particular party. The mid-century consensus of the-good-and-the-great has broken apart. The Robbins committee was able to regard the increasing influence of the state over higher education with equanimity, even with enthusiasm, because it had in mind the nation state, not the party state. It still seemed to be possible to argue that higher education should serve the nation, and of course that the nation should nurture higher education, without intending to deliver the universities and other colleges into the hands of the politicians. Even a generation ago there were difficulties with this distinction. Although, by and large, politicians continued to respect this arms-length concordat between higher education and the state through the 1960s and 1970s, there were operational inconsistencies. There was pressure on mediating institutions such as the University Grants Committee and on local education authorities. To what degree was it reasonable for the UGC to resist immediate political demands, when universities had become unambiguously public institutions and ministers through Parliament represented the authority of the democratic state? If polytechnics and colleges were designed to be more socially responsive than the universities, did local authorities have the right to influence or even determine their development? And to what extent should local authorities be able to qualify or interfere with policies determined by the national state? These questions, in concrete and detailed form, were asked again and again in the twenty years following Robbins. No satisfactory answers were ever provided. More recently, any pretence that a distinction can be drawn between the nation and the state has been abandoned. In one of the Official Secrets cases so common in the 1980s a judge explicitly rejected the notion that the public interest could be distinguished from that of the Government of the day. This doctrine, together with the notion of the absolute sovereignty of Parliament, has produced a democratic centralism which would probably have dismayed the Robbins committee – and perhaps made it less ready to advocate increasing state control of higher education.

The third difference is that the moral authority of the state has been compromised, just when its political authority has been enhanced. One reason for this, of course, is that the Conservative Party, in power throughout the 1980s, is committed to 'privatisation', a programme aimed at reducing the public sector by selling nationalised industries and by reducing general dependency upon welfare mechanisms. This programme undermines the moral assumptions that sustained the growth of state power in the past. The idea that the state, as well as intervening to correct and supplement the private market, represents the cultural and moral integrity of the nation has fallen for the moment out of fashion. It has been replaced by a crude dichotomy which suggests simply that public is bad and private is good. Nothing could be more distant from the aristocratic corporatism which informed the Robbins report or the democratic enthusiasms which were such a powerful force behind the creation of the polytechnics. Instead it is suggested that higher education's dependence on the state is evidence of its moral inadequacy, a failure to satisfy its customers. This polemical suggestion is not consistent with the historical record, which demonstrates clearly that the subsidy of universities and technical education was introduced to enable these institutions to undertake work of national importance, not to allow them to luxuriate in academic indifference. But its popularity in political circles makes it difficult to ignore.

A second reason for the declining moral authority of the state is that it is seen as authoritarian. Politicians and civil servants now decide upon policies which a generation ago would have been within the discretion of individual institutions. This accretion of bureaucratic power, part deliberate and part accidental, has radically adjusted the frontier between the public and private lives of higher education. Despite, or perhaps because of, the recent enthusiasm for 'privatisation', there is little academic privacy left in higher education. Almost everything has become a political question. There is also a tension, even confusion, between 'privatisation', which is designed to set universities, polytechnics and colleges free from the detailed regulation of the state, and the determination to make higher education more accountable to its customers. For the state is higher education's most important customer (and likely to remain so, however successful institutions may be in attracting private income). First, the state provides the bulk of the income of universities and polytechnics and will always provide their 'core' funding, so it is in a powerful position to determine the priorities of institutions. Secondly, the state is the direct or indirect employer of a high proportion of graduates. The public sector has always employed more graduates and other highly-skilled workers than the private sector, because of its professional structure and the range of services it provides. Thirdly, the state is the single most important sponsor of university and polytechnic research; in certain key areas such as weapons research it is the dominant customer. The experience of all other developed countries suggests that high-technology companies and other research-intensive enterprises are exceptionally dependent on the patronage of the state.

The perception of the state as an increasingly authoritarian entity has solidified as the good-and-great consensus has crumbled. As it no longer seems to embody 'national' as well as 'party' programmes, its moral authority has been diminished. The conventions which once obliged those members of the political class opposed to a particular Government to restrain their opposition within moderate limits have lost their force. At the same time, the idea of a loyal opposition, which is as much part of the democratic state as is the Government, has been difficult to maintain in the absence of an agreed consensus about 'national' goals. The outcome has been unprecedented politicisation.

The Conservative enthusiasm for 'privatisation', paradoxically, has contributed to this politicisation. It is part of an 'enterprise' ideology, a determination that Britain be born again into a new entrepreneurial faith. The intention is not only to modify the behaviour of institutions and individuals but also to change their attitudes. Accordingly, Britain needs to be kept under tight political control to prevent it sliding back into its bad old corporatist ways. This tension between the rhetoric of freedom and the reality of control has posed particular difficulties for Conservative supporters who wish to give the fullest scope to the free market, as well as for liberals and socialists who reject the assumptions on which 'privatisation' rests.

The development of British higher education in the last twenty-five years, therefore, has been marked by continuity of policies and discontinuity of values. The continuity must be emphasised because its force is not appreciated. The number of full-time students increased three-fold between 1960 and 1980, just as the statisticians employed by the Robbins committee had estimated.[10] Across the span of a quarter of a century – eight general elections, four changes of Government, two Middle East wars – such a close prediction suggests more than blind shooting which by chance has hit the target. Rather, it suggests an underlying symmetry between how Robbins saw the future evolution of higher education and its actual development. There has never been any serious attempt to reverse Robbins' endorsement of expansion. Just as at some time during the 1960s that crucial frontier between a private and a public system of higher education was crossed, so in the same decade an irreversible decision was taken to open up higher education to a changing Britain. As late as 1960 our universities and colleges made up an immature and inward system, underdeveloped by the standards of North America and of the rest of Europe and backward when compared to schools and the other social institutions of the postwar welfare state. Arguably, higher education was lagging behind and out of step. The greatest achievement of Robbins was to help it to catch up and march in step with the rest of British society. Over the past quarter of a century higher education *has* kept in step. Despite the pessimism of the late 1970s and early 1980s about the effect demographic decline might have on future student recruitment, there never was any chance that the size of the system would be reduced or opportunities to enter higher education diminished. The decision to plan for further expansion in the 1990s, announced in the 1987 White Paper, was really a foregone conclusion.[11] The die had been cast a generation earlier.

All the consequences of choosing an open rather than closed system of higher education have not yet been appreciated. In the 1960s, expansion was justified in terms of the need to meet the rising social demand for higher education, reflecting improved standards in postwar schools and increasing expectations among young people in the never-had-it-so-good society. But Robbins was careful to present reassuringly conservative arguments. The intention was to prevent universities becoming academic hothouses without a broader cultural role. Expansion without evident loss of standards could be guaranteed. The alternative was for universities to be superseded by other advanced training institutions. The radical implications of expansion were addressed only obliquely. More pass and general degrees should be encouraged. More postgraduate courses would be needed. In the 1980s, expansion was justified in terms of the need not only to meet rising social demand fuelled by higher standards in schools, but also to increase the supply of skilled manpower. The fear that expansion might undermine quality, apparent at the time of Robbins, was still there. In its White Paper, the Government insisted that it attached 'no less importance than previously to its policy of maintaining and raising standards. It believes that increased participation in higher education need not be at the expense of academic excellence; indeed the stimulus of change should help to sharpen awareness of the different types of achievement that properly form part of the output of higher education.'[12] That last qualification has the ring of an alibi. In the 1990s, unless there is a dramatic increase in the number of qualified school leavers or of able adults, the demand from candidates in many subjects will barely exceed the supply of places. By the end of the century many institutions, and more departments, will have become in effect open access. But this outcome was preordained long ago.

The standard account of British higher education since the 1960s emphasises its discontinuities rather than its underlying stability – the designation of the polytechnics as a separate sector rather than the creation of more universities; the incorporation of teacher education in this new sector rather than in the universities; the growing *dirigisme* of the University Grants Committee; the creeping nationalisation of the polytechnics and other colleges, first with the creation of the National Advisory Body in 1982, and finally with the rupture of their historic links with local government in 1988; the growing power of the Department of Education and Science culminating in the abolition of the UGC and the extinction of the special relationship which the universities had traditionally enjoyed with the state. A world turned upside down indeed.

Yet these changes obscure the enduring continuity of higher education's role in British society. A quarter of a century ago, Robbins envisaged an expanded system made up of large comprehensive multi-faculty teaching-and-research institutions organised within a coherent national framework. Of course, the committee believed that these institutions would be based on and share many of the characteristics of the existing universities. But its members would probably have had little difficulty recognising today's polytechnics or central institutions as the type of institution they had in mind. The average polytechnic at the end of the 1980s is much larger than the average university was at the beginning of the 1960s. It has equivalent or superior academic experience. If bureaucratic characteristics are put on one side, the polytechnics already are 'universities' in the Robbins sense. The report also emphasised the need for a national framework. It was already assumed a generation ago that a coherent system of 'higher education' had to be established which would break away from, or subsume, the older categories, like 'universities', 'further education', 'teacher training'. The 1988 Act established just such a system. Universities and polytechnics and colleges are now planned and funded by two parallel agencies, the Universities Funding Council and the Polytechnics and College Funding Council, both subject on almost identical terms to the Secretary of State for Education and Science. The differences in their respective administrative regimes are little more than residual anomalies. The pressure to merge these two councils and to establish a truly common system of higher education is already considerable. Few people expect the binary division of British higher education to continue, even in its present attenuated form, until the end of the century.

Although there has been a three-fold expansion of higher education since 1960, it has continued to be distinct from further education on the one hand and, on the other, from adult education; both demarcations are much less clear in the rest of Europe and absent entirely in the United States. In 1963, Robbins insisted higher education was different, its natural links not with schools and lower-level colleges but with research councils and similar scientific and scholarly bodies. A quarter of century later, the 1988 Act insisted on an equally clear division between higher education and other forms of postsecondary education. Perhaps this demarcation will break down during the 1990s as higher education moves rapidly towards open access. But for the moment it has been maintained and reinforced by the recent Act. The Robbins view of higher education as inescapably national in focus, and therefore directed mainly at full-time advanced students, has been preferred to the alternative view enshrined in the rhetoric of the binary policy, if not in the practice of the polytechnics, that higher education is also local, and therefore open too to part-time students on less advanced courses. The 1987 White Paper justified the removal of the polytechnics and colleges from the control of local education authorities in terms which would have appealed to Robbins: that they were national institutions; that they were firmly established (a direct comparison with universities was offered as evidence); and that they made 'a high-quality contribution to higher education'.[13]

The attachment to the exclusiveness of higher education is strong in Britain. One explanation is to be found in the social composition of the student population of universities and, to a lesser degree, of polytechnics, central institutions, and colleges. A second can be derived from the exclusionary instincts' of our culture. A *co-optative* meritocracy, which is perhaps a too benign description of late twentieth-century Britain, needs clear demarcations far more than does a *competitive* one like the United States. In the rest of Europe, similar social rigidities are qualified by the strongly civic and republican values that Britain lacks because of the underdevelopment of its democracy. A third arises from deeply-felt assumptions of academic propriety. The linking of higher education not with schools but with the world of science and scholarship clearly elevates the role of research and degrades that of teaching. The emphasis on the national rather than local standing of higher education not only has important social reverberations; metropolitan values once again are preferred to provincial ones. It also has important implications for the intellectual agenda, and for the relationship of academic study to both social action and industrial utility.

The 1988 Act confirmed the configuration of higher education established over the previous quarter of a century. It reaffirmed the assumptions about the relationship between higher education and the state, its role in society and its semi-detached position within the wider education system, on which these adminstrative arrangements rested. This continuity helps to explain why universities protested so little about the abolition of that celebrated buffer agency, the UGC. What appeared to many people outside the universities as their irreversible subordination to the state, and even the end of British university civilisation, seemed to be regarded by many university leaders as a pragmatic adjustment, the next logical step in an evolving relationship. By the 1980s it was already recognised that the old UGC constitution had become an anachronism which demanded reform.[14] The hope that the post-Robbins university system in all its complexity could be managed by an informal committee of academic members and their soul-mates or that such an arrangement could continue to command the confidence of government was recognised to be in vain. It was not felt to be in the interests of the universities to defend the indefensible (academic tenure was also relegated to this terminal category). The Mephistophelean bargain with the state had been sealed long before. It could not be repudiated now. Nor was there any great desire to do so if the Government still recognised the exceptionalism, no longer perhaps of universities alone but still of a higher education system, in which universities would continue to enjoy a dominant position.

If the universities were not unduly alarmed by the 1988 Act, the polytechnics and colleges offered it an indiscriminate welcome. It gave them freedom from local education authorities, final vindication of their full membership of the higher education club. Doubts about the effective freedom they would enjoy under the direction of the

Polytechnics and Colleges Funding Council and the DES were suppressed by joy at this symbolic coming of age. In practice, the focus of power had passed to the centre when the National Advisory Body for public sector higher education was created in 1982. After that, local authorities had only a vestigial role in the polytechnics and colleges for which they formally remained responsible. Indeed the very conception of the polytechnics rested on nationalising assumptions incompatible with genuine local control. Perhaps the Labour Government of the 1960s had only been able to reject the recommendation of the Robbins report that more universities should be established by agreeing to establish *ersatz* universities in the shape of the new polytechnics. Policies for the non-university sector of higher education may appear to have oscillated wildly during the past quarter of a century: the Robbins plan for the orderly extension of the university sector to include most major institutions was superseded by the binary policy which established an alternative and rival sector; this policy was in turn superseded by a creeping nationalisation of the polytechnics and colleges which has tended to reduce the sharpness of this binary divide. Yet underneath these superficial oscillations of policy there has been little change in the assumptions about what can properly be regarded as higher education.

Far from challenging these assumptions, the 1987 White Paper and the 1988 Act confirmed them. They represented not a programme of radical reform (except at the level of adminstrative routines and funding procedures) but a conservative, even reactionary, programme. The symbiotic relationship between universities and the nation's elite was once upheld by an informal concordat between two almost equal partners. It was a family understanding which could safely be administered through the anachronistic agency of the UGC. In the late 1980s, tighter policing of that relationship seemed to be necessary. In the eyes of government the rules governing that special relationship needed to be made explicit because the expanded university system which had grown up during the 1960s and 1970s showed signs of ignoring these informal constraints. In an important sense British universities have never been free. The mingling of their interests with those of the state made freedom both unthinkable and unnecessary. The genuine autonomy of the universities, their translation into a genuinely critical force in society, have perhaps always been fearful prospects. The replacement of the UGC by a UFC was not designed to build a brave new world but to uphold the old order of things. The 1988 Act was an attempt to keep a potentially wayward university system to the terms of its old engagements to the state.

A similar interpretation can be offered of the explicit nationalisation of the polytechnics and colleges brought about by the same Act. The lack of definition between higher, and further, and adult education, which flowed from local-authority management of these institutions, was a threat to the traditional integrity of higher education. Those thin clear streams of academic and professional excellence were being diluted, or even polluted. The involvement of local education authorities in higher education kept the frontier open – to wider opportunity and mass access, perhaps. But it also threatened to produce administrative incoherence and, worst of all in the eyes of upholders of a conservative academic order, ideological instability. Closing this frontier is not a radical act. For its unacknowledged intention is not to break away from an obsolescent past but to tame a turbulent future. Its true purpose is to protect the systematic hierarchy of education, with its confusing social, professional and cultural reverberations, by reasserting the separate and superior identity of higher education. Whether this is a feasible project on the brink of the twenty-first century is another question.

THE ACADEMY UNDER SIEGE

Why, when higher education is needed so much, does it seem to be wanted so little? Is it a paradox that puzzles many who work in universities, polytechnics and colleges. For its first part cannot be denied. Like all open societies and advanced economies modern Britain has never needed higher education more than in these last years of the twentieth century. The right to a higher education is woven into the expectations of the broad middle classes to a degree unknown a generation ago. Industry and employment are increasingly dependent on technological innovation, which in turn depends largely on research undertaken in universities and similar institutions. The quality of our nation's culture, indeed of all human civilisation, is deeply influenced by what happens in the private world of higher education within its constituent disciplines. The popularisation of ideas, science and intellectual fashions shape our values far more than can comfortably be admitted.

Britain could not survive as a healthy democracy, a liberal society or a thriving economy without a system of advanced education, training and research at least as extensive as that which it presently possesses. Indeed, those who look enviously across the Atlantic, or just across the Channel, argue that Britain needs a more extensive system of universities and colleges if it is to match the social, economic and cultural ambitions of other nations. The old fears that 'more means worse', still influential as late as the 1960s and always a brake on the expansion of higher education, are effectively dead. Expansion was inescapable. The elaboration of secondary education between the 1940s and the 1970s had stoked the social demand for university, college and, later, polytechnic places. That pressure could never have been resisted. More recent complaints that universities are prisoners of ivory-tower preoccupations and that scientists prefer the most abstract research are as deeply flawed. It is always possible to argue about the priorities of research. It is not possible to respect the assumptions which lurk behind such complaints, that Britain can get by with less research or that trained intelligence is less important than 'first-class minds' or entrepreneurial guts. It is hardly necessary to accept uncritically Daniel Bell's description of postindustrial society to understand that modern Britain is inescapably a knowledge-based society. The codification of theoretical knowledge may not yet have become our primary source of energy, as oil, coal or muscle-power were in industrial and preindustrial society. But like all modern nations Britain has become exceptionally dependent on high technology and its equivalents in the social and human sciences.

However, although it is clear that the need for higher education cannot be denied and will increase still further before the end of this century, higher education seems to be wanted less and less. It has lost the high and unconditional public esteem it once enjoyed. The budgets of universities have been reduced, departments and courses closed and academic staff made redundant.[15] But few people outside universities have complained. Polytechnics, central institutions and colleges have been forced to admit many more students without any corresponding increase in their budgets.[16] These gains in 'productivity' have undermined their efforts to offer a higher education equivalent to that provided by universities and to create a more satisfactory environment for student learning and staff research. Again, there have been few objections from outside the affected institutions. The research councils have been unable to fund all the attractive proposals put to them. The development in the 1980s of the pressure group, 'Save British Science', demonstrated the growing frustration of scientists, even in Britain's most famous universities.[17] Right across higher education morale has declined. The academy seems to be under siege.

Of course this distress can be exaggerated. Deep demoralisation can coexist with intellectual excitement. Judged in one perspective, the 1970s and 1980s indeed appear lean years for British higher education, in particular for universities – the years of cuts, more cuts and yet more cuts, a long painful hangover once the Robbins party was finished. But judged in other perspectives these same years have been a time of great academic success in discipline after discipline, a success which has continued up to the present. British universities may never before have flourished academically as they do today. The policies of successive Governments have made little contribution to this success, except to the extent that they provided or withheld the required resources. Some of the most interesting and exciting progress has been made in disciplines regarded with disfavour by politicians, while other disciplines that enjoyed their patronage have been marked by intellectual mediocrity. Some argue the success of British higher education has been built on accumulated capital laid down by previous political generations. The fear is that once this capital has been used up higher education will suffer an irreversible decline. There may be no more Nobel prizes in the pipeline. Perhaps this is too gloomy a view. But it is plausible, especially for particular institutions or disciplines. In many cases the glory days seem to lie in an irredeemable past. However, even if the success of higher education is acknowledged, it merely leads to another version of the first paradox: higher education has never been more troubled and never more successful. Why?

There are various possible explanations. The first is that this paradox reflects the inevitable condition of democratic societies, the chronic and inescapable crisis brought about by inflated expectations fuelled by the acquisitive logic of the market and the extravagant promises of politicians. Put simply, we want more than we can afford – or, more accurately, we want things which we are reluctant to pay for. At a banal level this first explanation is plausible enough. But its general application makes it an insufficient explanation of higher education's particular predicament. The crisis of over-expectations applies to everyone and everything. A second explanation is that it is all an ephemeral political accident. Society is not hostile to higher education, although many of its members may be indifferent. As a result, a particular Government has been able to indulge its own special hostility to higher education, which has been punished either because it is part of an unwelcome corporatist state or because it is a carrier of leftist values. The influence of high politics should not be underestimated. But this second explanation rests on the hopeful assumption that, had other political parties been in power in Britain in the 1980s, the experience of higher education would have been less troubled. Possible rather than probable, this assumption is not practically relevant. So this second explanation is no good either.

A third explanation is higher education has failed to sell itself properly – to politicians at Westminster and civil servants in Whitehall, to industry and business, to local communities, to the people. This failure is one of public relations or, perhaps, of institutional leadership. If only newspapers had printed and radio and television had broadcast more positive accounts of higher education, if only vice chancellors, directors and principals had been more charismatic performers, perhaps higher education would have been in a stronger position to resist recent assaults.[18] Of course in modern society where images and style are increasingly influential in shaping reputations, higher education is right to devote considerable resources to presentation. But it is hard to believe that bad communications are at the root of the system's present difficulties. First, it is naive to imagine that politicians, civil servants, industrialists, businessmen and others do not appreciate higher education because they do not understand it. Most are themselves graduates with direct personal experience of higher education. They may be unfamiliar with the most recent developments, so they undervalue the contribution of the polytechnics or disparage the new universities. But there can be little doubt about their overall understanding of the importance of higher education within modern society.[19] Secondly, the emphasis on effective public relations and purposeful leadership suggest that there is nothing wrong with the product itself – or nothing wrong that cannot be put right by adding a few hundred million pounds to the higher education budget. But this is too complacent a view. The academy's malaise cannot be reduced to an image problem.

A fourth explanation seems more persuasive. Because higher education has become so pervasive in modern society it can no longer expect to be treated with old-fashioned deference. Universities and other institutions have left the sacred realm and become part of the humdrum world. If higher education is no longer placed on a high pedestal and admired from far below, this is not because of the unfortunate consequences of student revolt in the late 1960s and early 1970s or the stuffiness of universities in the 1980s but because higher education has become a more common experience. Many people have had close personal experience of higher education, direct or vicarious, so it cannot be invested with the same sacred mystique. Higher education is largely a victim of its own success. Since the great expansion of the 1960s and 1970s it has become routine, at any rate among the middle classes. This has had two important consequences, one negative and one positive. First, it can no longer expect special treatment. Its claims cannot be unconditionally satisfied. They must be weighed in the balance along with those of schools or of the National Health Service. Secondly, no Government can diminish access to higher education, either by reducing the number of places for students or by raising the financial threshold for entry into the system. Britain has some way to go before it matches the social penetration higher education has achieved in the United States or in some other parts of Europe. In Britain, higher education is a routine commodity but not yet an essential one, which helps to explain the apparent mismatch between needs and wants.

So it is an exaggeration to say that higher education is the victim of its own success. There is still too much ambiguity about the place of universities, and polytechnics and colleges, in British society. Two aspects are worth emphasising. One, already discussed, is the demystification of higher education. Ever since 1964, when the present Department of Education and Science was created and the University Grants Committee made subject to it rather than to the Treasury, universities have become closely associated with primary, secondary and further education. The shift in university culture implied by this association was compounded by the contemporary movement towards a system of comprehensive secondary schools. The old elitist, or better still, paternalist, networks which had nourished the universities fell into disuse. Three factors came together to promote democratic change within higher education: the rapid expansion of the system, the closer association with 'lower' education, and the reform of secondary schools. All have been welcome. But, for universities in particular, these changes have had disturbing reverberations.

The second aspect is that higher education has been devalued. In the eyes of some conservatives academic standards have been allowed to slip. (In fact, entry to higher education is more competitive than it was a generation ago, if the A Level grades demanded by institutions are an accurate guide.) They have been dismayed by the introduction of unfamiliar subjects in unusual combinations. Higher education has lost its high cultural tone. This prejudice is felt rather than argued. But although inarticulate it is influential. Inside the more traditional parts of the system it is reflected in the suspicion that the academic enterprise has lost status and may be itself partly responsible. In a more direct sense, higher education has been devalued. Three times as many students are admitted as a generation ago and the proportion of graduates in the general population is rising remorselessly. To the extent that higher education is a positional good, its value determined by its scarcity, it is now less valuable to the individual – in extrinsic terms, at any rate.[20] In a culture such as Britain's, which delights in its exclusionary instincts, free and easy access to higher education is an ambiguous phenomenon.

A fifth explanation is that higher education has lost, or never gained, popular support because it is seen as irrelevant, even aristocratic. It favours the academic rather than the practical, the critical rather than the constructive, the pure rather than the applied, the individual rather than the team, and so on. There are two versions of this indictment of higher education. The first emphasises its impracticality, perhaps even its anti-practicality. Half-remembered passages from Martin Weiner's *English Culture and the Decline of the Industrial Spirit* are recalled as damning evidence.[21] Universities in particular are accused of being out of sympathy with the ethos of the market. The British intellectual tradition is stigmatised as fastidious, aloof and aristocratic. This is why, it is argued, the donnish UGC had to be replaced by a UFC dominated by lay voices, why all institutions of higher education must receive their budgets from the state in the form of 'contracts' for which they have to bid rather than 'grants' to which they feel entitled, and why they must be managed like business enterprises. Of course the assumptions on which such policies are based do not stand up to serious examination. If the examples of collaboration between higher education and industry are counted up, if the output of graduates in vocational subjects like engineering or business studies is recalled, if the scale of post-experience vocational education is remembered, the indictment for anti-practicality must be dismissed. But prejudiced feelings, sadly, are often more influential than sober facts.

According to the second version, higher education has failed to break away from the social exclusiveness which marked it in the past. Despite the new universities of the 1960s with their ambition to redraw the map of learning, despite the Open University which has done more than any other institution to provide opportunities for adults and is renowned in other countries for its pioneering work in distance learning, despite the polytechnics and colleges which have brought further education's open-door tradition right into the heart of British higher education, the system has remained essentially a middle class enterprise. The great expansion which followed the Robbins report has established higher education as the routine expectation of middle-class families. Unless their children are very much below average or positively unwilling they are now expected to continue their full-time education after leaving secondary school. But this expansion has done little to lift the low rates of participation by the working class in higher education. Those who argue in this way do not blame higher education entirely, or even at all, for its social failure. The roots of discrimination are recognised as going much deeper, back to early schooling or the class structure of British society. But whether higher education is blamed or not, it is placed outside the mainstream of educational reform and stigmatised as less relevant to any movement towards democratic education. Some, of course, take a harsher view of higher education's complicity. They see universities especially, and some universities in particular, as active instruments of social discrimination.

Is this second version of the indictment more convincing than the first? The social base of higher education has not been extended as far as many of the most enthusiastic supporters of university and college expansion had hoped a generation ago. The most important phenomenon influencing that expansion turned out to be a rapid rise in female participation. But this extension of educational opportunity for women has sometimes been disparaged because it does not fit into traditional notions of emancipation rooted in social class. Yet it remains a social phenomenon of outstanding significance and by any reasonable standard a progressive movement of society. The relative failure to increase working-class participation in higher education also has to be seen in the context of social and economic change. Since 1945 the middle class has expanded and the working class contracted. New ethnically-based groups have emerged as dominant social categories. The configuration of the underprivileged has undergone rapid change. The progress of higher education towards achieving greater equity must be measured by late twentieth-century criteria, not by those which reflected a now redundant social order.[22] Because higher education now enrols three times as many students as it did in 1960, in absolute terms there has been a substantial increase in the number of students from working-class families. Their proportion within the total student population may not have increased, and may even have declined since 1980. But, because the opportunities for young and older people from all social backgrounds to enter higher education have increased, working-class school leavers are now much more likely to continue in full-time education or to return to study later. Far more progress has been made towards opening up higher education than is sometimes acknowledged. More has been made in the polytechnics, central institutions and colleges than in the universities because their style of higher-education – more vocational subjects, more part-time degrees, more diploma and certificate courses – makes them more accessible to first-time students.

A sixth explanation is that higher education is out of touch with the free-market, entrepreneurial, materialistic and, in a broad sense, neo-conservative spirit of the age. Universities and other institutions are products of a dull, discredited, corporatist world. The system is both the sponsor and the beneficiary of a social paternalism embodying welfare values now out of favour. As it expanded during the 1960s and 1970s, higher education developed to meet the needs of a powerful welfare state within an expanding public sector. Higher education, far from being the ivory tower imagined by some critics, has always been closely identified with the values of the society and the practice of the economy in which it is embedded. So when the tone of society seems to change, as it may have done during the 1980s, higher education must adjust its style to match the new *zeitgeist*. But it is easy to exaggerate this change. Political rhetoric is volatile, social and economic change more gradual and less dramatic than the ideological gloss placed upon it. The kind of graduates higher education needs to produce and the type of research which it needs to undertake have not changed. Indeed, both have remained stable for more than a generation.

There is a more extreme version of this assertion that higher education has fallen behind the ideological times. Higher education is not so much out-of-touch as out-of-sympathy. The task is not simply to wean universities, polytechnics and colleges off the bad habits that come from over-dependence on the state and to make them stand on their own entrepreneurial feet; their ethos is actively subversive in terms of neo-conservative orthodoxy. They are citadels of leftish fashion that patronise the intellectual strivings of the new right. Their liberal traditions make them contemptuous of the merits of social hierarchy and of wealth creation. But this complaint cannot be taken seriously, even if it were based on an accurate description of British higher education. The tradition of a nation, especially of a democratic nation, can never be regarded as the possession of a particular Government, party or movement. The duty of higher education, and in particular, perhaps, of universities, is to defend that tradition while remaining fully part of contemporary society. It is its absolute duty, as it is of all education, to refine beliefs, prejudices, feelings and instincts in the sweet light of reason. Any system of higher education abandoning this duty denies its most solemn obligation not only to the democratic state and to a liberal society but also to itself, to the very values of science and scholarship.

A seventh explanation of this puzzling paradox is that it is an exaggeration, or even a misunderstanding. No sensible person denies the need for higher education, but politics are about establishing priorities. If higher education feels undervalued it is a measure of its own unreasonable expectations rather than of society's lack of appreciation. There is a sliver of truth here. Part of the pain felt in universities during the 1980s arose from a refusal to comprehend that a well-intentioned state could nevertheless deny some of their demands. But as a general explanation it is flawed. First, it is banal; our ambitions will always outrun our resources. Secondly, if uttered by representatives of responsible Government, it is disingenuous. If Britain cannot afford its present system of higher education it must be adapted to what can be afforded. Thirdly, it fails to explain the particular hostility to higher education during the 1980s.

None of these seven explanations of why higher education seems to be needed so much but wanted so little is satisfactory. All contain odd particles of truth. But even together they do not explain the puzzle, which needs to be approached from another direction, from inside rather than outside. These explanations are all concerned with the external aspects of higher education. The key lies with higher education's perception of itself. The lack of a sturdy vision of higher education is at the root of the unease and anxiety in universities, central institutions, polytechnics and colleges. Of course budget cuts and other external assaults have undermined the academy's self-confidence. But another source of unease is a deeper crisis of self-identification. The need is not only to be able to answer questions about the value of higher education in terms which convince those beyond the campus. The same question must be asked of higher education and answered in terms which it finds satisfactory.

In the past there have always been convincing models, or visions, of the university around which individuals and institutions could organise their ambitions. They were able, thus convinced, to present a confident face to society. The earliest and most famous of these models remains that embodied in Cardinal Newman's *The Idea of a University*, a mid-Victorian work not much read today but often appealed to in rhetorical argument.[23] At the centre of Newman's university were the liberal arts, although these are not the same as the modern humanities. He saw little place for what today would be regarded as the defining characteristic of the university: research. Newman's university is sometimes stigmatised as a finishing school for imperial rulers or for members of the politico-administrative elite which was being rapidly formed in the middle of the ninteenth century out of the debris of the 'Old Corruption'. Wrongly perhaps. The values prized by Newman were not those of aggressive leadership but of Christian civilisation. In nineteenth-century Scotland a different but equally liberal tradition of university education developed, which is generally summed up in the phrase 'the democratic intellect'. As this phrase suggests it was a more open tradition than that celebrated by Newman in his Dublin lecture. But its intellectual assumptions, and so the disciplines it chose to emphasise, were remarkably similar. Both owed much to idealist philosophy, although they rejected the excesses of post-revolutionary romanticism, and both were suspicious of the utilitarianism which dominated mid-Victorian thought.

The second model was that of the research university, most fully developed in nineteenth-century Germany and after the Civil War in the United States, but always an important influence on the development of London University and those other universities which looked to London rather than to Oxford or Cambridge. The all-powerful professor, a civil servant but guaranteed the right to teach and research freely, presiding over a seminar of assistants and students; the comparative neglect of undergraduate education, at any rate in terms of the paternalism practised by many British universities; a neutral, even amoral, approach to knowledge which at the worst of times (like Germany in the 1930s), could collapse into a terrifying illiberalism – these and other characteristics of the research university are well understood. But its most important quality was the sense of sheer intellectual power it conveyed.

A third model was provided by the composite university which grew up in the first half of the present century in the United States. 'Composite' is a better description than the usual term, 'comprehensive', because the latter suggests a degree of integration between undergraduate college, graduate school, research department and extension or extramural divisions only rarely present. In Britain this model was admired rather than reproduced. Its centrifugal diversity was peculiar to America. In an old country like Britain it was difficult to establish. But its influence was powerful, particularly over the founders of the new universities in the 1960s. Here was a model for a university which was genuinely open. It was not constrained by inherited notions of propriety. Across the Atlantic the composite university achieved a fit, a symbiosis even, with a rapidly evolving and increasingly diverse society. In most of Europe the university was still regarded as standing a little apart from daily routines. After 1945, and most decisively in the 1960s, the composite university became the multiversity, the vision celebrated by Clark Kerr in *The Uses of the University*.[24] Where Newman had seen a single idea, Kerr discerned multiple uses. Perhaps this shift of language demonstrated the movement towards utilitarianism and away from coherence, characteristic of modern systems of higher education. This fourth model, the multiversity, was beyond ideology in a formal sense. After all, this was the high tide of postwar pragmatism. But informally it seemed to gather up all the aspirations of mid-century society for scientific excellence, economic growth and efficiency, social reform, and individual advancement and fulfilment. At its highest point in the mid-1960s this was an intoxicating vision infused with a millenarian spirit.

The grandiose forms of the multiversity were never reproduced in Britain. Its campuses were too small and too inward. Higher education still stood aside from the bustle of society and culture. But the spirit of the multiversity crossed oceans and frontiers at will. It was an important influence over the development of British universities in the 1960s and remains a compelling model for the whole system in the 1980s. But its ambition to gather together all the threads of postsecondary education, to contain within itself diverse and even competitive roles, has been a disturbing prospect on this side of the Atlantic. In Britain a fifth model of higher education, that of the people's university which grew out of the open-door traditions of further and technical education, has been important.[25] In the United States this idea came to be subsumed in the wider vision of the multiuniversity. But not in Britain. Partly because the university tradition was more restricted in its social and intellectual ambitions and partly because, for political reasons, a rigid binary division between universities and other institutions was maintained for more than a generation, this fifth model has flourished independently in the form of the polytechnics and colleges of higher education. Diversity and flexibility are the main characteristics of this model. A much wider variety of courses, at different levels and taught in different modes, designed for a more heterogeneous student population is offered by these institutions than by traditional universities. In the 1980s the polytechnics have demonstrated a capacity that suggests that it is they which are likely to become the multiversities of British higher education in the next century. Even today the only role they have not assumed is that of fundamental and speculative research, a role which many universities have found it difficult to sustain.

Despite this polytechnic promise, British higher education as a whole lacks a satisfying vision of its own ambitions. The models or visions of the past have been exposed as either inadequate or overambitious. It sometimes feels, especially in universities, as if we have seen the future and are no longer sure that it works, or even as if we can no longer see the future clearly. This retreat into anxiety is a general phenomenon in the West. But it is felt with particular intensity in Britain. The most obvious reason is the budget cuts which universities, polytechnics and colleges have experienced in recent years. British higher education has suffered more than most other comparable systems. And, because in the past it enjoyed especially appreciative links with the national elite, its disenchantment is particularly intense. But a second more significant reason is the lack of a suitable language in which to re-express the goals of higher education. Britain's public culture is instinctive rather than articulate, composed of implicit values and silent beliefs. Within the tight-knit elites of the past this silence did not matter. It may even have been beneficial because explicit argument could have led to ideological rancour. Everyone understood the code, but it was better left untranslated.

In Britain, universities were part of this silent establishment until the 1960s or even later. Today they no longer are. In any case, the coherence of the establishment has been undermined by ideological explicitness; universities, and all institutions of higher education, now have to learn the language needed to explain themselves to the world beyond the campus and to themselves. But this is more difficult than ever because of the diversity of the system. A generation ago, at the time of the Robbins report, the creation of the new universities, and the establishment of the polytechnics, there was greater fluency. Redrawing the map of learning seemed feasible. Ambitious blueprints could be drawn up for individual institutions. And whole sectors, such as the new polytechnics, could be allocated an exhilarating mission. Today the language of higher education is managerial, not academic. A cadre of policy experts, embracing institutional and sectoral leaders, has been created. They stand aside from both the academic preoccupations growing out of various disciplines and the wider cultural interests which reflect the relationship between higher education and society.

There is a third reason why British higher education has failed to conjure up a vision of its contemporary goal as eloquent as those of the past. The difficulty lies with the very term 'higher education'. It is both restricted and incoherent – restricted because it suggests frontiers between higher and 'lower' education, that is, between higher education and other forms of postsecondary education described as further or adult or perhaps continuing; and incoherent because higher education is a bureaucratic amalgamation of different types of institutions, universities, polytechnics, colleges. England's higher education – Scotland may be different in this respect – is composed of incomplete or half-completed institutions. For a brief period in the early 1960s it was possible for the founders of the new universities to imagine they were designed as complete and comprehensive institutions. Perhaps the builders of the civic universities were offered a similar window of opportunity in the late ninteenth and early twentieth centuries. But for most of the time universities and, *a fortiori*, polytechnics and colleges have had restricted roles. Their ambitions have been arbitrarily restricted. Higher education in Britain is divided among, and often against, itself. The integrity and morale of the whole system have been undermined. There is little sense of common purpose, of shared expertise, except perhaps within the cadre of policy experts disinclined to draw the cultural conclusions so urgently needed. The central weakness of British higher education in these last years of the twentieth century is this moral incapacity to see its life steadily and to see it whole.

A RE-ENCHANTED VISION

What higher education needs most at the end of the twentieth century is re-enchantment. Re-enchantment because more is needed than a recovery of confidence. The process must go beyond the instrumentalities with which we are comfortably preoccupied to the world of idealism which so disturbs the expert equilibrium of the modern age. That process must start with the question, What is higher education for? A naive question that can never be properly answered, but one that each generation must try to answer in its own way. Why do we encourage almost 900 000 young, and not-so-young, people to study history or physics or sociology or engineering for three or more years at an annual public cost of more than three billion pounds? If we cannot supply an answer that is more than an accumulation of utilitarian arguments, the future development of higher education will have no direction. There will be no possibility of re-enchantment.

Instead, the goals of higher education will be defined by the inertia and the momentum of universities, polytechnics, colleges, research establishments and other institutions which make up the system. Future ends will be derived from past means. Or rival interpretations of the goals of higher education will be a projection of the prejudices and irritations provoked by what seems to lay people a complacent ambition to protect a self-interested status quo.

During the 1980s the debate about the future of higher education has been dominated by these rival instincts. The defenders of the system have rooted their arguments in a gloomy analysis of the damage likely to be caused by the lack of adequate resources for teaching, scholarship and science and by the centralisation of political power. Politicians, it is said, have given higher education less and less and wanted more and more in return. Of course, in their own defence they have alluded to both idealistic and utilitarian arguments for higher education. But these arguments have been deployed in rhetorical support rather than in front-line attack. Similar reticence has been apparent among the critics of higher education. They have argued that the system must become more cost effective, its quality improved and its teaching and research made more relevant. But they, too, have been reluctant to argue about the goals of higher education, which in their vagueness have gone unargued, and instead have confined their concern to how these goals can be realised more effectively. Of course their criticism of means has occasionally spilt over into doubts about ends, most notably in the case of social science. But as with the defence of higher education this argument about the ultimate intentions of the enterprise is a sideshow. This is the territory in which the skirmishers of the radical right – the Centre for Policy Studies, the Social Affairs Unit of the Institute of Economic Affairs and so on – fight, not the main battlefield of White Papers and Acts of Parliament.

Yet a generation ago Robbins placed its discussion of the aims of higher education first in its famous report. These aims it reduced to four – instruction in skills suitable to play a part in the general division of labour, the promotion of the powers of the mind, the advancement of learning and the transmission of a common culture. The difficulty today is not that we object to these four aims but that, through disuse, they seem insipid. For both the potency and the practicality of the Robbins definition of the aims of higher education were derived from an envelope of surrounding assumptions, assumptions which were liberal in the sense discussed earlier in this chapter and which reflected the strength of the postwar social settlement and the confident growth of consumer-led affluence. In the 1960s the Robbins Committee succeeded in rewriting the first principles inherited from a quieter academic age to take account of the power of science revealed during the war and of the spirit of social democracy that had become the keynote of postwar society.

The Robbins success has not been repeated in the 1980s. Many of the assumptions about society, culture and the economy which a generation ago were beyond challenge have been undermined. Higher education itself has grown three times over and taken on increasingly complex and contentious roles. The uncertainty of the ideological environment has been compounded by the incoherence of the system. The Robbins phrases, their eloquence unimpaired but their significance diminished, will no longer serve. Yet no serious attempt has been made to replace them. The three-year Leverhulme inquiry into the future of higher education in the early 1980s[26] failed to reconsider these first principles. Shying away from the need to establish a post-Robbins framework, it concentrated on filling in useful policy details. The subsequent attempt by the University Grants Committee to stimulate a debate about the future by inviting all universities to reply to a wide-ranging list of open-ended questions produced cramped results.[27] Its most positive outcome was a joint statement, with the National Advisory Body, on 'Higher Education and the Needs of Society', which attempted to modify the

Robbins principle by emphasising continuing education and a student's ability to benefit as the basis for qualification to enter higher education in addition to academic ability, attainment and motivation.[28] Neither the 1985 Green Paper nor the 1987 White Paper made any serious attempt to go back to first principles. Their efforts to define the purposes of higher education were banal and perfunctory.

This failure to answer the question, 'What is higher education for?, in these final years of the twentieth century is at the root of the system's incoherence. Arguing out particular roles for particular institutions is difficult without a framework of systematic intentions in which they can be placed. The relationship between the development of disciplines and of institutions has become obscure, even disconnected. The same failure is also a source of the disorientation felt in higher education described in the preceding section of this chapter. Above all, this failure is an obstacle to the re-enchantment of the academy. For out of the answers to this apparently naive question is fashioned higher education's sense of its place in the sum of the present. These answers, however provisional, matter. They are the starting point for an inquiry into not only the particular future of higher education but also the delicate relationship between knowledge and culture in modern society.

The past offers three possible answers. The first is rooted in utilitarianism. Higher education adds to the value of the economy, the community and the individual. The acquisition of knowledge is the means for gaining wealth, power and status. This is the answer on which Governments rely to justify public expense on higher education and which has fuelled the popular appetite for it. The goals of higher education are seen as extrinsic ones – the promotion of economic efficiency or the fostering of social development or the construction of national identity. This interpretation has appealed to governments of left and right in the developed and developing worlds alike. In 1987 a Labour Government in Australia and a Conservative Government in Britain published White Papers on higher education which were similar not only in their prescriptions but also in their assumptions.

That most modern systems of higher education have utilitarian roots can hardly be denied. Those who established the civic universities in Victorian Britain and the land-grant universities in Civil War America were practical people who intended these institutions to satisfy urgent social and economic needs, although they did not despise broader academic ambitions. But this first answer to the question, What is higher education for?, is unsatisfactory in a number of respects. It implies that safe distinctions can be made between more and less 'useful' subjects and more and less 'valuable' institutions using external criteria. But in practice both are difficult. The first distinction becomes more and more treacherous with the unpredictable advances of technology. Today's *cul-de-sac* becomes tomorrow's broad avenue.

Functional rationalism seems to offer an incomplete and inaccurate account of what higher education is for. Too much that is important is left out. The old argument about human capital, which is central to this interpretation of higher education, is left unresolved. Do advanced societies possess sophisticated systems of higher education because they need them or because they can afford them? There is a second difficulty with this utilitarian interpretation of higher education. Put simply, it fails to explain what the enterprise is for. The question is simply deflected. If higher education must serve the cause of economic efficiency, national power, social equality, individual welfare, what purposes do *these* serve? For, even without touching on the notion of transcendence, they cannot be taken to be goals in their own right. And what if economic efficiency and national power are defined, at least partly, in terms of a capacity to maintain elaborate or at any rate adequate systems of higher education? What if individual welfare is defined in terms of access to higher education? So the question of what higher education is for is difficult to answer satisfactorily in entirely materialist terms.

The second answer is rooted in idealism. Knowledge is regarded not as a means to good but as a good in itself. Like truth or beauty it is its own reward. So institutions that produce knowledge and promote learning do not need to look beyond themselves for justification. A good society benefits from their mere existence. They are the cocoons of uncorrupted philosophy. The demands of practicality, whatever form they take, tend to undermine the integrity of higher education and its ultimate value to human society.[29]

In an unadorned form, this answer is unacceptable. It is contradicted by the historical origins and development of institutions and disciplines. The former were designed to fulfill specific social and economic functions as well as academic ones, while the latter grew out of intellectual attempts to solve practical problems – which, of course, were as often cultural as technical. But in a less categorical form this second answer cannot be dismissed entirely. Curiosity, serendipity, even eccentricity have all played their part in the advance of science. Nor can it be denied that very many people in Britain, as in all societies, seek education for its own sake. While 900,000 students, full- and part-time, are enrolled in higher education, almost twice that number attend adult education classes that lead to no recognised qualifications and have no visible utilitarian purpose.

The third answer is rooted in the idea of culture. Higher education is not subordinate to civil society but a component of it. Its responsibility is to a culture that it helps to form and by which it is formed. This answer is best described as a compromise between the utilitarianism of the first and the idealism of the second. For culture combines both. It arises out of the material world of the present but aspires towards the ideal world of the future and celebrates the universal world that belongs to both past and future. Culture, in the definition which Matthew Arnold made famous, is both means and end. It is 'a pursuit of our total perfection by means of getting to know, on all matters that most concern us, the best that has been thought and said in the world; and through this knowledge turning a stream of fresh and free thought upon our stock notions and habits'.[30] It is this balance between idealism and materialism that gives Arnold's notion of culture, akin to the contemporary German idea of *Bildung*, its power and penetration. On the one hand he saw it as 'an inward operation'; on the other he insisted on a direct link between culture and society.

> This is the social idea and the men of culture are the true apostles of equality. The great men of culture are those who have passion for diffusing, for making prevail, for carrying from one end of society to the other, the best knowledge, the best ideas of their time; who have laboured to divest knowledge of all that was harsh, uncouth, difficult, abstract, professional, exclusive; to humanise it, to make efficient outside the clique of the cultivated and learned, yet still remaining the best knowledge and thought of the time, and a true source, therefore of sweetness and light.[31]

This third answer is attractive in two respects. First, it transcends utilitarianism because, if culture is the goal, knowledge is not only the means to other ends but, provided it is the best knowledge, an end in itself. It is part of culture. But only part. Secondly, because culture is more than knowledge, higher education cannot be regarded as a closed system capable of justifying itself without reference to external criteria. It cannot stand alone in principle, any more than in practice it can resist the political, social and economic demands of the democratic state. It is the responsibility of higher education to diffuse the knowledge it produces, to make it prevail, to make it efficient, to humanise it. There is no conflict between knowledge for its own sake and knowledge which serves other goals. It is because it is the best knowledge that it must be diffused. Or even that it becomes the best knowledge by being diffused.

Of course there are difficulties in rooting the justification of higher education in the notion of culture or *Bildung*. The first is that only the best knowledge counts towards culture. But who is to define this and how is this to be defined? Historically, the best knowledge has been determined by the preferences of elites. Certain kinds of knowledge have been celebrated; others, stigmatised. The debate in the 1960s about the 'two cultures', arts and science, highlighted by C.P. Snow, and the perennial allegation that in our intellectual culture there is a strong anti-practical bias reflect the hazards of defining the best knowledge. This difficulty will only increase. With the development of advanced computers and the complex systems they feed the present distinction between knowledge and information will become more diffuse. The former will be seen as simply an intelligent aggregation of millions of impulses of the latter. The knowledge society and the information society will become virtually interchangeable categories. Under these conditions the notion of the best knowledge will be difficult to sustain. Yet this notion is crucial to culture or *Bildung*, and in turn allows higher education to escape from the utilitarian cage in which it would otherwise be imprisoned. The advance of information technology is as grave a challenge to our ability to discriminate between the best and other knowledge as was the commercialisation and vulgarisation which so worried F. R. Leavis and his followers in the middle of the century.

The second difficulty is that the best knowledge, once defined, must be diffused. This process, the socialisation of the best knowledge, also requires careful definition. Who is to judge, in Arnold's terms, how and whether the best knowledge can be made efficient without its ceasing to be 'a true source of sweetness and light'. Arnold, of course, saw no difficulty. His social project was straightforward. Education, provided by the state, was to replace the aristocracy as the sponsor of culture. Indeed it was superior to aristocracy because it spread culture to the democratic masses.[32] If this project failed the result would be anarchy, which he interpreted not as revolution but as, in the words of *The Scholar Gipsy*, 'this strange disease of modern life with its sick hurry, its divided aims, its head o'ertaxed, its palsied hearts'.[33] A century after Arnold's death his project must be rewritten. But not ignored. His emphasis on the central importance of education in sustaining culture in a democratic world, his refusal to see the school (or the college or university) as 'a mere machine' for the transmission of information or the acquiring of skills, his belief in the state as a moral institution, ourselves in our 'collective and corporate character', none of these convictions has lost its relevance or resonance.

What then should be higher education's project at the end of the twentieth century? The first objective is to widen the social base of higher education. It must become a mass system, not one which confines itself to the education of elites, however extended, and the training of experts. Its thin clear stream of excellence must become a broad river. A postindustrial society requires not only a greatly increased supply of highly-skilled workers but also a better educated population at large. The full potential of education will never be achieved so long as it culminates in a selective higher education system more concerned to exclude than to include. How can standards be raised when so many pupils must inevitably be discarded or rejected? Finally the best knowledge, in order to deserve that title, must be diffused, made efficient, humanised. So economic, educational and cultural imperatives come together to support the case for opening up higher education.

The second objective is to protect that best knowledge, to safeguard it in teaching and to promote it in research and scholarship. But that is not necessarily or best done by maintaining a set of closed elite institutions within an otherwise open system. Modern higher education must develop a diversity of institutions, some preoccupied with high-quality research and others designed to teach large numbers of students. But, except where scientific and logistical reasons compel concentration, rigid segregation into research-led and teaching-led institutions, closed and open sectors, is not the best way to foster the best knowledge. One reason is that the best knowledge must be made to prevail outside the clique of the cultivated and the learned. Only by prevailing can it establish its claim to be the best. The most open systems of higher education sustain the highest levels of academic excellence. This is not only because mass systems command greater resources and closed systems restrict the free flow of talent. The United States has a more extensive system of universities and colleges than any other nation. Yet America also possesses the world's finest universities. Wide access and high quality are allies, not rivals.

The third objective links the first two. It is to widen the intellectual base of higher education, enabling it to appeal to a much broader constituency while at the same time enriching the best knowledge. The frontier must be kept open to new kinds and styles of knowledge. There is no reason why women's or Black studies, defined with sufficient rigour, should not be incorporated into the common curriculum of higher education. Some of the disciplines regarded as central to the university experience today, like English or history, were seen as newfangled a century ago. All subjects were newcomers once. It is more important than ever to be openminded in the face of the evolution, even revolution, of knowledge. The need for flexibility is accepted in science and technology, which so rapidly transform our perceptions of knowledge's validity and utility. But the need is as great in the human and social sciences.

There is also a need to re-establish the integrity of our intellectual tradition, to fight against the divisiveness of academic specialisation. Specialisation is the begetter of silence, of cultural muteness. The privacy, the inwardness, the exclusiveness, the clubbability of disciplines inhibit the search for Arnold's best knowledge because they intimidate those who seek wider understanding. The *Geist* and *Bildung* beloved of the Enlightenment have been sacrificed to the divisions of academic labour. So the field has been left to the Foucaults and Marcuses who could not be shamed into silence, although their popularity has transformed intellectual life into a branch of the mass media. Their jargon, generated within specialised disciplines, has been deployed as a quasi-religious language with as great a capacity to intimidate as the chilly disapproval of the specialists. There has to be a better way to generalise intellectual experience, to explain the interconnectedness of different branches of knowledge without abandoning exacting standards. It is only by curbing the inwardness of the academic tradition that higher education can generate the best knowledge, in a moral sense as well as in the material sense demanded by modern postindustrial society, and that universities and other institutions can reach out into our democracy to touch the whole people.

6

NATIONAL EDUCATION

This chapter is about education – education in schools and colleges rather than universities, English and Welsh polytechnics, Scottish central institutions and colleges. Its territory is the entire apparatus of government and institutions, the diversity of values and practices, the accumulation of past traditions and the assembly of future hopes that make up British education a century or more after the 1870 Act which first established compulsory education, half a century or less after the 1944 Act which established universal secondary education, almost exactly a quarter of a century after the progressive school reforms of the 1960s and the great expansion of higher and further education that was their contemporary, and at a time when far-reaching changes in the organisation and curricula of schools have been ordained by the present Government.

The chapter is informed by two perspectives which may also help to explain its intentions. The first is that higher education, indeed the 'highest intelligences' of the whole intellectual system which has been the subject of the first part of this book, sits on top of but at the same time apart from schools and colleges. In one sense, higher education has an imperial relationship with the rest of education. It attracts the brightest pupils from schools and colleges and so deeply influences their structure and practice. Also, it both judges and articulates the values expressed through the wider education system. But in another sense higher education is isolationist. Maybe its three-fold expansion since 1960 has increased this sense of apartness from the schools. Once university and school teachers were quite close; today they inhabit more distant professional worlds. In the eyes of many, higher education has become a different kind of enterprise from the education system in which it is rooted. Advancing the frontiers of knowledge and serving the demands of intellectual and industrial culture have tended to dominate and perhaps even degrade the older business of teaching.

The second perspective is that education – school education – is an absolutely *fundamental* process within British society, which higher education for all the advances of recent years has not yet become, although it clearly has in the United States. It is not simply that education is a mass political arena in which votes, maybe millions of them, are won and lost. It is that it holds up a mirror to our society and ourselves which offers an undistorted image of our beliefs and hopes, our ambitions and fears. The mirror that higher education holds up is different – more brilliant perhaps but also more opaque; selective, certainly. Education addresses the whole nation; higher education only its most privileged and cerebral part. So what is happening in schools, with their millions of pupils, shapes the possibilities in higher education, with its hundreds of thousands of students. This is true not only in an obvious and direct sense, such as the number of school leavers with appropriate entry qualifications or the pattern of subject specialisation in schools. It is true also because schools help to shape the political, social and cultural environment in which higher education must do its work. However imperfect our democracy, numbers count; even the most influential elites must pay attention to this mass arithmetic. Universities, polytechnics and colleges may be the most powerful intellectual institutions in British education. But they are overpowered by the cumulative influence of our thirty thousand schools.

YOUTH IS A FOREIGN COUNTRY

Young people live in an all-consuming present. Unlike the old and the middle-aged they have no lengthy personal memories on which to draw. Their individual integrity has to be constructed out of contemporary sensation. In a society already oppressed by the instant and the immediate, their oppression is particularly intense. Nor is this inevitable lack of personal memories compensated for by shared family memories. The structure of family life, the pattern of work, the centrifugal character of leisure and culture mean that in modern Britain different generations, even within happy and settled families, often live quite separate lives. Parents who both work, parents who are both unemployed, family break-up, single-parent families, the absence of grandparents, the decline of authority and the rise of child-centred 'parenting', the giddy turnover of youth culture – all these phenomena inhibit communication across generations. Perhaps the only (transitory) exceptions are young parents with young children; early childhood is innocence in every age.

Nor are the lack of deep personal memories among the young and the unreliable transmission of family memories across generations compensated for by a rich social memory. Britain may be dotted with beautiful cathedrals, quiet country houses and deserted castles, many of them crowded with summer visitors, but it has become an ahistorical society. The weight of our traditions is unacknowledged except as leisure (the National Trust), commerce (the 'heritage' industry), or, sometimes, politics (the Falklands war and the miners' strike of the mid-1980s). As in most advanced industrial societies, with the possible and peculiar exception of Japan, our past is not much in our present. We have lost it as surely as our religion. Of course, a distinction has to be drawn between individuals and institutions. For the former, the power of the present is unchallenged. Our history has been reduced to the slumbering giant of the nation's subconscious mind. But in our institutions there is almost too much history. We are ruled by a Parliament that continues to be mesmerised by its Victorian heyday. We join trade unions that still live off the moral capital of working-class solidarity accumulated in the industrial revolution. We work for companies dominated too often by an old-fashioned mercantilist rather than a modern productive ethos. And we are served by, or subject to, a public administration that is paternalist and amateur.

For the young this is confusing. They are thoroughly modern and live in a society apparently obsessed by instant fashion. Yet they also live in an old country dominated by institutions which seem to owe too much rather than too little to the past. Perhaps this awkward contrast between a one-dimensional present and an entrenched past helps to explain why so many British institutions are under-performing – or, more significantly, why the British believe they are under-performing. Our elderly institutions find it difficult to engage the support of, or even be understood by, the new generations which they continue to mould and serve. They cannot easily be adapted to the volatility of each new generations' peculiar culture. Yet the incestuous character of each generation's unique experience is a remarkable feature of twentieth-century culture in the West. Every decade since the Great War has carried its own distinguishing marks. The hedonism of the booming 1920s, that nervous attempt to recall prewar solidarity; the stoicism of the depression decade of the 1930s when the pride of Victorian industrialism came tumbling down; the high moral seriousness of the 1940s, the product of a just war against evil enemies and as just a struggle for a fairer society; the 'enrich-yourselves' mentality of the 1950s when affluence and cold war came to Britain; the high hopes and high rise of the 'swinging sixties'; the pendulum years of the 1970s when the postwar social democratic consensus first began to falter; the hard-faced prosperity and mass unemployment of the 1980s.

It has become commonplace to argue that young people are influenced more heavily by their peers than by their parents, by present opportunities more than past traditions. Our material civilisation cannot tolerate too much continuity or allow too many backward regrets. Perhaps these succeeding generations, characterised decade by decade, have acted as peer groups on the large scale. Certainly the dominant pattern of each has been more powerful and exclusive than that of the one before. What in the early part of the century could be characterised only tentatively as 'the spirit of the age', from which there were many exceptions and exclusions, has become by the late twentieth century a set of values and attitudes, a view of the world, from which it is difficult to escape. So young people in Britain today live in a sometimes suffocating present. Their elders, too, generally live in one-dimensional 'presents' too, only different ones. Their parents probably live in the 'present' of the 1960s to which they may look back with guilty nostalgia, while the people who run the country value an even more distant 'present', perhaps the high-minded 1940s or the brittly materialistic 1950s. But the difficulties that young people face go beyond the confusion of 'presents'. Generational change is as old as the world. Theirs is a more intense 'present', because it is real rather than imagined and because the pressures of peer-group orthodoxy are stronger and the countervailing influence of non-peer authority weaker than ever before.

What is their present? Two features above all must be emphasised. First, the young are growing up in an ageing society, something which no generation in Britain has experienced for more than half a century, and perhaps for half a millennium.[1] Second, the threat of nuclear war, environmental peril, mass unemployment and other omens of late twentieth-century Britain mean that young people cannot find in hope for the future compensation for their dissatisfaction with the present or ignorance of the past. The first phenomenon will have an incalculable influence over the way young people regard the world. Theirs is an almost unique experience. In pre-industrial society, high mortality ensured the youth of the population, while in industrial society high fertility more than made up for longer lifespans. But that centuries-old balance has been overturned. The future will no longer belong so triumphantly to the young. They will become an unregarded minority. They will be affected by two great changes which will flow from this demographic shift. First, a far-reaching redistribution of resources within the welfare state, which will continue to exist even in a privatised disguise, is already under way. At present its long-term significance is masked by emergency programmes to reduce high levels of youth unemployment as the postwar baby boom's second wave searches for work. But the shift of resources is inexorable. School rolls fall and house building is cut back, while the demands upon the health service increase year by year and the social security budget is only kept under control by the parsimonious repackaging of benefits. The effect of this redistribution of effort is that the welfare state is now less concerned with building the infrastructure of the future than with maintaining the fabric of the present. This will have important political consequences. A welfare state that services the present rather than imagines the future is a much less exciting prospect. It may also be a less radical enterprise in the eyes of reformers and a less deserving cause in the eyes of voters. The welfare state has changed its nature. It is no longer a moral project designed to build a good society; it is a routine bureaucracy designed to patch up an indifferent one.

The second change that will flow from an ageing society is closely related. The modern state has developed over the past two centuries when society was young. Its growth has been fuelled by the demands of this youthful population for a better future. Its forward horizon has extended over half a century or more, across a whole life time. This has been reflected in the responsibilities it has adopted and the institutions it has built – in industrial development, improved public administration, the growth of the welfare state. Twentieth-century British society has been built round growth and the future. All its institutions of government, its organs of administration, its instruments of industry depend on this ultimate simplicity. But what happens when society has become as much retrospective as prospective, when its forward horizon shrinks to not much more than a decade? What will happen to the institutions designed to satisfy the old imperatives? What will it be like to be young in such a society? The practical difficulties of adjustment will be great, although there will be benefits, too, like reduced competition for higher education or for jobs. But the psychological adjustment may be more difficult still. It is difficult not to believe that there will not be a rise in the level of pessimism, or anxiety, linked perhaps to a retreat into political quietism.

The second feature of the culture of the 1980s – the threat of unemployment, the spectre of the bomb and similar omens of ill fortune – are surely likely to feed this incipient pessimism produced by the structural consequences of an ageing society. A common belief is that young people in the 1990s are more pragmatic than those who were young in the 1960s and 1970s, that they are more utilitarian, and that theirs is a 'me' generation. But this may be a shallow interpretation of their mood. Once the best and brightest among the young were able to dream their dreams, at any rate for an essential while; the middling sort was able to pursue coherent careers around which they could build worthwhile lives; and even the less fortunate mostly found decent jobs. Today the best and brightest cannot risk those dreams, out of which hope and imagination arise. So they make money instead. The middle mass of young people has been forced to take jobs rather than build careers. The less fortunate are being formed into a frightening underclass, their narrow world bracketed by youth training at the best and at the worst heroin and hooliganism. Hardly a change for the better.

Young people today live in a world in which there are more sticks than carrots, more penalties than opportunities. How will they adapt to this harsher environment? One obvious strategy is to retreat from the public world of jobs and politics and invest their more powerful energies in a private world of pop, fashion, lifestyle. This, of course, will intensify the generational apartheid. It could also lead to a disengagement of work from social value and personal identity. In the 1980s, jobs may have become more essential for young people (if they can find any), as they have for many women. But work may have become less important. It no longer builds community, confers status or fosters self-confidence in the manner imagined by those who believed in a puritan work ethic. This is not only, or mainly, because the ethos of individual responsibility has been undermined (by affluence? by the welfare state?), but because the pattern of work, insecure part-time jobs with a rapid turnover, is inimical to such an ethos.

A second strategy is for the young to refuse to accept that the hopeful future which previous generations had confidently expected has been foreclosed for them, however utopian such a refusal may appear to a cynical adult world. Paradoxically, the young may therefore appear old-fashioned, even reactionary and romantic. They may refuse to accept that 'the party's over' in the welfare state, that a nuclear balance of terror has become inevitable, that uneconomic factories must be closed and redundant communities dispersed, that human relations can be reduced to some utilitarian calculus of narcissistic pleasure. Either or both strategies are possible, cynicism or utopianism, the extinction of ambition or the rejection of the diminished world accepted by their tired elders. As Dr Johnson observed: 'Young men [he was not a feminist] have more virtue than old men; they have more generous sentiments in every respect'.[2]

THE SCHOOLS REVOLUTION

Still the sharpest image of the divided world of (English) education after almost a century is Thomas Hardy's description in *Jude the Obscure* of Jude's first sight of the distant spires of Christminster (Oxford) from the bleak Berkshire downs which were his narrow poverty-stricken home. Scotland has its own more hopeful images, perhaps myths, of educational progress. Already in that first glimpse, and the lines that describe it, the rest of the story is contained – the hopelessness, the vanity, the failure of Jude's ambition.[3] The distance between Jude's world, the late-Victorian world of rural poverty in which village schools where Sue Bridehead taught struggled for a secure foundation, and the world of Jowett's Oxford in the middle of its passage from Barchester to *Glittering Prizes* was too great for all but those with the greatest determination and the best luck to travel. Jude, like every man, had insufficient of either.

When it was first published in 1896 *Jude the Obscure* was denounced as an obscene work for reasons that have lost their capacity to shock in the late twentieth century. Yet today it remains a shocking book. Its bleak story of unrealisable hope, frustrated ambition, social failure and finally moral degradation is too dark even for the present age. Obscurity, failure and the other disturbing elements in the book's message are just as unpalatable to us as they were to the most naive Victorian optimist.

Even within the narrower frame of eduation the thoughts provoked by *Jude* are sombre ones. After all, Christminster is still there, not so very much changed. The Judes of today may have a closer view of its spires, from the council estates of Cowley rather than the distant downs, but the university has not changed very much either. This is despite a century of reform in which the dominant preoccupation has been to reduce these ancient divisions, to create a common system of education that embraced both the Christminsters and the board schools and to establish a united teaching profession that included not only the Jowetts, but also the Sue Brideheads of Hardy's village schools.

So much of this generous project has been achieved. But these advances are not assured, as the reactionary provisions of the 1988 Education Reform Act in England and Wales have demonstrated.[4] The old ghost of Jude perhaps haunts those who struggle to abolish the divided world of education more than it does those who are content to see it continue. The incompleteness of the educational revolution is taken as proof that it can never be completed. Sadly, Jude's ghost is less likely to shock the fortunate out of their moral complacency than it is to confirm their belief in a settled inequality. How much happier Jude would have been if he had never travelled to Christminster: that is the insinuating conclusion that many will draw. Reformers therefore cannot afford to falter. They must exorcise Hardy's gloomy ghost.

The securest advance has been made in primary schools. The progressive pattern conceived in the 1940s and 1950s and authoritatively endorsed by the Plowden report in England in the 1960s still seems to command widespread support.[5] Within a system divided by sharp controversy, primary education seems to be an area of amiable agreement or, at the worst, civilised disagreement among parents, teachers, children and even politicians. Mixed-ability teaching and multiracism flourish without serious challenge. The exodus of the children of the anxious upper middle class into private schools is often delayed until the end of primary education, or a little earlier if entrance examination timetables require it. Even the difficulties that primary schools face seem to be mild. Some people complain older children are not sufficiently challenged and demand the more systematic introduction of homework or of French. But middle schools for nine- to thirteen-year-olds, which arguably could help to introduce this extra rigour, have not proved a popular model. The most common complaint is that they tend to extend the 'primary' ethos rather than introducing at an earlier age a 'secondary' environment. Some believe that national tests of achievement at the age of seven are the answer. This has been provided for in the Education Reform Act. But few expect such tests to be effectively applied. At the pre-primary level there has been a significant failure to develop nursery schools. Among the reasons for this have been a shortage of resources, the reluctance of teachers to become 'child-minders' and a social conservatism which holds that more comprehensive child care undermines the institution of the family and the ethos of personal responsibility.

There are several possible explanations for this surprising lack of controversy about the progressive arrangement of the first seven years (more than half the total) of compulsory education. The first is that the radical challenge to academic and selective secondary schools presented by the growth of 'extended' elementary schools, the first attempt to establish comprehensive schools based on modern practical values, was defeated in the early years of this century. This meant that when this challenge inexorably was renewed it would not come from below. The political quietism imposed on elementary schools by the 1902 Education Act was reinforced after 1944 when compulsory education was extended to the secondary stage. Future battles would be fought out between the competing traditions within secondary education – the later years of elementary education organised under the 'secondary modern' label, and the grammar schools. Finally, in the 1960s, the abolition of secondary selection removed the shadow of the eleven plus examination which had lain over the last years of primary education. But the most convincing explanation is also the simplest. The break between primary and secondary education marks a natural break in the development of children or reflects, at any rate, the conventional adult interpretation of that development that has persisted even after Freud – a break between childhood and adolescence, between a Rousseauan world of natural innocence and a social world in which inequalities of birth, achievement and status are an inescapable reality.

The real battle is over secondary schools. But it has become a battle of oblique skirmishes rather than of direct confrontation. The pattern of comprehensive schools established in the 1960s is not under serious challenge. Ninety per cent of all secondary pupils are now enrolled in comprehensives. An irreversible change has taken place in the pattern of British education. The future may bring new types of comprehensive schools (like 'magnet' schools?) but it is unlikely to see the open restoration of selective schools on a significant scale. The establishment of City Technology Colleges, national schools sponsored by business under the direct patronage of the Department of Education and Science; the ability of schools to become independent of local education authorities; the spread of the technical and vocational education initiative (TVEI) designed to offer less able fourteen- and fifteen-year-olds a more practical curriculum – none of these recent developments is likely to disturb the present pattern of comprehensive schools. Other recent measures, such as the development of a national core curriculum and the imposition of a battery of national tests, will confirm this pattern. So the retreating roar of a rearguard should not be mistaken for the cry of a battle still in doubt.

If the battle for the comprehensive principle has not been lost, neither have the detailed arrangements for the organisation of secondary education become a source of damaging controversy. Perhaps twenty years ago anxious parents and conservative politicians (on the left as well as right) feared that an inflexible pattern of gigantic comprehensives, American high schools with all their alien difficulties, was about to be imposed across Britain. But the comprehensive school has shown itself to be a highly variable model. Big schools had already fallen out of fashion before the declining number of secondary-school-age children forced a rethink on organisation. Mixed-abillity teaching, setting, even streaming have all found a respected place within the comprehensive tradition. A more common complaint in the 1980s is about the diversity of comprehensive schools. Their organisation, teaching methods and curricula are too varied, it is alleged. What is needed is greater national uniformity. Much less is heard today about 'black-board jungles', as early disciplinary problems have been overcome by the reassertion of more traditional patterns of pastoral care (and as standards of acceptable behaviour in schools, and in society, have changed?). Even the idea of a secondary education which stretches from the primary school through to higher education has been challenged by the growth of sixth form and tertiary colleges for sixteen- to nineteen-year-olds. Perhaps the growth of a more coherent tertiary sector will take the ideological heat off secondary schools, which would then be left alone like primary schools. The comprehensive school has demonstrated that it is a broad church in its ruling ethos, its internal arrangement and its external organisation.

The sharpest controversies about comprehensives concern two points. The first is academic achievement. The common-sense prejudice is that comprehensives fail their brightest pupils compared to the former grammar schools and that they encourage a kind of mass mediocrity. In fact, the contrary seems to be the case.[6] Comprehensives have competed rather well with the grammar schools in terms of the academic achievements of their more able pupils. The simplest evidence is that at a time when most British secondary schools were becoming comprehensive, higher education was able to treble its intake of students. Far from falling, entry standards edged up during this period. But comprehensives may have been less successful with the less able and the less motivated – today's Judes. Their more relaxed environment make it more difficult to counteract the levelling pressures of the peer group. The truly disadvantaged, socially and academically, comprehensive schools have served well. But it may be that so much effort has been put into reassuring middle-class parents, nostalgic for their grammar or public school days, that less energy has been available with which to tackle the broader social mission for which comprehensives were designed. The second is the social message which comprehensive schools, despite their cautious practice, carry. It is a disturbing message in the closed meritocracy which Britain has remained, although in North America and large parts of Europe the anxiety it creates is difficult to understand. That message is that there is a need to go beyond the formal equality of citizenship which (nearly) everyone has to accept in the late twentieth century, to try to achieve a richer social equality. This means not just a cultural equality that extends beyond the temporary solidarity of youth, but also an equality of social and economic opportunities and even outcomes. Education is embroiled in this question because schools play such an important part in forming the division of labour and so in settling the hierarchy of society.

To some that is a disturbing message and to a few an intolerable one. Guiltily for the first group and defiantly for the second, private education offers an escape. In recent years the social situation of private schools has undergone a paradoxical shift. Never more popular, as those who despise civic solidarity regard the education they provide as a good to to be purchased, they have drifted away from public education into a closed world.[7] A slippage in terminology reveals this important change. As late as the 1960s the title 'public schools' was still a common (as well as proper) description of the top private schools. Maybe in this usage some shrivelled sense of public responsibility survived, a patronising but nevertheless intimate association with the rest of education. Today the preferred title is 'independent schools', on the grounds that it is important to emphasise their freedom from the state. That secret sense of public responsibility has been finally abandoned. In the late 1960s a window of opportunity for a redrawn relationship between public and 'public' schools opened, and as quickly closed.[8] Only a few, more perceptive, private schools even noticed its quick flash of hope.

The shape of the teaching profession has changed as much as the pattern of schools since the days of Sue Bridehead (probably pre-1870 despite the much later publication of *Jude*). It has ceased to be a two-class profession, divided into an upper stratum of public and grammar school teachers closely linked to the universities in which nearly all of them had been educated, and a lower stratum of minimally-qualified board school teachers oppressed by a mean 'payment by results' regime and an inquisitorial inspectorate.[9] Some may say that all teachers are now in the same category – the lower one. But such cynicism, although understandable in the light of the poor pay and shabby treatment of school teachers in Britain in the 1980s, seriously underestimates the professional gains of the past century. A few teachers remain outside today's united teaching profession. Those in independent schools now find themselves in a ghetto. University dons, too, in the first half of this century succeeded in establishing a higher professional identity, although in the second half they have found it difficult to maintain.

Teachers in polytechnics and other higher education colleges now enjoy the (somewhat reduced) prestige of the dons. But the bulk of school teachers share a professional unity. Old divisions between grammar and secondary-modern have been swallowed up by comprehensive reorganisation. Those between graduate and certificated teachers have disappeared. The divisions which have succeeded these earlier gulfs, between primary and secondary schools and between teachers with professional degrees and those with academic qualifications, are much milder. The contrast between the academic values of 'upper' teachers and the more practical values of 'lower' teachers has also been softened. Within teacher education the trend has been to give the academically qualified a firmer professional grounding, while upgrading the academic knowledge of teachers with more practical skills.

But teachers have not been able to secure an absolutely assured professional status. The underdevelopment of English schools in the nineteenth century and the power of the public schools with their near-monopoly of the education of the national elite have both contributed to a cultural memory in which teachers are not treated with respect. This instinctive degradation of the teaching profession, of course, is not as pronounced in Scotland with its tradition of the 'dominie' and of the Democratic Intellect, nor in Wales where teachers along with ministers made such a vital contribution to the recovery of Welshness in the nineteenth and twentieth centuries. These differences remain, despite vociferous complaints about the 'anglicisation' of Scottish education. But in England schools and teachers have never seemed so central to the achievement of national purposes. Remember Shaw's, 'He who can does. He who can't teaches'. Unlike university dons, school teachers have not been able to ensure the corporate independence of their institutions, and unlike doctors they have been unable to establish their individual and collective autonomy within public institutions. But teachers, especially head teachers, are much the most influential group in determining the character of schools, whatever the small print of Acts of Parliament, DES circulars, the advice of Her Majesty's Inspectors or local authority regulations may say. The professional autonomy exercised by the classroom teacher may not seem as awesome or as final as the clinical freedom exercised by the surgeon in the operating theatre. But it is of the same order and may have greater consequences.

So it may be that while teachers are angered by their apparent undervaluation by society (and their indisputable underpayment!), society is frightened by the extent of the teacher's effective freedom. This fear is sometimes expressed through unreasonable, because they are unrealisable, demands for greater accountability. Here there is an interesting contrast between the practice of local education authorities and of central Government, whether represented by the DES, the Scottish Education Department or HMI. Local authorities generally respect the professional independence of teachers, except in limited areas either of high political visibility, like equal opportunities or multiracism, or of administrative action, like the appointment of head teachers and the organisation of the pattern of local schools. Central government is much more suspicious of the autonomy of teachers, although in Scotland the SED has sponsored the professionalisation of teachers – on its own terms, of course. From the Board through the Ministry to the Department of Education (and now Science) the consistent policy has been one of accelerating intervention to control schools and teachers. Often this accumulation of power has been justified on the grounds that central government is acting as a proxy for 'parents' or 'industry'. Yet there is little evidence that these groups are especially unhappy with standards in schools, or hostile to the professional autonomy of teachers. Yet as the responsibilities of local education authorities are progressively eroded (for political as much as for educational reasons), and the power of central government is allowed to increase, the freedom of teachers will be called into greater question and the advances towards professionalism made since the days of Jowett and Jude may be put at risk. However these dangers can be exaggerated. The traditional partnership between central and local government in education has always been something of a myth, its ambiguity summed up in that delightfully opaque phrase 'a national system locally administered'. All the decisive initiatives, most of them beneficial, from the 1870 Act to the comprehensive reorganisation of the 1960s, have come from the centre. Yet there must be concern that the 1988 Education Reform Act, with its alarming lurch towards national control of schools, may have upset the historical balance.

What has been achieved a century after Jude first saw the spires of Christminster? Where we were two educational nations, we have become almost one. Of course the missionary emotions of nineteenth century school teachers like Sue Bridehead, or the 'New Jerusalem' hopes of the 1940s, or the social ambitions of 1960s reformers remain unsatisfied. But that is perhaps how it should be. The education revolution is a permanent revolution. In one of his less well known books, *A French Eton*, Matthew Arnold, who himself knew both worlds, that of Christminster and of the obscure Jude, wrote:

Children of the future, whose day has not yet dawned, you, when that day arrives, will hardly believe what obstructions were long suffered to prevent its coming! You who, with all your faults, have neither the aridity of aristocracies, nor the narrow-mindedness of middle classes, you, whose power of simple enthusiasm is your great gift, will not comprehend how progress twoards man's best perfection – the adorning and ennobling of his spirit – should have been reluctantly undertaken; how it should have been for years and years retarded by commonplaces, by worn-out clap-traps. You will wonder at the labour of its friends in proving the self-proving; you will know nothing of the doubts, the fears, the prejudices they had to dispel; nothing of the outcry they had to encounter; of the fierce protestations of life from policies which were dead and did not know it, and the shrill querulous upbraiding from publicists in their dotage. But you, in your turn, with difficulties of your own, will then be mounting some new step in the arduous ladder whereby men climbs towards his perfection; towards that unattainable but irresistible lode-star, gazed after with earnest longing, and invoked with bitter tears: the longing of thousands of hearts, the tears of many generations.[10]

CIVIC AND VOCATIONAL LITERACY

In 1976 the then Prime Minister James Callaghan opened a 'Great Debate' about standards in schools with a speech at Ruskin College, Oxford.[11] In the eyes of those who delight in historical symbolism, Ruskin may have been an unfortunate place to launch such an initiative. For there was nothing in Mr Callaghan's speech to encourage the view that the submerged populist tradition of workers education represented by Ruskin, liberal in its intentions and politically engaged, should be given belated emphasis. Instead, the Prime Minister talked of the need to make education more relevant to the economic life of the nation and to maintain, or even restore, traditional standards. Some have regarded the Ruskin speech as the signal for a counter-revolution, an implicit rejection of the exaggerated liberalism encouraged by progressive school reforms in the previous decade, a kind of grammar school's revenge. Yet almost as plausible is the alternative view, that the Ruskin speech marked the next stage in the comprehensive revolution, the attempt to substitute a modern curriculum relevant to social and economic conditions for the watered-down academic curriculum inherited from the old grammar school. In any case, the debate begun at Ruskin with its twin themes of standards and relevance has endured. It was carried forward by the Conservative Government elected in 1979. Keith Joseph, Secretary of State for Education and Science in the early 1980s, attempted to improve standards in schools by measures designed to produce better teachers, efforts which were summed up in his *Better Schools* White Paper.[12] Kenneth Baker, who succeeded him at the DES, adopted a more direct and aggressive approach in the 1988 Act designed to increase competition between schools.

Despite Mr Baker's Act the focus of education policy in the 1980s has switched from the external organisation of schools, the dominant preoccupation in the 1960s at the high tide of comprehensive reform, to their internal organisation. Despite the creation of City Technology Colleges, the new right of schools to 'opt out' of the control of local education authorities and the imposition of school boards in Scotland, the present pattern of comprehensive primary and secondary schools is not under serious challenge. The main area of institutional fluidity is the tertiary sector, ignored in the recent Act. The traditional sixth form looks unlikely to outlive the present century. But perhaps the greater freedom that has now been given to secondary schools will allow them to resist the inevitable rationalisation of sixteen-to-nineteen education for a little longer. In any case, present arrangements for the education of five- to sixteen-year olds will not change. No local education authority is going to reintroduce selective secondary schools on a significant scale, partly because this is opposed by public, parental and professional opinion but also partly because the shortage of resources will always discourage the setting up of a wasteful system of parallel schools. Nor is there likely to be significant expansion of the independent sector. To the extent that the 1988 Act encourages greater differentiation in public education, independent schools will become less attractive.

The action has moved elsewhere. The quality of teachers, the content of the curriculum, the reform of school examination – these are now the areas of most active policy. Here, not in the reorganisation of schools, is to be found today's volatility. Part of the reason may be that, precisely because the structure of schools established in the 1960s looks so impregnable, those who opposed comprehensive reform must find another arena in which to attempt their counter-revolution. But a more important reason is that everyone, conservatives and liberals alike, recognises that the experience of pupils is moulded much more decisively by the practice of education – the subjects they learn, the quality of classroom teaching, the examinations or other measures of achievement by which they are judged – than the shape of the institution, still less the name over its door. In education, as elsewhere, there has been a shift away from a preoccupation with structure to a renewed concern with the culture of schools. Clearly the curriculum itself is the most important component of that culture, although it is doubtful whether a national curriculum will unlock the door into this secret garden. This phrase became the favourite post-Ruskin metaphor to describe the curriculum. It is a revealing phrase which sums up most picturesquely some powerful prejudices about that curriculum. The 'secret' part of the phrase reflects resentment at the professional autonomy of teachers and dissatisfaction about the resistance of schools to lay influence, whether social or industrial. The 'garden' part suggests a great diversity of knowledge and skills but also their organised (and traditional?) arrangement, happily separate from the wild wood outside the classroom.

The dilemma of modern education is that it must attempt to create two quite different beings, economic man (and woman) and the educated citizen. To pretend that these two intentions, and their supporting curricular paraphernalia, are the same is wrong. The economic achievement of men and women does not encompass their civic and personal development. Each is a necessary but hardly sufficient condition for the other. Work, of course, will remain an important source of social status and personal identity, as well as a crucial means of creating wealth. A system of education which did not produce school leavers or graduates with practical skills would be utterly deficient. But work and life are not the same. First, more than half the population of modern societies does not 'work' in a narrow industrial sense. They are too young or too old, unemployed, chronically ill or disabled, or responsible for looking after young children. Many of these, of course, work much harder than the conventionally employed but are not regarded as being engaged in productive work. Secondly, the industrial revolution produced an irreversible separation between work and non-work. It introduced a sophisticated division of labour, which incorporated the bulk of the working population into a centralised market economy and disenfranchised those left outside. Thirdly, twentieth-century affluence has tended to widen the gulf between work and non-work. Working hours have been reduced and the time available for leisure has increased. Work has become a minority occupation even for those in jobs.

So the school curriculum has to wrestle with this fundamental ambiguity. It must try to produce competent workers and good citizens. This has become more difficult now that secondary schools are comprehensive in their intake and have pupils of all abilities and from all social classes; centrifugal intentions have to be balanced within a comprehensive curriculum. In the bad old days of the two-tier system, grammar schools as opposed to first elementary and then secondary modern schools this difficult task could be evaded. The former could offer a curriculum which attempted to provide an education for citizenship, even if that curriculum was academic rather than liberal and the citizenship it aimed at reflected upper class culture rather than popular democracy. The latter could offer a curriculum confined to training in economic skills with only the thinnest of civic veneers. It is the academic education inherited from the grammar school which has predominated over the practical education inherited from the secondary modern in the curriculum of most comprehensive schools. The reasons are simple. The new comprehensives have had to try to match the grammar schools in the academic honours game, and the oppressively utilitarian education provided in many secondary modern schools was long overdue for liberal reform.

But this inevitable bias may have led to a reactionary longing for the curricular simplicity of a two-class school system. This longing may explain the resonance of Mr Callaghan's Ruskin speech. The prejudice persisted that, by aiming at an integrated curriculum, comprehensives would inevitably fail the academically able while stigmatising those young people with more practical inclinations. Keith Joseph certainly believed that schools were failing what he called 'the bottom 40 per cent'. The TVEI initiative is designed to motivate pupils who despite their intelligence are not attracted by the academic studies which continue to dominate the curriculum of the upper secondary school.[13] Sadly, the emphasis on the twin themes of standards and relevance since the Ruskin speech has made it more difficult for schools to devise an integrated curriculum that bridges the gap between the academic and the practical, although Scotland's 'action plan' is a brave attempt. However much effort is devoted to devising new approaches to excellence and to emphasising that 'fitness for purpose' must be the decisive criterion, the call for higher standards will be interpreted by many as a code for the restoration of a traditional academic curriculum and the call for relevance as a code for renewed emphasis on a practical, utilitarian, skills-based curriculum.

Means and ends are extricably confused in the school curriculum. Its objectives and its methods cannot be disentangled. One positive outcome of the post-Ruskin climate has been a renewed interest in objectives. This has stiffened the debate about the curriculum. It is no longer regarded as a hidden agenda that cannot easily be made explicit, nor, at the permissive extreme, is it imagined that objectives will emerge spontaneously. On the contrary, objectives need to be stated with some care. It is not enough to say that schools must teach skills that are economically relevant. Does this mean down-to-earth training in useful skills which can be applied immediately to the world of work? Or a much broader vocational literacy which provides a blend of skills and attitudes that can survive the alarmingly fast turnover of jobs and occupations? If the first is the aim, this suggests a return to the old skills-based curriculum, at any rate for the less academically able. But it is doubtful whether schools are equipped to provide training in highly specialised skills, except at the most meagre level. Even if they were, it would often be a waste of time and effort because many such skills are likely to become quickly redundant. In modern Britain, as in all advanced societies, high-level professional skills have a much longer shelf-life than lower-level occupational skills. So the less able may need more flexible skills than those pupils who go on to further and higher education.

However, if a narrow skills-based curriculum is unsuitable for most young people, the alternative, a curriculum aimed at producing broader vocational literacy, is difficult to design. Should it concentrate on developing positive attitudes and fundamental skills in basic industrial and business practice, such as good time-keeping or the ability to work in a team? Or should it teach core skills like literacy, numeracy, communication (human and electronic) to try to provide a firm base on which a superstructure of specialised skills and knowledge can later be built, probably on the job? Or should such a curriculum be designed to foster those transferable intellectual skills, like the ability to analyse and argue logically, which will be needed in any sustained professional career? One answer, of course, is that a curriculum for vocational literacy must do all three. The least able would concentrate on learning good industrial job habits; the most able on high-level intellectual skills; and the middle band on core developmental skills. But this is an unsatisfactory answer because it fails to recognise that these three objectives may point to three quite distinct curricula – a practical education with few academic frills for the first group; something close to the traditional academic/liberal education for the most able; and a core curriculum high in quality but low in variety for the rest. If the present attempts to write a national curriculum are to result in more than a crude share-out of time among different subjects, and if the devising of national tests is to produce useful and universal measures of achievement, the systematic difficulty of translating objectives into content must be confronted.

The other main objective of schools, to promote civic literary, must be pursued with equal care. The difficulty here is that liberal education, the obvious vehicle for promoting such literacy, was hijacked long ago by academic education. It was Huxley, not Arnold, who won the celebrated nineteenth-century debate. An academic curriculum heavily influenced by the entry requirements of a selective and specialist higher education system has stood proxy for liberal education for most of the twentieth century. Yet the two are very different. Academic education is organised around the commanding concept of knowledge, and liberal education around that of culture. These two words, knowledge and culture, suggest contrasting ways to recognise truth. Their conflict has led to two difficulties for those concerned with the school curriculum. First, an academic curriculum must give its undivided allegiance to distinguishing truth from falsehood. It has no choice but to accept the division of academic labour that is the most effective means for making such distinctions. So its ethos is necessarily amoral, and its techniques, reductionist. Liberal education, in contrast, is moral and integrative, at any rate in its intention. Its aims to sustain a common culture. Of course there is a danger that liberal education can degenerate into a polite form of propaganda, or the facile 'cultural literacy' favoured by some conservatives in the United States. The line between interpretation, which is central to the idea of a liberal education, and propaganda, which is its opposite, is very thin indeed.

The second difficulty is linked to the first. Today it is a truism among teachers, inspectors and other experts that the school curriculum must concentrate on process as much as product, that how pupils learn is as important as what they learn. They study history not so much to learn about the Tudor or Stuart kings or the causes of the Second World War as to learn how to collect and analyse evidence, how to construct interpretations that are logical and persuasive, and to develop other cognitive skills.[14] But clearly this emphasis on the process, problem-solving, rather than on the product, the accumulation of knowledge, can be carried too far. First, the content is rarely irrelevant to the method. Secondly, civic literacy requires a minimum common knowledge. Those without such knowledge are effectively disenfranchised. Thirdly, employers want to know what their prospective recruits have learned as well as how they have learned it. But the most powerful objection is that in a society that runs on professional expertise, and in an economy driven by science and technology, knowledge occupies a decisive position. Even a century ago Arnold's 'sweetness and light' of humanist culture had been overborne by Huxley's imperatives of modern science. How much more unequal the contest has become in the course of the twentieth century. Many trends in education since Mr Callaghan's Ruskin speech are welcome – the emphasis on higher standards and on social and industrial relevance, a new clarity about the objectives of the curriculum, a determination to improve the quality of learning rather than to simply perpetuate the accumulation of thoughtless knowledge. But there is a danger that those worthy aims will be perverted into a restatement of the old British conceit that 'first-class minds' and entrepreneurial guts will see us through. They won't. The task for schools is to develop interpretations of vocational literacy that are sufficiently broad to meet the demands of a postindustrial future and to define a civic literacy that aims to produce educated citizens, not cultured conformists.

'FIRST-CLASS MINDS AT BAY'

British education today seems to be the victim of the unfairest of paradoxes. On the one hand, schools are the focus for popular discontent, even if the intensity of this discontent has been exaggerated. The nation's leaders, right, left and centre, argue that schools (and higher education is often included in the indictment) are failing to develop the talent of young people to its fullest potential. Parents feel a parallel unease, although their instinct is to blame the politicians rather than the teachers. They invest the highest hopes in the present achievements and future happiness of their children, and if these hopes are frustrated the schools are often blamed. On the other hand, the evidence to explain this tangible unease is slight. Since the comprehensive reform of the 1960s, Britain has enjoyed a sensible pattern of schools for pupils aged five to sixteen and beyond. The teaching profession is better qualified, than even before, and however shaky its collective morale the dedication of the great majority of individual teachers is not in doubt. Few British secondary schools, even in the most deprived districts, encounter the overwhelming remedial and discipline problems faced by some American high schools. Levels of achievement are measurably higher than in the United States. There is almost no evidence that French, German or even Japanese pupils are educated according to a more modern curriculum. By most sensible international indices, whether the output of graduate engineers or the levels of residual illiteracy, British education seems to be performing at an above-average level.

One reason for this puzzling paradox is that schools and teachers are handy scapegoats. Some parents are alarmed by some of the phenomena described at the beginning of this chapter – the inward culture of the young, the crumbling of authority before the remorseless pressure of the peer group, the invasion of family privacy by consumerism and the mass media – and they are tempted to blame the schools and their teachers. A few who have become so used to the idea that the 'state' will provide everything expect schools to do the impossible, to educate their children into a rich literacy when they themselves provide a virtually non-literate environment at home. The old expectation that education depends on a partnership between family and school is difficult to sustain today, however hard some parents and most teachers work to that end. But another explanation of this paradox is that the values of education are much too close for comfort to our self-image as a society, our evaluation of the British present and assessment of the British future. Schools hold up a mirror to society. If their contemporary reputation is fragile the most important reason is that we do not like, or even understand, what we see in that mirror. The complacent, even arrogant, solidity of Victorian and early twentieth-century Britain has been dissolved; the fuzzy postimperial postindustrial image that has succeeded it creates instead a sense of unease in which education is implicated.

This close relationship between the reputation of our schools and the state of national morale is not hard to understand. Of all social activities education touches individual lives and cultural values most closely. In contrast the regulation, or deregulation, of industry, the social security system, even the health service have more limited intentions. They are concerned with improving and civilising our means of living; education is concerned with the ends of that living, the quality of our lives. Their purpose is to promote socio-economic wealth or physical health; the purpose of schools, although it certainly embraces these practical goals, extends in the secular twentieth century to the moral well-being of the individual and of society. Only a limited amount of information can be discovered about the quality of a nation by examining its employment structure, its industry, its health services or its foreign policies, but an examination of its education provides a recognisable portrait of its ultimate values. It goes to the heart of the matter. France's Cartesian tradition and Revolutionary/Napoleonic inheritance are written on the face of its schools. That curious amalgam of Jeffersonian liberalism, frontier populism and patriotic religion is still a commanding presence in American education. And in Britain? Maybe that is the difficulty. Fifty, even thirty years ago, a settled national identity seemed to be available – at home, a liberal welfare-state democracy still in touch with a more aristocratic past, and abroad a great power if no longer a world empire. But today? Britain's domestic identity is fiercely contested territory; its social-democratic majority beleaguered by a militant free-market minority. Its international status is inexplicably confused, one moment on first-name terms with the world's superpowers and the next the odd man out in a humdrum European Community.

Another reason is that education is the most future-directed of all the activities undertaken by modern societies. Not only does it address ends as well as means and engage individual hopes as well as social and economic ambitions, but the future is its territory as much as the present. The character of schools not only offers an almost too honest insight into the quality of contemporary society, but also provides a powerful statement about society's desired future. What goes on in schools today is as much directed to twenty-first-century Britain as to the routines of the 1990s. As the distant future is more sharply contested than the immediate future, because it seems an open question rather than a preordained outcome, schools have become embroiled in these intense controversies. They are the most conspicuous arena in which we argue about our future. The impact of education's future-direction on its present reputation is difficult to assess. Of course in a troubled and ageing society with abbreviated ambitions the future seems less enticing. But the restlessness modern Britain shares with all similar societies, and its obsession with novelty and style, may put a higher premium on future-directed activities like education. The frenetic quality of modern life, also undermines the capacity of schools to validate a hopeful future. The accelerating accumulation of knowledge, the destabilising turnover of technology, the apartheid of generations, the collapse of community tradition, the rise of ephemeral consumerism – none of these creates the conditions for a confident reach forward into the future.

This fissiparous future is difficult to contain within the traditions that still govern British education and the impressions in the mirror schools hold up to society. Two dominant traditions can be distinguished. The first is that of liberal education, a package of pedagogy and curricula organised around the principle that the most important task of schools is to develop the potential of the individual child to the full within a humanist culture. This can take both elitist and populist forms. The best example of the latter was the extensive educational programmes developed in the armed forces during the Second World War. The second tradition is that of a modernising, science-based curriculum organised around the principle that the purpose of schooling is to produce socio-economic man (and woman), competent and effective in our modern age. The revered prophets of liberal education have always been Arnold and Newman. But this stuffy identification with high-minded Victorian classicism can be misleading. Much of popular education in the last century and in the early years of this, including much of the work of the often misunderstood mechanics' institutes, was as deeply liberal in its intentions as Oxford 'Greats'. Indeed it can be argued that the mechanics' institutes, motivated by the desire to enlighten the industrial and democratic masses, were more 'liberal' than Oxbridge, which offered an apprenticeship in government. Today liberal values permeate British schools. The emphasis on process, on the quality of learning, on active discovery – all are elements in this liberal project. Most arts subjects, and some social and natural sciences, justify their intentions in the language of liberal education.

Yet that language has remained deficient in two respects. First, liberal education has failed to incorporate natural science and technology adequately or sufficiently. Literature and history, not physics or biology, have continued to be the principal channels through which liberal values flow in British education. In a society shaped by science and technology this is an unhealthy imbalance. Of course some argue that this anti-science bias is inevitable. Reductionist disciplines cannot compete with summative ones in their contribution to the liberal project. But who can reasonably claim that in the age after Einstein and the unravelling of DNA physics and biology are not summative subjects? Who can also deny, at a time of triumphant specialisation in so many of the arts, that English or history often betray a distressing bias towards reductionism? But this weakness remains in our definition of liberal education. Beyond the General Certificate of Secondary Education or Scottish ordinary level, science, with the possible exception of mathematics, is excluded from any serious role in promoting general education in schools. 'A' level or Higher Grade chemistry is not regarded as a course that stretches the imagination. So the natural enthusiasm that science excites among young people in an industrial society has not been recruited into the service of liberal values. As a result, both liberal and science education lose something of their intellectual vitality. Rather as a common European civilisation is divided into two armed camps, C.P. Snow's 'two cultures' cut through what should be a common liberal project.

Secondly, despite the mechanics' institutes in the last century and the Workers Educational Association and the university extramural departments in this, liberal education has too often remained predemocratic as well as prescientific (or preindustrial?). Many people at the top of British society do not believe it is desirable to educate the mass of young people in accordance with such liberal intentions. For those who make up in Eric Ashby's phrase, 'the thin clear stream of excellence' or who are said to possess, in that revealingly ambiguous phrase, 'first-class minds', an education that promotes high-level intellectual skills within a settled humanist tradition is regarded as entirely appropriate. But this cannot be a reasonable ambition for the mass of pupils. It would encourage an intellectual autonomy which in an unequal society could not be matched by an equivalent personal autonomy and so become a source of frustration and discontent (as in the fictional case of Jude). And were this liberal project to fail the outcome would be that many pupils, denied any finer compensations, would leave school vocationally illiterate. Such are the arguments which, discreetly articulated, decisively inhibit democratic education in Britain. But the difficulty goes even deeper. The pragmatism of the British intellectual tradition, which sometimes shades off into philistinism, values a solidarity of manners at the expense of the explicit coherence of ideas and expertise. Initiation into this informal but exclusive society of intellectual manners can easily be confused with the intentions of liberal education, so reducing the latter to the indefensible clubbability of 'first-class minds'.

The failure to develop a persuasive model of civic literacy and this cramped definition of liberal education are both aspects of the same phenomenon, the incomplete modernisation of British society. Two centuries ago Britain was arguably the most modern society in Europe. Today it is among the most traditional. Until the mid-nineteenth century the development of a liberal society and the growth of an industrial economy both proceeded without serious check. Then modernisation seemed to falter, maybe because of the counter-attractions of empire, maybe because the middle classes had been incorporated with too slight a struggle into the structure of national power and had responded by uncritically adopting a semi-aristocratic cult of gentility. The causes are less important than the consequences. The liberal tradition, in education as elsewhere, became associated with intellectual conformity (even philistinism), social exclusiveness and an anti-vocational amateurism. Its anachronistic footprints are still to be found everywhere in British education in these last years of the twentieth century. All Souls man has to compete with the *Polytechnicien*. His intellectual ability may be as considerable, his professional expertise as great but his mental priorities belong in that predemocratic pre-industrial world produced by Britain's aborted modernisation.

So much for the liberal tradition. Its importance in debates about culture and education should not conceal the fact that its claim to be the dominant tradition within British schools is weak. It is the second tradition, that of a modernising science-based education, which has animated the movement for educational reform, improvement and expansion since 1870 and, with increased emphasis, since 1945. The intention all along was to implement Huxley's not Arnold's, programme. Certainly most nineteenth and twentieth century Governments have justified additional public investment in schools in these terms, to produce a scientifically-educated and vocationally-trained population, although the argument that enfranchised citizens must be educated up to their democratic responsibilities was influential between 1870 and 1902 and again in the 1940s and 1960s. The core sciences like physics, chemistry, biology and, of course, mathematics have superseded the classics as the key disciplines. Today they provide the essential intellectual equipment for an educated life.

Yet two obstacles have stood in the way of the easy success of this second tradition. The first is the inwardness, even the scholasticism, of science. Often this tradition has been dominated by notions of expertise. Scientists have been content to remain loyal servants of industry or the technical advisers of the state. They have rarely attempted to develop alternative cultural codes to those inherited from the prescientific past. So the impact of science, although deep, has been confined in its extent. Education which seeks to speak to ultimate ends has to rely on an extra-scientific or even meta-scientific vocabulary. The second is that this modernising, science-based curriculum has always been vulnerable to a Gradgrind-style utilitarianism. This is compounded by that conspiracy of intellectual manners which in Britain often substitutes for high ability and is summed up in the phrase 'first-class minds'. For the politically powerful class a modern curriculum can only be accepted if it is unlikely to challenge the older culture on which this class even today bases its authority. So this curriculum is reduced to training high-grade specialists or teaching narrow industrial skills or even promoting an unthreatening trainability.

These are a few of the blurred images that can be glimpsed in the mirror which British education holds up to British society. The inconsistencies they reveal must not be exaggerated. They are minor and benign indeed, compared with those suffered by all but a handful of the most fortunate nations. What is particular about the long-contemplated British disease is not its intensity but its intractability. It is a knot of cultural and social attitudes which is difficult to untie, but it does not bind tightly. In a society which since the eighteenth century has solved its public dilemmas by crabwise accommodation and, until very recently, by pragmatic consensus the power of ideas has always been subordinate to the older solidarities of instinct, affection and loyalty. Our moral conception of Britain and Britishness grew out of the latter rather than the former. So today we seem to lack the intellectual means by which we may analyse our present dilemmas and propose alternatives, while the instinctive moral order which was once so strong has crumbled into relativism and conflict. Education is caught in the middle – able to reflect these baleful images which disturb us but, because of the intellectual silence of British culture, unable to take an active part in modifying our perceptions. What cannot be reasonably discussed is what is most deeply felt. As Jane Austen, still in many ways the keenest observer of the British character and in many others its archetype, wrote in *Northanger Abbey*: 'From politics, it was an easy step to silence'.[15] Amid the shouts and cries of modernity Britain remains a silent society.

7
THE BRITISH WAY

The portrait of any nation in any age is difficult to draw. Maybe it can be attempted successfully by a confident historian, like G. M. Young, of a confident age like the Victorian.[1] But the confusions, anxieties and divisions of the late twentieth-century Britain resist portraiture. Instead, we must make do with snapshots and rough sketches. One difficulty is simply that our present age will not sit still long enough to be painted. It was the nineteenth century that first had to accept that restless change had replaced organic growth as the motion of society, that an unknown future might be, would be, discontinuous with the familiar past. J. A. Froude wrote in 1864:

> From the England of Fielding and Richardson to the England of Miss Austen – from the England of Miss Austen to the England of railways and Free-Trade how vast the change; yet perhaps Sir Charles Grandison would not seem so strange to us as one of ourselves will seem to our great-grandchildren. The world moves faster and faster; and the difference will probably be considerably greater. The temper of each new generation is a continual surprise.[2]

Perhaps Froude was misleading about the past. We can now recognise the disturbing novelty, even modernity, if not of Richardson's *Sir Charles Grandison* then certainly of his *Clarissa*. The eighteenth century saw a sea-change in sensibility that marked the emergence of a distinctively modern consciousness. Victorian historians, however, showed little interest in the psyche. But Froude was right about the future. As those great-grandchildren we can confirm the accuracy of his prediction. To us the Victorian age seems strange and more remote than the eighteenth century appeared to the Victorians. Change has become remorseless – but also routine. Today it is stability that shocks.

But Froude may have been wrong to write of the temper of each new generation. Today a generation is much too long. Social change is so rapid that it takes place *within* rather than *between* generations. In the hurrying last years of the twentieth century a single generation must absorb changes which once would have been spread over two or three, or ten. Into a single decade are crammed changes that once would have been enough to absorb the attention of an entire generation. So any easy symmetry between the generations of man and the ages of a nation has disappeared. But if the velocity of social change has increased its direction has been dispersed. Froude's contemporaries may have found it difficult to judge how much further down the road each new generation would explore, but they were sure they recognised the road. From Cardinal Newman to Karl Marx their views of human society had a teleological simplicity irrecoverable today. In the 1980s detailed predictions of the extent and direction of change – scientific, economic, cultural, even personal – have become so sophisticated that broad generalisations have become impossible. All sense of a coherent trajectory, of continuity across a total national culture, has been abandoned. There is no longer time or space for portraits of a whole age, only snapshots – badly composed, soon forgotten.

However, there is a further difficulty. Even if there were time to paint a portrait it would be difficult to know where to begin. The outline has been lost. The images of Britain from which these outlines were derived have faded away. Britain is no longer a great imperial or industrial power. It has shared in the secular decline of the West. Our national identity cannot be imagined in terms of a manifest destiny to spread British civilisation round the world – Shakespeare and Milton, Parliamentary democracy and the rule of law. This civilising mission has been reduced to the British Council's commercially-minded 'cultural diplomacy'. Nor is the alternative image of Britain as the workshop of the world any longer available. Our great industries are closed down. Britain's economy more and more resembles that of a republic of bankers, another Venice or Antwerp. Our affluence is defined by the possession of consumer goods and stylish status symbols, many manufactured or designed abroad. Britain's former achievement in industry, engineering and technology is now recalled only by the precarious excellence of our science. Instead Britain is commonly described as a postimperial and postindustrial nation, both disturbing epithets which suggest past loss more powerfully than future opportunity. The sheet is blank. No images here except, perhaps, of regret.

Even the myths have gone. That of Britain as a middle-class nation, or at any rate a nation that long ago curbed the claims of aristocratic privilege and produced a relatively open society within which the talented poor could rise. A Britain that rose above the necessity of revolutions, a land of quiet shires and companionable towns. A happy nation ruled for three or four long centuries by liberal and patriotic gentlemen, perhaps in their last days with a little help from the professional bourgeoisie and the *arrivistes* entrepreneurs of the great industrial cities. A national idyll that stretched from before Shakespeare to after Trollope or, in a Scottish idiom, from William Dunbar to Hugh MacDiarmid. Or Puritan and Nonconformist England, the world of

Pilgrim's Progress or *Adam Bede*, of stern moral values that animated both evangelical Christianity and the Labour movement. All gone – not, of course, in every detail but as convincing metaphors to describe the essential genius of Britain. Once-firm outlines have been replaced by a few nervous scribbles.

Despite these difficulties, the aim of this chapter is to paint a portrait of our age, of Britain at the end of the twentieth century. It is written, of course, in the full knowledge that such a portrait can never be achieved but in the belief that it must be attempted. In a centrifugal culture and a diverse, even dispersed, society, synthesis and perspective have become more and more difficult to achieve. Yet identity, meaning, even morality grow out of synthesis and depend on perspective, both in the world of ideas and in personal experience. And definitions of nationhood and perceptions of patriotism remain central to our notions of knowledge and value.

EMPIRE AND PROVINCE

Britain is an invented nation, not so much older than the United States. Only sixty-nine years separate the Treaty of Union from the Declaration of Independence, less than the Biblical span of man's life. Of course this new nation was formed from three very old nations, England, Scotland and Wales, with identities as ancient as any in Europe. Nor was the idea of a British nation a radical adventure. It had been prefigured in rhetoric and literature since the Middle Ages, and in the practical political world since at least the union of the English and Scottish crowns in 1603. An earlier attempt to establish a full union had been made in the time of Cromwell. But the artificiality of British nationalism is worth recalling. It helps to explain two of its two most significant but apparently contradictory components – its imperialism and its provincialism. From its beginning in 1707 Great Britain contained an imperial idea. Under the Hanoverian kings it grew into an imperial state, a rising power in Europe and the centre of a worldwide empire.[3] After the French revolutionary wars and the defeat of Napoleon the accent on empire increased until by the end of the ninteenth century imperialism, in a dutiful as well as predatory form, was elevated into almost a national religion. Even in the twentieth century Britain's part in two world wars continued the theme of a great nation engaged in great events.

A simple proof of the significance of empire in British nationalism is provided by a quiet stroll through one of our many great churches or cathedrals. On every wall there are memorials to the dead – soldiers and sailors, bishops and clergy, mayors and members of Parliament – which demonstrate the fusion of Christian faith, classical learning and patriotic duty within a heroic vision of an empire holding sway over foreign enemies, inferior races, and over men's souls. Another less pleasant proof is to recall the savagery with which the enemies of this imperial Britain were sometimes treated, especially internal enemies like the Scottish Jacobites in the eighteenth century and Irish nationalists in the nineteenth and twentieth. This uncomprehending harshness cannot be understood if the ideological threat posed by such dissent is not appreciated. We sometimes congratulate ourselves on avoiding the extreme passions of nationalism that have gripped other nations. The truth, perhaps, is that there have been few occasions on which the challenge to Britain's national identity has been extreme enough to call forth such passions.

Now the empire has gone. Certainly the visible empire of colonies, the great-power charisma, and perhaps too the heroic idea of empire embedded in the notion of 'Great Britain'. Since the Suez adventure of 1956 we have had to come to terms with the idea of Britain without empire. This has not always rested easily on the nation's mind. The last flare of the old imperialism during the Falklands war in the early 1980s demonstrated not only how incongruous imperial passions had become but also how seductive regression to attitudes of empire remained. Great Britain in all its raucous rhetoric was on display in the House of Commons the day after the Argentinian invasion of the Falklands. The British obsession with defence, as pronounced among supporters of the Campaign for Nuclear Disarmament as it is among enthusiasts for the cold war, may be another relic of imperial nostalgia. So may be our endless ambivalence about Britain's relationship with the United States. Both pro- and anti-American sentiments silently assert a claim to a vanished imperial status, the former claiming a special influence in the American empire, Britain's Greece to America's Rome, the latter expressing resentment at Britain's relegation from the superpower league.

The contrast with the rest of Europe is marked. In France too there have been signs of the same anxiety at withdrawal from empire, but slighter ones. Our neighbours seem to regret much less the loss of their various empires – of power, culture, colonies. They are more content with the pragmatism and provincialism of postwar Europe. Perhaps their need for clouds of imperial glory is less because their national identities are organic rather than artificial, deeply rooted in their land and histories, earthy rather than ethereal. Somehow it is easier to imagine the Scots and the Welsh, or even the English, at ease in modern Europe and the modern world. The difficulty is with the British. And one reason may be that British nationalism has little of that 'blood and soil' quality which, for better or worse, has animated feelings in other nations. It remains a literary, cerebral, elitist, perhaps even anaemic movement.

Provincialism is as important a part of Britain's mentality as imperialism. Indeed it is imperialism's antiphony. For all its pomp and circumstance, its outbursts of jingoism in the nineteenth century and its carefully-crafted media monarchy in the twentieth, Great British nationalism has never really been a popular movement.[4] Rather it has remained the approved ideology of the ruling establishment. It is their tombs and memorials that clutter cathedrals; the graves of the common people are to be found in city cemeteries and country church yards. Perhaps this official nationalism has only been able to survive for so long because older, organic nationalisms persisted in England, Scotland and Wales, satisfying more primitive and personal needs for a reassuring identity. Well into the nineteenth century for most Britons, and into the twentieth for a substantial minority, loyalties were local. The regional patriotisms within the many communities of Britain, defined by creed and class as well as geography, fulfilled subtle moral functions which in our modern age are difficult to recall.

These many layers of national feeling may help to explain the tension, but also balance, between prosaic Little England-ism and heroic imperialism. But provincialism has not simply acted as an antidote or additive to imperialism. Provincial Britons have often made good imperialists, from Joseph Chamberlain in the 1890s to Margaret Thatcher in the 1980s. Provincialism also possessed its own rival identity. It offered more than an alternative view of the British experience; until the mid-twentieth century or even later it reflected the real government of Britain. This was largely a local affair, justices of the peace at their quarter sessions, mayors and provosts, county and city councils. Parliament may always have been sovereign, and the state all-powerful in law. In practice, government remained in the hands of local elites. For a long time local and regional loyalties were more powerful than British nationalism. Imperialism was never intended to be re-imported. Only since the middle of the present century has this balance between local and national power been upset.

Today, like imperialism, provincialism is in decline. The growth of the administrative state in the nineteenth century and of the welfare state in the twentieth (and of the 'enterprise' state in the twenty-first?); the nationalising influence first of compulsory education and, more recently, of the mass media; the decline of the traditional industrial regions which so strongly sustained provincial feeling – such factors have undermined the old local and regional loyalties of the British. Another reason for the decay of provincialism has been the parallel decline of Britain as an imperial power. The latter has had two consquences which have deeply affected domestic Britain. First the national elite can no longer be preoccupied with foreign glory. A day-trip to Brussels or Paris to haggle about agricultural surpluses or European energy policy is more typical of their business today. So their attention has been forced inwards to home affairs, while foreign relations have been domesticated. Second, this elite's imperial mentality, its commitment to heroic ideology, have been applied to domestic policies once guided by a pragmatic provincialism. The achievements of the nation have to be rewritten and regional, civic and even individual goals redescribed in a sub-heroic vocabularly derived from the days of empire. The word 'excellence' has a curious ring in Britain. At times it seems to announce an attempt to reimpose an anachronistic imperial code, to recall Trafalgar or D-Day, rather than to describe the process of achieving and excelling in the humdrum modern world. In a puzzling inversion, the British in the late twentieth century seem to be refighting the battle of Waterloo, if not on the playing fields of Eton, then in our schools, laboratories and factories. Britain's domestic pragmatism has succumbed to an imperial ideology that can no longer be kept safely busy abroad.

It may not be a coincidence that the imperial Great British state and provincial England (and Scotland and Wales) have lived and are now dying together. The imperial idea always had to share its dominion with these older organic loyalties. It could never have taken the strain alone. In the late twentieth century imperialism has collapsed in on itself while provincialism has lost its former vitality. The clearest outcome is an overload on national government. Just as Britain's ambitions must now be focused on domestic affairs or unglorious foreign relations, so local initiative has been stifled by the transfer of talent and power to London. Neither the political system with its traditional emphasis on consensual policies (until Mrs Thatcher!) and its antipathy to formal constitution-making, nor a bureaucracy committed to an inward administrative culture rather than to professional expertise is really designed to bear this concentrated burden.[5] So a state which a century ago ruled a worldwide empire now struggles to control the expenditure of local councils. But the overload is moral as well as administrative. The loss of empire has diminished the credibility of British nationalism. Our national religion must now survive without its imperial god. But the decay of local and regional loyalties and of family and community attachments makes Britishness, whatever it has become, more important than ever. In the global village of the modern world, and in a Britain increasingly divided by region, race, class, generation and gender, the need for some unifying identification has become more urgent.

One outcome, of course, could be failure – the break-up of Britain, to borrow the title of Tom Nairn's book.[6] Certainly the present vigour of nationalism in Scotland and Wales, which extends far beyond the party boundaries of the Scottish National Party and Plaid Cymru, should not be underestimated. It is not a superficial political eruption but a response to a deeper crisis of national identity. If the idea of Britain as a whole is in doubt, how much more insecure are definitions of North and West Britain. But the break-up of Britain, at any rate in the form of a regression to its constituent nations, looks unlikely in a world of economic integration and cultural homogeneity. A more hopeful and more likely outcome could be a redefinition of Britishness, the reconstruction of our nation on pragmatic and democratic lines purged of postimperial dreaming. There are those obscure but resonant lines from G. K. Chesterton, often but perhaps mistakenly interpreted in proto-fascist terms as an appeal to the 'blood and soil' feelings so conspicuously lacking in our national spirit: 'Smile at us, pay us, pass us: but do not quite forget. For we are the people of England, that never have spoken yet.'[7] A purged patriotism would probably owe more to Britain's provincial roots than its heroic imperial past. It might give greater weight to older constituent nationalisms, regional loyalties and local attachments which have been so important in the history of our nation. But whatever the prescription or indeed the outcome, the need for a reformation of our national religion cannot be denied.

THE CODES OF CLASS

Class is the language of British society. It is the language in which very many people recall their lives and ambitions, the language in which whole communities describe their moral identity, the language in which we as a nation contemplate the possibilities of social action and the limits of individual achievement. But it is an obscure language. On one reading, Britain is a class-crazed country; on another it is an open, liberal and democratic society. Both cannot be right, but neither can be effectively denied. This ambiguity defines our deepest national experience. The evidence of our obsession with class is overwhelming. Politics is dominated by class-based parties that are not ashamed to exploit the rhetoric of class. In intellectual life the categories of class remain a favourite currency, even when they seem a doubtful analytical tool. In literature and the arts, contested symbols of class retain their creative impulse more than a century after the birth of D. H. Lawrence or Lewis Grassic Gibbon. Where would postwar theatre be without an acutely-developed class consciousness? A Britain denied the use of references to class would be a Britain without a lively soul. Yet the evidence for the openness of British society is also difficult to discount. Social mobility is high, not perhaps as high as in the United States or Australia, but impressive by European standards. Despite the sharpening of feeling in the last decade class antagonisms are mild. The snobberies of manners and style are strong but effective social taboos are weak.

Several explanations have been offered. One is that Britain may once have been a comparatively open society, in the eighteenth century when our rivals were the caste societies of Europe's *ancien régime* and in the nineteenth when the British working class was integrated more quickly and thoroughly into established society than in many industrial nations, but that this has ceased to be true in the present century. Other countries have overtaken Britain on the open-society index. For a long time this sombre fact was concealed by the levelling experience of two world wars and by the exceptional social mobility generated by rapid postwar economic growth. Only now with the increasing unevenness of economic rewards and the abandonment of the mid-century political consensus have serious doubts about the openness of British society come to the surface. Inequality is no longer something to be ashamed of.

But there are serious objections to this first explanation. Lawrence Stone's painstaking analysis of the ruling elites of three English counties between the sixteenth and nineteenth centuries casts doubts on this comforting picture of Britain's past. He shows that many of our most cherished beliefs about openness – the permeability of the gentry, the rise of new men and the decline of old families, the easy incorporation of commerical and professional elites – rest on shaky empirical foundations. Although not exhibiting as extreme an obsession with exclusiveness as their French or German peers, Britain's pre-industrial elite had a consciousness of rank that was a formidable barrier to social mobility. In Stone's account the families that scrambled to power between the 1540s and the 1660s, during the difficult years of the Reformation, the dissolution of the monasteries, the consolidation of the Tudor and Stuart monarchy, and the civil war, were left largely undisturbed in possession of that power until the mid-nineteenth century. Their grip was only broken by Parliamentary and church reform, which eroded their moral and ideological power, and by the repeal of the corn laws and the easy import of American corn, which destroyed their economic power.

There are suggestive parallels between Stone's empirical account and the more polemical accounts of historians of a very different school who have argued that the British *ancien régime* ended not in 1642 or 1688 but only in the crisis of 1828–32. On the other hand, re-examination of French society before the revolution has shown that it was more open than its hard veneer of rigid caste suggested. The status of many aristocrats was insecure and many noble privileges had been sold or mortgaged to the more successful members of the bourgeoisie long before 1789. Taken together, these recent accounts cast serious doubts on the suggestion that pre-industrial Britain was an exceptionally open society in which mobility between classes was commonplace. The difference between Britain and France was less than the conventional Whig interpretation suggested. But, of course, this difference cannot be dissolved away entirely. To Voltaire, to the American colonists, to Britain's own political elite it seemed remarkable – but it was defined more readily in terms of traditional ideas of 'liberty' than by anachronistic twentieth-century notions of social mobility.

The degree to which industrial Britain was and is an open society can also be questioned. More than half a century after it began the debate about whether the living standards of the working class rose or fell during the early stages of the industrial revolution remains unresolved. Certainly in the mid-nineteenth century the apparent impoverishment of the new proletariat formed an important element in Marx's scheme of society. Even in the later nineteenth and twentieth centuries, when the absolute improvement in the material condition of all classes was beyond doubt, the degree of social mobility remains difficult to measure. The accounts offered by David Glass in the 1950s[8] and by the Oxford mobility project in the 1970s suggest that social mobility in modern Britain has been largely intergenerational, fuelled by the increase in middle-class jobs and the decrease of working-class ones, a phenomenon that will be discussed later. In other words, mobility is a function of the changing shape of society produced by economic growth, rather than of the greater equality of opportunity enjoyed by individual citizens. Mobility, arguably, is therefore a matter of economics rather than of equity, perhaps a difficult conclusion for social-democratic reformers to accept.

A second explanation is more subtle. It is that sensitivity to class is strongest in open societies. The 'have-nots' resent inequality because it seems arbitrary and artificial (and so temporary?), while in more traditional and hierarchical societies inequality appears to be part of the natural, organic and so unchallengeable order (except in truly revolutionary circumstances). The 'haves', on the other hand, are most preoccupied with status and privilege when the social order is unstable and advantages of family and wealth easily undermined. On this account, Britain's obsession with class is back-handed evidence of a reluctant openness.

According to this second explanation, the fraternity and solidarity on which many foreign observers of Britain have often enviously remarked, are closely linked to our sensitivity to class. Far from reducing broader national cohesion, class consciousness reinforces it by offering most Britons with a reassuring identity. But this class-based identity is not necessarily antagonistic or separatist in spirit. It does not exclude people from established society. So the British sense of class is intense but not exclusive, cultural in origin as much as socio-economic. It is more about 'belonging' to a family, a street, a community or a region with a shared experience than about membership in a caste that constrains ambition and achievement. Class consciousness may even be a kind of local patriotism, a nationalism of social condition not necessarily in conflict with the broader nationalism that embraces all classes.

This benign and tranquil interpretation of British society has never been captured as well as by George Orwell's famous wartime description:

England is not the jewelled isle of Shakespeare's much quoted passage, nor is it the inferno depicted by Dr Goebbels. More than either it resembles a family, a rather stuffy Victorian family, with not many black sheep in it but with all its cupboards bursting with skeletons. It has rich relations who have to be kow-towed to and poor relations who are horribly sat upon, and there is a deep conspiracy of silence about the source of the family income. It is a family in which the young are generally thwarted and most of the power is in the hands of irresponsible uncles and bedridden aunts. Still, it is family. It has a private language and common memories, and at the approach of an enemy it closes its ranks. A family with the wrong members in control – that, perhaps, is as near as one can come to describing England in a phrase.[10]

Today the young have been thrown out of the house and told to 'get on their bikes'; the bedridden aunts are pampered in private hospitals or wait in draughty queues to be cared for by a crumbling National Health Service; the source of the family income is the proceeds of international finance rather than the plunder of global empire – but still the private language and the common memories survive. Orwell's remains the ruling hypothesis about the British character, perhaps because it is what we want to believe. But is it true? Even more than the attempt to measure the openness of British society, this is a hypothesis that resists empirical proof.

Since Orwell wrote in the 1940s, two powerful phenomena have reworked the face of Britain – the erosion of traditional working-class culture and proletarian solidarity, and the decline of that powerful code of manners to which the upper and middle classes subscribed. Both were evident long before the 1940s. Perhaps for a majority of the working class solidarity had never been possible. Servants, farm labourers, sweated home workers were never able to make a common cause and develop a shared identity in the 1780s or 1880s, any more than in the 1980s the growing army of part time and casual workers in our emerging postindustrial society are able to do. That intense impression of solidarity created by Nonconformity, the Labour movement and the accidental proletarian concentrations that reflected the economy's transitory domination by heavy industry never touched more than a minority of the working class.

The middle-class code may have been another myth. Even in the Victorian age the Christian gentleman, the Smilesian entrepreneur devoted to the Protestant work ethic, the enlightened public servant, the social reformer and other code carriers made up only a small part of the spreading middle class. Their sense of public duty was not shared by most of their peers. They were perhaps no more typical of the middle class than self-conscious proletarians were of the working class, although both embodied compelling models of behaviour. In any case, well before the middle of the present century both working-class solidarity and middle-class code were being undermined by that popular sub-bourgeois culture so well described in its postwar form in Richard Hoggart's *The Uses of Literacy*, which was to develop into the mass entertainment culture of today. In the long quarter-century that followed the end of the Second World War these two traditions were regarded with benign neglect. Their modification was seen as an inevitable outcome of the democratic influences that were building a classless society. The working class was coming out of its ghetto, geographical and cultural. The middle class was abandoning its stuffiness and snobbery. Postwar man (and woman) stripped of old-fashioned class obsessions was being moulded by a new culture of mass entertainment (with its many sanitised glimpses of American 'openness'), social optimism, scientific promise and economic growth. There seemed to be no room for sentimental regret. The rough work of the world was being made smooth.

Today the feeling is different. What had seemed a welcome movement towards a classless society can now be redefined as the prising away of the cement that holds society together. The decline of traditional working-class culture is more likely to be seen as having produced a rootless, divided and perhaps demoralised proletariat. The decay of the old middle-class code has undermined the self-confidence of the great-and-good, making them timorous and cynical. 'You've never had it so good' materialism typical of the late 1950s, the 'Do your own thing' individualism of the 1960s and 1970s and the 'loadsamoney' greed of the 1980s have overriden older altruisms. But the almost Faustian crisis of over-expectations that followed, and perhaps ran ahead of, postwar economic growth bred anomie and dissatis-faction, which have grown more bitter during the 1980s as the gap between expectations and resources, ambitions and achievements has widened.

The decay of the working class has two aspects. First, its relative shrinking as the occupational pattern has shifted from manufacturing to better-paying service jobs has opened up the promise of a middle-class lifestyle to a growing proportion of the population. Second, a qualitative change in the character of the working class has undermined its cultural cohesion. The first has produced the un-Marxian result that the classic proletariat formed by the industrial revolution is no longer a majority. Sheer numbers are no longer on its side. However keen the nostalgia of intellectuals on the left, the Marxian, or Methodist, working class is not going to reform. The skimming of talent, represented exceptionally in the postwar years by the upward progress of the 'scholarship boys', has now become institutionalised in our comprehensive schools and our much-expanded systems of further and higher education.

Some will object to this brief sketch of educational change. The principal beneficiary of successive school reforms – the elaboration of secondary education after 1944, comprehensive reorganisation in the 1960s and, no doubt, the recent changes made in the 1988 Education Reform Act in England – has been, in the Oxford mobility project's phrase, the 'service class'. It is the professional middle class which has gained most from improvements in schools, while the burden of these improvements has fallen on the whole community. The relative disadvantage of the working class has changed little.[11] But, *relative* is an important qualification here. In absolute terms many more able young people from working-class homes have been taken out of the social and cultural environment into which they were born by the action of progressive education. In one sense, the 'scholarship boys' may be the exception that proves the rule. In another, they *are* now the rule. In any case working class communities have greatly changed. The old concentrations of skilled manual workers in steel, coal and shipbuilding have been broken up. The cost of labour and the advance of technology, to different degrees in different sectors, have pushed industry beyond mechanisation. The new industries repel labour as surely as the old industries depended on mass manpower. We are already over the brink of Bell's postindustrial society.[12]

But the second aspect of the decay of working-class culture is more decisive. This culture is changing more rapidly and thoroughly than at any time since the decisive move from an agrarian and mercantile economy to an industrial society two centuries ago. The break-up of the old proletarian concentrations has weakened the fierce, self-confident class consciousness that reached its climax in the early years of this century. The swing-back of national power to the southern English majority, as the north, Wales and Scotland have lost the electoral influence they possessed between 1832 and the 1970s, has also helped to undermine the proud values of the old working class. The north–south divide, so much remarked on since 1979, is far more than a psephological phenomenon. It is uncomfortably aligned with the two nations of our cultural imaginings. Working-class solidarity too has been undermined by the new heterodoxy of employment, the growing number of working women and the increasing presence of ethnic minorities. Traditional working-class culture was a masculine and inward affair. A large part of the modern working class is again servile, as it was before the industrial revolution. They are not personal servants, of course, but servants of the all-powerful consumer (themselves, perhaps, in another guise) and of the state in its many forms. The new working class is divided by race, gender and region. It has lost its proletarian pride. Part of it has been depressed, to form a dangerous but apolitical 'under-class', which for most of the time is sunk in dependency, resignation and despair but is capable of spasmodic riot.

The eighteenth-century mob, absorbed by crime and fascinated by violence, is being recreated in a postindustrial Britain.

These changes may seem comforting news to those rulers of Britain who have spent the last two centuries frightened that social change might run out of control and undermine the hierarchy on which an ordered state depended. But a class is never more dangerous than when it is in decline. It was the self-assurance of the working class, not its weakness, which worried a ruling establishment into reforms that, ultimately, have benefited the whole nation. Now that a divided and diminished proletariat can be safely ignored that worry will ease. So the pace of reform too may slow or even cease – one day perhaps to be overwhelmed by revolutionary change. The mass unemployment of the 1980s, which Britain seems to have tolerated with less concern than other advanced nations, has imposed no serious penalties on its perpetrators – yet. But those who assume that there will never be a reckoning for the wasted years of millions should recall Gerard Manley Hopkins's poem on the unemployed of a century ago, 'Tom's Garland': 'This, by Despair, bred Hangdog dull; by Rage, Manwolf, worse; and their packs infest the age.[13]

The old self-assurance of the working class was important for the whole nation in a second sense. It was a means by which the underprivileged could imagine a securer future in a fairer world. It was a powerful force for social integration. Today, with that self-assurance undermined, no happy futures can be glimpsed, only a dour defensive struggle to protect what little privilege and prosperity has been accumulated. One result could be a retreat by the remnants of the old proletarian working class into its last redoubts. The strikes of steel workers, miners, seamen and railwaymen in the past decade can be seen in this light. Immense damage can be done to the fabric of society, and to the nation's civic culture, even if in political and economic terms these retrospective, even reactionary, proletarian challenges can be brushed aside. Another more speculative outcome could be an eventual recoalescing of a working class that sees its salvation in terms of opposition to established society rather than of progressive reform. It is too early to speculate what form a 'rainbow' coalition, to borrow an American phrase, of Britain's dispossessed might take. But it would not necessarily be a benign phenomenon.

Meanwhile, the middle classes have changed almost as much. The rich have got richer, not so much through their own entrepreneurial effort or even with the help of friendly Governments selling windfall shares in public utilities and opening up tax loopholes but because inflation has overvalued property and undervalued earnings and because financial services have become more important than manufacturing effort in the new British economy. All forms of speculation have flourished, legitimate and not-so-legitimate. The *rentier* has again become an important figure. As a result, an upper section of the middle class has split itself off and formed, rather like a new aristocracy, a *noblesse* without the *oblige*. Statistics on the changing pattern of income demostrate this growing division within the middle class, a division more significant than the obvious gap between the super-rich and the 'under-class'. But this new aristocracy is unlikely to act like the old. Its diverse (even democratic) social origins, the dubious (and insecure?) sources of its wealth, are unlikely to inculcate a strong sense of public duty. This is no longer the solid sober world of the professional bourgeoisie, or even of the tough entrepreneurs who engineered our industrial economy. The individualism of the 1960s has been transformed into an aggressive hedonism a generation later, and the rediscovery of capitalism as a moral enterprise has chopped away the supports of old-fashioned paternalism. Pampering the poor is bad for them. But this crude utilitarianism is not modulated as it was in the nineteenth century by the sobriety of Evangelicalism and its secular equivalents. Instead, we are witnessing the revival of an almost rakish aristocratic code such as has not been seen in Britain since the Regency gave way to the Victorian age.

The middle class is also more divided. Alongside this new aristocracy is the old service class of doctors, lawyers, civil servants, dons, and a new class of professional workers in local government, the big corporations and quangoland. There is also an immense salariat which staffs the bureaucracies of modern business and is perhaps the most powerful social group in modern Britain. The old service class and the new professional workers are the groups that should continue to carry the traditional middle-class code. But neither is a reliable code carrier. In the old service class the sense of a common administrative culture has almost gone, undermined by the demands of technical expertise and the lack of agreed national goals. The empire of the good-and-great has declined. Among the public sector professionals 'duty' has been replaced by 'caring', a very different idea. Moral obligation has been transformed into political engagement or professional responsibility. Technical expertise, radical advocacy, political relativism and bureaucratic welfarism are mixed together in an administrative tradition indifferent, even hostile, to the old middle-class code.

Mid-century Britain was benignly divided into a declining aristocracy, tolerated for its antiquarian whimsies, a growing middle class whose code was close to becoming our civil region and a working class determined to pursue its claim to full citizenship. The composition of late twentieth-century Britain is very different – a revived and less responsible aristocracy, a divided middle class dominated by a salariat mesmerised by mass consumer culture and a working class reduced in numbers and morale. Hardly a more hopeful configuration of society, or a more modern one. Today it is difficult to describe Britain as a civilised meritocracy, qualified on the one hand by an aristocratic openness that allows the best and brightest of all classes to be co-opted into the national elite and, on the other, by social democratic values that insist efficiency must be matched with equity. Perhaps that is how we still like to see ourselves – but it is no longer how we are.

THE BRITISH DISEASE

A spectre has been stalking the British economy since the end of the last war, or possibly the war before, or the 1880s or even since the Great Exhibition of 1851 closed its doors. That spectre is the so-called British disease, which has sapped the economic vitality of the nation and created the disturbing phenomenon of chronic underperformance that has preoccupied every Government, left and right, certainly since 1945 and probably for much longer. It is a brooding presence in British politics, its bedrock issue. Ideological differences take second place to the question of which party or Government can tackle the British disease more effectively.

But this disease is such a confused collection of causes and symptoms that its main value during the long years of comparative economic decline (and actual economic advance) has been to serve as a defeatist alibi. For some, the disease is a cultural phenomenon – the centuries-old condescension to 'trade' that the achievements of the industrial revolution never quite suppressed. Of course there is a wealth of literary and anecdotal evidence to support this thesis, much of it almost too effectively deployed in Martin Weiner's *English Culture and the Decline of the Industrial Spirit*. But perhaps a more contemporary and convincing illustration can be found in the regional imbalance of late twentieth-century Britain discussed in the last section, the decline of the north with its industrial values and the renaissance of the south with its mercantile culture. For others, the British disease is a matter of national psychology, of the instinctive fraternity of the British which has encouraged an uncompetitive solidarity inimical to enterprise. This interpretation is strongly believed, particularly by the radical right, but difficult to prove. Are the British less entrepreneurial because they are more fraternal, or is it that having fallen behind in the economic race we emphasise our fraternity as a kind of consolation prize? Both questions, of course, presume that the British are more hostile than other nations to entrepreneurial values, which must remain a doubtful proposition. Others again prefer an almost mystical interpretation of the British disease. They like to see it as a rejection of modernity. We, it is said, are still in love with our past, our dreams of an agrarian, proletarian or suburban idyll, while other nations have been divorced from theirs by war or revolution.[14]

Then there are accounts of the British disease that focus on the weakness of our institutions. One emphasises the peculiar structure of the British economy – the subordination of industry, often in the midlands, north, Wales or Scotland, to London capital. Money, not goods, is the primary product of Britain's capitalist economy, pre-industrial in its ethos and postindustrial in its practice. So the City of London reaps the benefits of the 'Big Bang' of high finance, set off by deregulation, while manufacturing industry continues to decay. A second account emphasises the idealism and anti-practicality of British education – the preoccupation of schools and universities with the liberal education of the whole person if need be at the expense of training in essential skills.[15] The failure of the family to foster a stronger sense of vocational responsibility is also seen as an aspect of the British disease. None of these accounts is convincing, although all contain slivers of useful explanation. The dichotomy between 'good' industrial capitalism producing goods and creating jobs and 'bad' finance capitalism speculating in money is a naive description of how an advanced and integrated economy works. It is a moral statement, with honourable antecedents that go back to mediaeval prohibitions of usury, rather than serious economic analysis. Both forms of capitalism, if any sensible distinction can be made between them, are complementary rather than competitive. The more crazy the speculation the more rapid the growth of the real economy, as has been demonstrated in the 1970s and 1980s in several Far Eastern nations. As for the effect of old-fashioned values transmitted through schools, other educational systems are just as anachronistic yet they have proved to be no obstacle to economic growth. Nor is the argument about family weakness blocking the transmission of traditional values of sobriety, hard work and individual responsibility more convincing. The British family is no weaker than the American or the European.[16]

So the British disease is not one phenomenon but many, not one interpretation but many. These phenomena are more or less plausible, the interpretations more or less suggestive. Everyone can believe in the British disease as an explanation for disappointing economic performance, or at any rate perceptions of such disappointment, because everyone can believe in different diseases. A few on the 'Green' fringe dispute the term 'disease', preferring to regard slower growth as evidence of sound economic health. Far from offering a general explanation, the British disease itself may be a symptom of underperformance, an invented excuse rather than a directing cause. At best, it is impression rather than analysis. It waxes and wanes without apparent regard for the performance of the economy. In the 1960s and 1970s it was a baleful presence, although economic growth was rapid. In the 1980s it seems to have retreated, although the economy has been slow to regain its productive momentum.

As well as suffering from this mysterious malignancy, the British economy has had to face the same challenges as those of other advanced industrial nations. The British experience, far from being unique, is commonplace. Within the global economy the balance of manufacturing power has tilted away from the developed countries of Europe and North America and towards the rapidly industrialising countries of Asia. The latter have lower labour costs, which attract the investment of multinational companies. Their governments are eager to encourage industrial development, to provide jobs for the large number of workers squeezed out of the countryside by successive agricultural revolutions and to end their semi-colonial dependence on the West for the supply of manufactured goods. At the same time, the high-wage, high-productivity enconomies of the West have stimulated a consumers' revolution, which has encouraged the rapid expansion of service industries. The same advanced nations have also built up sophisticated superstructures as demonstrated by defence expenditure to maintain their virility as great powers or important allies, large-scale industrial interventions to check regional imbalances which threaten social disturbance, and the spreading welfare systems of health, education and social security.[17] Finally, the West in the third quarter of the twentieth century established a technological hegemony, based on its science and education, which was more complete than the industrial hegemony and colonial supremacy it established in the nineteenth century.

The behaviour of the British economy has not been at all exceptional when judged against this broad pattern. Our old manufacturing industries have declined, as they have in Lille or Pittsburgh.[18] Because these industries were labour-intensive many hundreds of thousands of jobs have been lost. Much higher routine levels of unemployment have been built back into the economy than would have been considered acceptable a generation earlier. It is a sad coincidence that just when the economic case for increased intervention to sustain employment was strengthened in the late 1970s a party came to power in Britain ideologically opposed to such intervention. But Britain's record is fairly average. Our poor productivity has accelerated industrial decline while our low wage rates have slowed it. If manufacturing industry has declined more slowly in the rest of Europe it is because governments there subsidised its survival. If they have been able to combat unemployment more successfully it has been because these governments have taken more deliberate efforts to encourage the growth of the service industries and to sustain the public sector.

On other counts, too, the experience of Britain's economy has not been exceptional. Lower living standards mean that the postwar consumer revolution has been less impressive in Britain than in many of our peer nations. But it has been spectacular enough to change the face of Britain in little more than a generation. Britain has been a highly successful producer of 'invisible' services like banking, culture and tourism, which in the 1980s have become major contributors to national wealth. Admittedly, the British record for producing consumer goods is less good. Bad design, indifferent quality and uncompetitive prices have encouraged the growth of anti-patriotic buying habits, although with the increasing integration of the global economy the national origins of particular products have become more difficult to establish. The British superstructure is also broadly similar in scale, although the balance is a little different (too many weapons, too few hospitals).[19] Finally, British science and technology are better than can be expected from a now medium-sized industrial base. The differences between Britain and other advanced nations are ones of degree rather than of substance. The British economy is not a freak. We have faced broadly the same challenges and constraints, confronted the same opportunities and penalties as other nations of the industrialised 'north'. Perhaps the *British disease* is just a label we attach to the mixed economic fortunes which have been the common experience of much of Europe and large parts of North America.

Four broad conclusions can be drawn from this analysis of the British economy. The first is we should cease to think in terms of a peculiarly British disease. The phrase is messianic or diabolical, depending on whether the politicians using it are in or out of power. It encourages the denigration of the substantial economic achievements of Britain in the second half of the twentieth century, while proposing sweeping and hopelessly simple miracle-drug solutions. (It is no accident that *miracle* is a word that is often used when politicians talk about the economy.) When Mrs Thatcher came to power in 1979 she was obliged to dismiss the not-unsuccessful adaption of the British economy to the colder climate of the later 1970s. But it was then that the changes in socio-economic attitudes occurred that were a precondition of the changes in industrial practice in the 1980s. Anthony Crosland's warning that 'the party's over', the various attempts at wage restraint, the so-called social contract, the cuts in public expenditure ordered by the International Monetary Fund, even the much misunderstood 'winter of discontent' – all were part of a painful adjustment to new economic constraints. The decisive break with the psychology of the 1960s happened before, not after, 1979.

Mrs Thatcher was also obliged by electoral politics to promise that the British disease could be cured by taking bitter-tasting medicines – strict monetary discipline, an attack on the assumed monopoly power of trade unions, breaking up and selling off nationalised industries, and so on. These medicines have not had the desired effect, although some on the radical right argue this has been because the doses were not sufficiently concentrated or were not administered for a long enough period. Manufacturing production in Britain in the late 1980s is no higher than it was in the late 1970s. If there ever was a British disease –

which is doubtful – it has persisted if objective economic indices are to be trusted. Yet despite this failure to fulfill its economic promises the Conservative Party has won three consecutive general elections. This suggests the British disease is a political phenomenon rather than an economic condition. It may appear to be cured when the performance of the economy has been indifferent, while it may seem to worsen during periods of comparative economic success.

Perhaps these two phenomena, the persistence of the economic conditions which seem to justify the notion of the British disease and the electoral success of the right during the 1980s may be linked in another way. In the present decade, Britons have become more prosperous as individual consumers, but as a society Britain has lowered its expectations. A nation that has come to accept mass unemployment is a nation that has learned to live with social failure. So the prosperity of Britain in the late 1980s, a prosperity that a substantial minority of Britons is forbidden to enjoy, may cover up an unacknowledged disappointment. The problem for the liberal left is that many Britons would like to believe in a New Jerusalem, the good society which the Labour Party even in its most revisionist mood is dedicated to building. But they find they no longer can. This may be why during the 1980s the British have thought left and voted right. Surveys of social attitudes continue to demonstrate deep-rooted support for public education, a National Health Service and all the other paraphernalia of postwar corporatism. Yet the political parties which support these policies and institutions, Labour and the shifting permutations of the liberal left, have failed to command enough support among voters to overcome the vagaries of the British electoral system. The right wing's supremacy during the 1980s may reflect its success in controlling the British disease (which is not the same as curing it!). The stigma of economic inadequacy that has been felt in Britain since the 1950s has been removed – but at the price of checking those wider social ambitions which have played such a conspicuous role in the growth of our nation in the past two centuries.

The second conclusion is that there are no miracle cures that can transform Britain's economic prospects. The deep structure of our economy is not affected by the tax cuts, the privatisation of nationalised industries and the tight monetary policies preferred by Conservative governments no more than would be by the national and regional planning and the post-Keynesian fine-tuning preferred by Labour oppositions. Such policies are significant only at the margin. The economy may even be influenced less by investment in science and technology than is commonly supposed, although politicians of all parties belive this is the most powerful panacea of all. So all of them, right, left and centre, want to over-equip primary schools with computers, distort the secondary school curriculum in favour of mathematics, science and technical subjects, push higher education into producing more engineers and founding more science parks even when market signals do not encourage such developments, and subsidise high-technology industry despite the failure of earlier efforts to subsidise the old-technology industries of the nineteenth century. Their common aim is to modernise the economy.

These priorities are difficult to contest. The continuing growth of the industrialised and urbanised 'north' depends crucially on the progress of science and its application through technology. It is our last and greatest advantage. But the relationship between science, technology, the economy and material civilisation cannot be reduced to a simple linear sequence. In his great three-volume study of civilisation and capitalism from the fifteenth to the eighteenth century, Fernand Brandel discussed this subtle relationship between technology and growth in the following terms:

> Nevertheless, having pointed out the obvious limitations and circumstantial problems of technology, we should not underestimate its role, which was a vital one. Sooner or later, everything depended upon its necessary intervention. As long as daily life proceeded without too much difficulty in its appointed pathway, within the framework of its inherited structures . . ., there was no economic motive for change. Inventors' blueprints (for there always were some) stayed in their drawer. It was only when things went wrong, when society came up against the ceiling of the possible that people turned to technology, and interest was aroused for the thousand potential inventions, out of which one would be recognized as the best. . . . For there are always hundreds of possible innovations lying dormant; sooner or later, it becomes a matter of urgency to call one of them into life.[20]

This stately Braudelian assessment of technology with its longest of long views is worth placing alongside the perhaps naive technological determinism which dominates British political attitudes to economic growth. It is civilisation that calls technology into life. Science cannot build an economy unaided. It needs the foundations of an advanced culture.

The third conclusion is that, once the apocalyptic vision of an incurable British disease has been discarded, the rigidities of the British economy should be discussed in more pragmatic terms. Seen in this softer light, these problems, while still serious, are no longer so daunting. Perhaps Britain's politicians and planners lack the technocratic skills which many of their peers in the rest of Europe seem to possess. Perhaps many of Britain's business people lack the entrepreneurial guts and flair which seem to mark out the Americans, or the ability to motivate and organise which, in very different ways, appear to characterise the Germans or the Japanese. But these differences are exaggerated. Britain's comparative disadvantage is more likely to be reduced by pragmatic policies, particularly in education (not only narrow vocational training), rather than by dramatic acts of ideological enlightenment. The overriding difficulty facing the British economy is uneven, rather than low, growth. In some industries, especially those on the advancing frontier of technology, growth has been very rapid – in some instances too rapid for the balanced exploitation of the nation's resources. Other industries, of course, face the prospect of slower growth or even actual decline. Acute skill shortages coexist with mass unemployment. The difficulties associated with uneven growth are partly social ones; while some regions and industries are impoverished, intolerable strains are placed on the infrastructures of others. They are also economic; in an integrated economy some industries need to be restrained and others encouraged to produce balanced and sustainable growth.

The fourth conclusion concerns the affordability, of the good life. Despite the free-market rhetoric of the right, which sees inequality as a spur to economic ambition, and the semi-revolutionary messianism of the left, which spurns all references to markets, affordability is the issue running along the main fault line in British politics. The moderate right thinks that social programmes, although desirable, cannot be afforded, or that premature social expenditure will undermine the economic base; the moderate left believes they can be afforded without damaging that economic base and *must* be afforded to underpin the foundations of an advanced society. If a nation's culture is as important as its economy in determining its wealth, the latter has a strong case. The issue of affordability can also be elaborated into an overarching theory about the character of late twentieth-century Britain. Britain, it is said, is trying to operate a first-class society on the back of a second-class economy. One result is that institutions of acknowledged excellence, like theatres, orchestras and universities, and those of arguable excellence, like hospitals or railways, are being inexorably undermined by economic weakness. But this theory is perhaps just another version of the British disease with all its dubieties.

Certainly this preoccupation with affordability in late twentieth-century Britain underestimates what has been achieved since 1945, and so what can reasonably be achieved in the future. In the past generation our cities have been rebuilt, not always successfully in aesthetic terms but with a thoroughness that matched the enthusiasm of our Victorian ancestors; a vastly extended system of secondary, further and higher education has been developed; our cultural life has enjoyed a sparkling renaissance. Many of the institutions which embody the qualities of excellence and achievement we value most highly have been developed in the years when the British disease is supposed to have been wasting our nation. This strange paradox should encourage those who insist that the good society, however it is defined, cannot be afforded to pause for reflection. Affordability is as much a state of mind as a measure of physical capacity. It is as variable a concept as the British disease. Perhaps a more general point can be made. Economics, it has been argued, dominate British politics. They seem to shape and limit our society. Yet according to any objective account Britain today possesses great wealth – wealth which would have dazzled the most enterprising nineteenth-century industry-builder, wealth which to most early twentieth-century radicals and socialists would have seemed ample to create a new society through its painless redistribution. But for us it is not enough. International comparisons alone are insufficient to explain our discontent. These are countered by intergenerational comparisons more dramatic. Maybe the real explanation is that after the deaths of the old gods of religion, nation, social justice and individual duty only the god of prosperity remains. Economic success has become the only reliable measure of man's genius, in which we dare not lose faith.

WALLINGTON AND WANDSWORTH

Around the walls of the roofed courtyard at the centre of Wallington Hall in Northumberland is a series of Pre-Raphaelite paintings by William Bell Scott. They begin with the building of the Roman Wall, which runs across England a dozen miles south of Wallington, and end with a shipbuilding scene on the industrial Tyne. Once they made favourite illustrations in childrens' history books. Too sentimental for the taste of the late twentieth century, these pictures nevertheless affirm a surety, a moral conviction, a faith in the continuity of our nation. Aesthetically they may be objected to as examples of Victorian mawkishness, but as an expression of Englishness, that quiet belief that hierarchy and reform can be reconciled within an organic tradition, that the past flows naturally into the present and the future, these pictures remind us of a civilised confidence achingly unavailable today.

Wallington is crowded with the symbols, actual and associative, of that essential England. It is an expression in Northumbrian stone and Italian stucco, in borders of old-fashioned flowers under the grey northern sky, of a pure Whig interpretation of our national identity. Tradition and reason, manners and instinct, property and progress, community and conscience held together in delicate but powerful harmony. Indeed, *interpretation* seems too tentative a term when these symbols are so solidly realised as they are at Wallington. The hall itself was built at the end of the seventeenth century for the Blacketts, a family enriched by coal and remembered in the name of one of Newcastle's principal streets. The plainness and assurance of its architecture seem to mirror the new order that succeeded the Glorious Revolution of 1688. In the next century, Wallington was embellished in the best taste of that Augustan age. This is hardly an accident. At nearby Kirkharle, where the moors meet the cultivated land, Capability Brown was born. More than any other man, he educated the eye of England through his ideal landscapes, informing the romantic imagination of the late eighteenth and nineteenth centuries and still unfolding for us today in their mature beauty. So Wallington, by association at any rate, is at the root of an aethetic vision of England which is more seductive than ever in the industrial and urban roar of the late twentieth century.

Later, Wallington passed by marriage to the Trevelyans, a Somerset family that moved north to their new and more substantial inheritance on the Border. The Trevelyans were to form a dynasty of high-minded men and women for whom public service was an imperative, even religious, duty. The most famous among them helped to mould the modern civil service which emerged in the mid-nineteenth century to replace Cobbett's 'Old Corruption' of placemen, sinecures and patronage. He was the archetypal Victorian administrator. His brother-in-law was the historian Macaulay, the Whigs' highest priest. The desk at which Macaulay wrote his *History of England* is in the library at Wallington. The next Trevelyan, his son, was a distinguished Liberal politician and also a historian. One grandson, who took his middle name from his famous great-uncle, was the Whiggest historian of them all. His *English Social History*, published in the same year as Orwell's characterisation of England as a quarrelling family, became the most influential work of popular history in this century. In so many ways it was the literary analogue of Scott's paintings at Wallington.

G. M. Trevelyan's life and work reflected an important shift in the Whig tradition, away from the activist administrative style typical of Victorian and, arguably, Edwardian England towards a more inward and aesthetic sensibility which flourished between the wars. Reforming Indian education, creating an open and competitive civil service and writing grand public history were gradually displaced by walking in the Cheviots, helping to found the National Trust (to which Wallington, very properly, now belongs), and even out-of-town membership of the Bloomsbury *avant garde* (another more recent Trevelyan was a conspicuously liberal censor of British films). Political ambitions were slowly superseded by cultural interests. But it was a slow transition. G. M. Trevelyan's cousin, the last in the Wallington line, continued the family tradition of progressive politics, sitting first as a Liberal MP and later becoming a Labour cabinet minister. So in this small corner of England almost at its northern edge the symbols of a powerful national personality are marvellously compressed. Everything is here. The Whig mentality is displayed. The descent from proud family portraits of the eighteenth century to photographs of Ramsay MacDonald's first cabinet is laid out in a grand, almost apostolic, succession of public virtue and private piety.

'Welcome to Wandsworth – the Brighter Borough' proclaim the stylish notices scattered apparently at random throughout south-west London. They offer a curious image. Sandwiched between the green of the parks and the blue of the sky, the city landscape of power stations, churches, schools and houses is presented in reverse silhouette. It is blank. Perhaps some confusing memory of *rus in urbe* rumbling away in the English psyche is being unwittingly expressed. These notices are encountered crossing the Thames bridges south from Chelsea and Fulham, or driving east into the inner city from suburban Richmond, or north from Wimbledon, Mitcham, Merton and other Surrey villages swamped by interwar urbanisation. To the east the notices mark a ragged frontier with Lambeth, geographically capricious but politically significant. In more than one Conservative party political broadcast during the 1980s self-conscious ministers have tramped down the middle of a nondescript street close to Clapham South underground station, comparing the Tory thrift of Wandsworth on their right with the spendthrift socialism of Labour-run Lambeth on their left.

Wandsworth, like the other thirty-odd boroughs into which the capital is divided, is an almost arbitrary administrative unit. Thomas Cromwell may have been born in Putney. Huguenot settlement may be marked by the French graves in an East Hill cemetery. Charles James Fox may have gone to school by the banks of the Wandle. George Eliot may have lived for a brief and anxious while in Southfields. Thomas Hardy may have spent an unhappy few years in a draughty Victorian terrace close to Wandsworth Common. A few years later David Lloyd George may have moved into a more substantial house half a mile away. Clement Attlee may have been brought up in the borough in the last days before the Surrey countryside was banished from memory and sight. But Wandsworth had no real history before it was created by the urban sprawl of Victorian and Edwardian London, mean tenements for the poor and terraced houses for the respectable classes in fog-filled streets. The final bits of the borough were filled in between 1920 and 1960 by the London County Council's overspill estates, by the clearance of slums and their replacement by neat rows of council houses and by the mixed mock-Tudor and sub-Bauhaus streets typical of private development between the wars. The occasional Queen Anne house and the churches and villas of the eighteenth and early nineteenth centuries seem like relics of a lost civilisation. Far more typical are the concrete-slab flats of the Doddington estate in Battersea, built in the 1960s as an unintended monument to the unfortunate alliance of comprehensive urban development and municipal corruption, and the box-like executive-style houses that swarm over the land once occupied by hospitals, an ironic monument to the triumph of credit-borne consumerism over community improvement.

For this the modern city – the new under-cover shopping centres and the declining parades of local shops, the crush of commuting cars and the anxious bus queues, the plate-glass comprehensives and the tall brick of the old Board schools, the pubs dressed up as wine bars and the bed-and-breakfast hotels which shelter the homeless, the gleaming teaching hospitals and doctors' dingy waiting rooms. The experience and environment of Wandsworth are shared by millions of people in Britain today who live far from London and further from the inner city. Wandsworth is typical in three ways. First, it is a confusion of communities. Not all are poor. In some parts, family houses start at £180,000 (once rising by more than ten per cent a year) and soon reach more than a third of a million; across the street they may be building flat-sized houses for first-time buyers; a road away there is a forest of estate agents' signs in a recently privatised council estate; a short distance off may be an estate of unsaleable flats where the rents are high and repairs endlessly delayed. The truly poor are a minority, the victims of unemployment or underemployment or of family break-up. Part-time low-paid jobs are plentiful in the city, just as human relationships are often fragile. Or the poor are simply the old or families with too many children. Although the poor are a minority, a much larger number of Wandsworth's inhabitants enjoy only a precarious prosperity and lack the reassuring security of reliable resources. The population, of course, is not all white. Many people in Wandsworth are Black or Asian. Revivalist churches, mosques and reggae add to the confusion of the borough's communities.

Second, Wandsworth's economy is highly dependent on the service and public sectors. Most of its middle-class inhabitants work in the West End and the City as high or low clerks in administration or the media, banking or business. Or they are professional workers in the many local branches of the welfare state. The factories along the Battersea waterfront or up the Wandle valley, once one of London's most important industrial districts because of its mill power, have all closed. Industrial employment, on a much smaller scale, is concentrated in backstreet workshops or purpose-built factory units. It is an artisan economy which recalls the preindustrial London of Dickens. But the big employers are public or semi-public enterprises – the borough council, the Inner London Education Authority (until it is abolished), the police, the electricity and gas boards. The public sector is the sun around which the private economy circles; this is as true of cleaning companies seeking local authority or health service contracts as of freelance plumbers or electricians who work for public utilities. The centre of London is much too close to allow substantial growth of office jobs in the private sector. Companies that desert London go far beyond Wandsworth. Its private sector is not dominated by large companies but by small enterprises. Up-market delicatessens, down-market video shops with nightly grills and all-market corner shops open all hours – these are typical of the thriving enterprise economy in Wandsworth. Its visual giants, of course, are the national brands which dominate the urban landscape of Britain in the 1980s, the superstores, the do-it-yourself hangars, the discount warehouses.

Third, Wandsworth displays great vitality – despite its confusion of social and ethnic communities and its unproductive economy. The inner city is far from being the anomic place of sociological prediction (or political ambition?). Perhaps this is a better description of the suburbs beyond. Voluntarism is a vital force, stimulated by the volatility of the modern city. Because communities are constantly forming and reforming, because the population of the borough is constantly changing, because the economy is volatile, there seems to be a greater urge to construct institutions that help to create at least the illusion of order and meaning. So parent–teacher associations, churches, Scouts and Woodcraft Folk, amenity and conservation groups, orchestras and choirs, agitprop campaigns, community health councils – all have flourished in chaotic profusion. These initiatives and organisations cannot easily be categorised. In one sense they represent a revolt against bureaucracy and officialdom; in another they have been called into life by the very forces which built the postwar welfare state. The culture of Wandsworth, as of Britain's urban civilisation, is both more open and more anxious than ever before. Unlike the traditional working-class culture of mill, steel works, pit, ship-yard or factory, and unlike the upper-class Whig culture preserved at Wallington, it cannot take community for granted. It has to invent its own definition, without the benefit of the silent rhythms of a settled society and without the endorsement of a mythic history. Perhaps that is why the urban landscape portrayed on Wandsworth's notices is a blank silhouetted between the green grass and the blue skies.

But is there any connection between Wallington, now a museum house to be enjoyed by discerning tourists, and Wandsworth, the inner-London borough with its quarter of a million inhabitants? Are there any links between the Whig mentality so dominantly displayed at Wallington and the diverse, even disintegrative, culture of urban and (post?) industrial Britain? The impulsive answer must be no. Wallington represents a fascinating site for the cultural archaeologist but its charisma has passed away into history. Whig culture died because it failed to develop. It never came to terms properly with industrial Britain. It was an ideology of great houses, non-conformist tradesmen and Matthew Arnold's 'liberal practitioners'.[21] Wandsworth, on the other hand, is the way we live now – although to fill out the picture other sample areas from the suburbs and the country, from the north and Scotland and Wales also need to be reviewed.

Certainly public and intellectual life in modern Britain seems to rest on anti-historical assumptions. Any sense of the continuity of our culture, the endurance of our civilisation, grows weaker year by year.

For many the past is an enemy not a friend, the seed-bed of national failure, or an irrecoverable dream, the memory of national success. Either way there seems little point in staying in touch. The past is regarded as irrelevant not because it is unappealing (the growth of the heritage industry suggests the contrary) but because it seems to be beyond effective recall. The British, for all the cajoling of Margaret Thatcher, still feel themselves to be a nation in decline. The old imperial arrogance, national assurance, social optimism and community pride have been lost. No satisfying new roles for Britain appear to have been discovered. Materialism has become a substitute for mission. Dean Acheson's celebrated aphorism, 'Great Britain has lost an empire and has not yet found a role', has applications far beyond foreign policy.[22] For some, of course, the racket of contemporaneity ceaselessly broadcast by the mass media, the instant style of a global consumer society, drown these quieter regrets and so serve as an unstable placebo to our anxiety. For others this sense of national decline is translated into a belief in the inevitable decay of high culture, Lawrence Durrell's 'doomboat of our culture', reinforced by apocalyptic fears of ecological disaster and nuclear holocaust. Our whole civilisation adrift.

Both the committed right and the committed left in Britain tend to see the past as an enemy. The right, with more power and influence than the left, is determined to reverse that current of reform which has flowed through our history from before 1832 to after 1945. Its timid adherents attempt to argue that this process of reform was hijacked by corporatists towards the end of the nineteenth century and by full-bloodied socialists in the twentieth, that instead of leading onto economic democracy political reform was diverted into the treacherous shallows of social democracy where Britain beached. According to this interpretation the Conservatives since 1979 have been struggling to refloat the nation by dragging it off the sand bank. Bad history, certainly, but probably good politics. Others on the right, more rigorous intellectually but politically reckless, admit the underlying continuity of the Whig–Liberal–Labour succession from Earl Grey to Mr Attlee, two prime ministers of rather similar temperament. This leads then to challenge the values of political democracy as well as those of social welfare, and to long for an *ancien régime* they themselves have half invented. For both these groups the historical mentality displayed at Wallington is to be despised, not praised.

The committed left, too, tends to regard the British past as an enemy, and the same Whig tradition of reform as a confidence trick that allowed the ruling establishment to maintain its power by making minimal concessions to the rising radical tide. But underneath the left's semi-Marxist analysis of British history and its rhetoric of class confrontation lies on older moral tradition, the influence of which is frequently betrayed by appeals to memories of the General Strike and

'Red Clydeside', to the Chartists and the Levellers. Even the far left in modern Britain seems to have far more in common with the radical agitators of the eighteenth and nineteeth centuries than with the revolutionary proletarian movements so important in the rest of Europe. The revolution eagerly anticipated by the British left has often appeared a moral as much as a political one. Nor is it right to regard this radical tradition as separate from the main liberal stream. Certainly in the 1790s the young Charles Grey, as a member of the aristocratic Friends of the People, was not as far from Thomas Paine and *The Rights of Man* as later Whig hagiography suggested, and forty years later when he was prime minister the radical turmoil of the early 1830s enabled him to impose the Reform Bill on the reluctant ruling class into which he had been born. There are many other examples of symbiosis between radicalism and liberalism later in the nineteenth century. In our own century, Ernest Bevin, a stalwart of the General Strike, became a key figure in the 1940–45 war cabinet and the architect of the Atlanticist foreign policy which has been the basis of Britain's postwar security.[23] Even in the age of Arthur Scargill and *Militant* it may be wrong to exaggerate the discontinuities on the left in Britain. Just as the right means more than it says the left may say more than it means. Its enduring characteristic remains its cross-grained patriotism, a sentimental radicalism rooted in old-fashioned British ways.

Another reason for lack of respect for our famous history is to be found in our much-misunderstood pragmatism. Alongside a nagging sense of national decline goes, however incongruously, a down-to-earth conviction that any difficulties faced by late twentieth century Britain can be reduced to the mechanical. The common view is that we face intractable economic or political crises but that British society is sound and our sense of nationhood is undisturbed. So public debate is dominated by socio-economic arguments, the cultural reverberations of which are often ignored. The interpretation offered in this chapter, and the theme of this book, is that the condition of Britain should be looked at the other way round. Our difficulties are more social than economic and still more cultural. At their root is a failing of national identity, a waning of patriotism.

It is in this context that history is important, and the Whig tradition may remain a creative mentality for modern Britain. This liberal descent offers the surest means for the revival of our civil religion, for the redefinition of our essential patriotism. What are the essentials of that tradition? A citizenship based on a Lockeian reciprocity of rights and responsibilities; a commitment to reform without the pain of revolution; a belief in the progress of mankind, which is built on, not opposed to, the improvement of the individual; a capacity to embrace, even subsume, competing ideologies within a broader community of interest; a sense of public service as a moral responsibility; a view of the state and the nation as ethical rather than utilitarian institutions. Out of these enduring values it is possible to fashion a moral and modest Britain – one which values social welfare and devalues class antagonism, at home egalitarian to foster patriotism and abroad peaceable to secure a safer world, a nation austere in its material promises but devoted to the enlargement of democracy. Perhaps here there is some link between Wallington and Wandsworth. The former may inform and even discipline the latter. Its objects, images, values can encourage us, who live in the turbulence, chaos and vitality of the late twentieth century, to reflect on what they meant and what they mean and what they will mean. Out of such reflection perhaps may come a more civilised patriotism built on T. S. Eliot's 'easy commerce of the old and the new'.[24]

But perhaps Eliot's is too austere a note on which to end this book which, for all its doubts, is intended to be hopeful. His studied equation of ends and beginnings, his belief that 'the moment of the rose and the moment of the yew-tree are of equal duration',[25] deny the very possibility of this book's project. This has been to relate, by suggestion, association and even anecdote rather than by proof, knowledge to nation – knowledge both in Arnold's sense of 'the best that has been thought and said in the world' and in terms of the reductionist disciplines which make up the modern academic enterprise, and nation, those unthought routines, undisciplined instincts and inherited values that make up the unpatterned fabric of the modern world. Eliot's response, for all its penetration, was a kind of giving-up and turning-away, another form of silence – and perhaps a less English form than Jane Austen's ironic reticence. For the most powerful objection to reinterpreting the Whig tradition is precisely *that*: its silence, its inarticulacy, even its banality or, more fairly, its privacy and inwardness. Its weakness is its lack of great events that 'make possible the social reconstruction of reality, the reordering of things-as-they-are so that they are no longer experienced as given but rather as willed, in accordance with convictions about how things ought to be'.[26] The Whig tradition is anti-heroic; its great events designed to avoid greater ones, as in 1832 or 1945. Perhaps therefore it is unable to match, in Robert Darnton's phrase 'possibilism against the givenness of things.'

But the English experience offers no enduring examples of raised revolutionary consciousness that allows us readily to imagine ideal worlds beyond the givenness of our present condition, of romantic intoxication that makes everything seem possible. We have to reach the same heights of what is humanly possible, and therefore necessary, by other routes, through reflection, stillness and – yes – maybe even banality and ordinariness. So in another sense Eliot's 'easy commerce of the old and the new' can be aligned with Arnold's quiet hope:

We have not won our political battles, we have not carried out main points, we have not stopped our adversaries' advance, we have not marched victoriously into the modern world; but we have told silently upon the mind of nation, we have prepared currents of feeling which sap our adversaries' position when it seemed gained, we have kept up our communication with the future.[27]

It is not possible to hope for more in a culture that listens to the silences more than the ideas, to the stillness more than the words, to nation more than knowledge.

NOTES

NOTES TO CHAPTER 1

1. 'But it moves', attributed to Galileo after his recantation in 1632, but it first appeared in Baretti, *Italian Library* (1757), 52.
2. Jacob Cats, *Proteus ofte Minnebeelden* (Amsterdam, 1628) quoted in Simon Schama, *The Embarrassment of Riches: an Interpretation of Dutch Culture in the Golden Age* (London, 1987), 383.
3. Matthew Arnold described the state as the 'organ of the national reason' in *The Popular Education of France* [London, 1861], in R. H. Super (ed.), *The Complete Prose Works of Matthew Arnold* (Ann Arbor, 1962), vol. 2, 157.
4. Robert Lowe, the vice-president of the Privy Council committee for education much criticised by Arnold and a determined opponent of the second Reform Bill, nevertheless asserted in 1867: 'I believe it will be absolutely necessary to compel our future masters to learn their letters', in A. Patchett Martin, *Life and Letters of the Right Honourable Robert Lowe Viscount Sherbrooke* (London, 1893), II, 323.
5. Daniel Bell, *The Coming of Post-Industrial Society* (New York, 1973). In this book Bell argues that the axial principle of postindustrial society would be the codification of theoretical knowledge just as the exploitation of energy sources was the key activity in industrial society.
6. Matthew Arnold, 'Dover Beach', line 25, in Kenneth Allott (ed.), *Poems* (Harmondsworth, 1985), 181.
7. F. W. H. Myers, *Century Magazine*, XXIII (1881), 62–3, quoted in Gordon Haight, *George Eliot: a biography* (Oxford, 1968), 464.
8. George Steiner, *Real Presences* (London, 1989). This book will be discussed in Chapter 3.
9. George Eliot, *Adam Bede* [1859] (Harmondsworth, 1980), 81.
10. Matthew Arnold, *Culture and Anarchy*, ed. J. Dover Wilson (Cambridge, 1932). In this collection of essays, first published in 1869, Arnold argued that the choice was between culture – 'the best that has been thought and said' – and anarchy, which he interpreted in spiritual as much as political terms.
11. Thomas Carlyle, *Shooting Niagara: and after?* (London, 1867). This gloomy pamphlet was written by Carlyle when he was seventy-two and after the death of his wife Jane. Nevetheless his pessimism can be compared to the Earl of Derby's celebrated remark that the second Reform Bill was 'a leap in the dark'.
12. Matthew Arnold, *Culture and Anarchy*, 70.
13. George Davie, *The Democratic Intellect* (Edinburgh, 1961) and *The Crisis of the Democratic Intellect* (Edinburgh, 1986). Both books discussed attempts by the Scottish Education Depart-

ment, in the 1880s and 1920s respectively, to make university education, in Davie's view, less democratic and more utilitarian.

14. Allan Bloom, *The Closing of the American Mind* (New York, 1987). A bestseller with a foreword by Saul Bellow, Bloom's book castigated the intellectual and moral relativism which he believed was endemic in American higher education. His solution was a return to Socratic values.

15. Paul Kennedy, *The Rise and Fall of the Great Powers: Economic Change and Military Conflict from 1500 to 2000* (London, 1988). Kennedy's argument, that the military greatness of nations is closely linked to their economic resources, commanded particular attention in an America concerned about its large trade deficit and international competition.

16. Emmanuel Le Roy Ladurie, *Montaillou* (London, 1978). Ladurie used the archives of an inquisition into Cathar heretics to penetrate the mental world of medieval France. The affection of a Norman for the lost world of the *pays d'oc* combined with the intellectual exuberance of French historiography to produce a bestseller, inside and outside France.

17. Lawrence and Jeanne Fawtier Stone, *An Open Elite? England 1540–1880* (Oxford, 1984). Based on the art of the cliometrician this book questioned the assumption that England's elite was exceptionally permeable.

18. Jonathan Clark, *English Society 1688–1832* (Cambridge, 1985) and *Revolution and Rebellion* (Cambridge, 1986). In these books Clark disputed the claims of 'Whig', Marxist and radical historians about the nature of England's historical development. He denied that the Civil War could be regarded as a form of bourgeois revolution and asserted that England's *ancien régime* survived until 1828–32.

19. Ralf Dahrendorf, *The New Liberty* (London, 1974), the published version of his Reith Lectures for the BBC, and *Life Chances: Approaches to Social and Political Action* (London, 1979), 40–42.

20. Alfred Noyes, 'His Burial', *The Manchester Guardian* 17 January, 1928, quoted in David Ayerst, *The Guardian Omnibus 1821–1971* (London, 1973), 444.

NOTES TO CHAPTER 2

1. Francis Bacon, 'Of Heresies'.
2. Job 28:18.
3. Francis Bacon, 'Of Truth'.
4. Phil. 4:7.
5. Matthew Arnold, 'Shakespeare', line 5, in Kenneth Allott (ed.), *Poems* (Harmondsworth, 1985), 123.
6. Thomas Kuhn, *The Structure of Scientific Revolutions*, 2nd edn. (Chicago, 1970) 43–51.
7. Henry James, *The Portrait of a Lady* (London, 1881 and Harmondsworth, 1963), 474.
8. J. H. Newman, *The Idea of a University* (London, 1852).
9. Martin J. Weiner, *English Culture and the Decline of the Industrial Spirit 1850–1980* (Cambridge, 1981).
10. T. S. Eliot, *The Wasteland* (London, 1922).

11. S. T. Coleridge, *On the Constitution of Church and State* (London, 1837), and *J. S. Mill on Bentham and Coleridge*, introduction by F. R. Leavis (London, 1950).
12. C. P. Snow, *The Two Cultures* (Cambridge, 1959).
13. T. S. Eliot, *Notes Towards a Definition of Culture* (London, 1948).
14. F. R. Leavis, *Mass Civilization and Minority Culture* (London, 1930).
15. George Steiner, *In Bluebeard's Castle* (London, 1971).
16. Daniel Bell, *The End of Ideology* (Glencoe, Illinois, 1960).
17. Donald Schön, *The Reflective Practitioner* (London, 1983).
18. Everett Hughes, *The Scoiological Eye* (Chicago, 1971).
19. Stefan Collini, Donald Winch and John Burrow, *That Noble Science of Politics: A Study in Nineteenth Century Intellectual History* (Cambridge, 1984).
20. Robert Dingwall and Philip Lewis (eds), *The Sociology of the Professions* (London, 1984), 10.
21. Ralf Dahrendorf, *Class and Class Conflict in Industrial Society* (London, 1959), vii. [Preface to the 1st (German) edn.]
22. A. H. Halsey in Martin Bulmer (ed.), *Essays in the History of British Sociological Research* (Cambridge, 1985).
23. Talcott Parsons, *The Structure of Social Action* [1937] (New York, 1968), and Talcott Parsons and Gerald Platt, *The American University* (Cambridge, Massachusetts, 1973).
24. Ralf Dahrendorf, op. cit., xi. [Preface to the revised (English) edn.]
25. Karl Popper, *The Logic of Scientific Discovery* (London, 1959), and *Objective Knowledge; An Evolutionary Approach* (Oxford, 1972).
26. Quoted in Norman Page, *A. E. Housman: a critical biography* (London, 1983), 68.
27. Henry James, *Princess Casamassima* (Harmondsworth, 1986), 35. [Preface to the 1909 (New York) edn.]

NOTES TO CHAPTER 3

1. *Higher Education*, report of the committee appointed by the Prime Minister under the chairmanship of Lord Robbins (London, 1963), 7.
2. *Ibid.*, para. 28.
3. George Orwell, *Homage to Catalonia* (Harmondsworth, 1966), 220.
4. Of Jane Austen's novels *Mansfield Park* is often regarded as most open about the conflict between old and new worlds. This aspect of the work is discussed by Tony Tanner in his introduction to the Penguin edition (Harmondsworth, 1966), 11, 12, 33–5.
5. Sir Walter Scott's *Waverley*, published in 1814, was immensely popular and established itself as the archetype of the historical novel in nineteenth-century Britain. As a firm Tory, Scott looks back on the conflict between Hanoverian establishment and Jacobite insurgency with a wistful ambivalence.
6. George Eliot's first work of fiction, *Scenes from Clerical Life*, three short novels published in 1858, was openly autobiographical and the ready association of characters with living people caused controversy. But many of her other novels, most notably *Adam Bede* (1859), *The Mill on the Floss* (1860), *Felix Holt* (1866) and, of course, *Middlemarch* (1872) contained autobio-

graphical fragments and were inspired by personal memories. The novels which are most detached from her Midlands roots, like *Romola*, are generally regarded to be her least successful.

7. A. E. Housman, 'Into my heart an air that kills', *A Shropshire Lad* XL, in Christopher Ricks (ed.), *The Collected Poems and Selected Prose*, (London, 1988), 64.

8. Richard Hoggart, *The Uses of Literacy* (London, 1957).

9. R. A. Butler, *The Art of the Possible* (London, 1971).

10. Alec Douglas Home [Lord Home of the Hirsel], *The Way the Wind Blows* (London, 1976).

11. Richard Hoggart's main works include *The Uses of Literacy*, already cited; *Speaking to Each Other*, 2 vols. (London, 1970); *Only Connect* (London, 1972); *An Idea and Its Servants* (London, 1978); *An English Temper* (London, 1982); and *A Local Habitation: Life and Times 1918–1940* (London, 1988).

12. Thomas Carlyle, 'Signs of the Times', *Edinburgh Review* 1829, in *Selected Writings* (Harmondsworth, 1971), 67.

13. J. M. Keynes, *General Theory of Employment, Interest and Money* (London, 1936), book VI, ch. 24.

14. Karl Popper, *Unended Quest: an intellectual biography* (London, 1976), 33.

15. Lionel Trilling, *The Liberal Imagination* (New York, 1950).

16. George Steiner's main works include *Tolstoy or Dostoevsky* (London, 1958); *The Death of Tragedy* (London, 1960), *Language and Silence* (London, 1967); *In Bluebeard's Castle* (London, 1971); *After Babel* (London, 1975); *On Difficulty* (London, 1978); *The Portage to San Cristobal of A.H.* (London, 1981); *Antigones* (London 1984); and *Real Presences* (London, 1989).

17. Talcott Parson's main books have already been cited in a note to Chapter 2 and David Riesman's will be noted below. Daniel Bell's main books are *The End of Ideology* (1960), *The Coming of Post-Industrial Society* (1973) and *The Cultural Contradictions of Capitalism* (1976).

18. Anthony Crosland, *The Future of Socialism* (London, 1956).

19. Ralf Dahrendorf, *Life Chances: Approaches to Social and Political Theory* (London, 1979), 107.

20. David Riesman's main works are *The Lonely Crowd: a Study of the Changing American Character* (New Haven, 1950) and *Faces in the Crowd* (New Haven, 1952), both in association with Nathan Glazer. He has also written extensively about American higher education.

21. Roger Scruton, *The Meaning of Conservatism* (Harmondsworth, 1980).

22. Michael Harrington, *The New American Poverty* (New York, 1984).

23. James Wilson, 'The Rediscovery of Character: Private Virtue and Public Policy', *The Public Interest*, 81 (1985).

24. Allan Bloom, *The Closing of the American Mind*, (New York, 1987).

25. Ibid., 337–79.

26. John Dewey, *Democracy in Danger* (New York, 1916); Robert Hutchins, *The Higher Learning in America* (Chicago, 1936); *General Education in a Free Society*, the Harvard report (Cambridge, Massachusetts, 1945).

27. Allan Bloom, op. cit., 271–3.

28. *A Return to Grand Theory* (London, 1984) considered John Rawls, Thomas Kuhn, Jürgen Habermas and Louis Althusser.

29. Thomas Kuhn's main works are *The Copernican Revolution* (New York, 1957); *The Structure of Scientific Revolutions* (Chicago, 1962); and *Sources for the History of Quantum Physics* (New York, 1967).

NOTES TO CHAPTER 4

1. Peter Scott, *The Crisis of the University* (London, 1984), 21–80. Harold Perkin, 'The Historical Perspective', in Burton R. Clark (ed.), *Perspectives on Higher Education* (California, 1984), 17–55.
2. A. B. Cobban, *The Medieval Universities: Their Development and Organization* (London, 1975).
3. Lawrence Stone (ed.) *The University in Society* vol. 1 (Oxford, 1975). Many of the essays are relevant here. Lawrence Stone, 'Social Control and Intellectual Excellence: Oxbridge and Edinburgh 1560–1983', in Nicholas Phillipson (ed.), *Universities, Society and the Future* (Edinburgh, 1983), 1–29.
4. Charles Camic, *Enlightenment and Experience*, (Edinburgh, 1984) offers an intriguing account of the links between socialisation, education and cultural change in eighteenth-century Scotland, with particular emphasis on key figures like Hume and Smith.
5. Laurence Stone, 'The Educational Revolutions in England, 1560–1640', *Past and Present*, 28 (July, 1964), 41–80.
6. Margaret Archer, *Social Origins of Educational Systems* (London, 1979).
7. Talcott Parsons and Gerald Platt, *The American University* (Harvard, 1973). Despite its title this is a theoretical account of the modern university.
8. Tony Becher and Maurice Kogan, *Process and Structure in Higher Education* (London, 1980), discusses the tension between academic and managerial values in the university.
9. Daniel Bell, *The Cultural Contradictions of Capitalism*, already cited, and Roland Inglehart, *The Silent Revolution* (Princeton, 1977).
10. Harold Perkin, *The Rise of Professional Society: England since 1880* (London, 1989).

NOTES TO CHAPTER 5

1. In the winter of 1980 the University Grants Committee warned the Government that any attempt to reduce public expenditure on universities too rapidly would lead to diseconomy. This warning was ignored and cuts of fifteen per cent spread over three years were imposed the following July.
2. In an opinion poll conducted among university, polytechnic and college teachers by Market and Opinion Research International (MORI) for *The Times Higher Education Supplement*, eighty-four per cent agreed with the statement, 'Cuts in higher education have reduced opportunities to enter universities and polytechnics, undermined the quality of teaching and research and produced chaos in many institutions.' Only seven per cent agreed with the statement, 'The Government has pursued

effective policies to promote efficiency and quality in higher education. As a result institutions are now much stronger than at the beginning of the decade.' *The Times Higher Education Supplement*, 5 June, 1987, 9.

3. The Alvey programme began in 1983. It was a collaborative programme in advanced information technology between industry, higher education and Government which was spread over five years and to which the Government contributed £200 million.

4. *Higher Education*, report of the committee appointed by the Prime Minister under the chairmanship of Lord Robbins (London, 1963).

5. *Higher Education: Meeting the Challenge* (London, 1987).

6. While the Robbins committee was deliberating and immediately after its publication there was vociferous opposition to the expansion of the universities, generally summed up by, in Kingsley Amis' phrase, 'more will mean worse'. *The Times* played an important role in this opposition.

7. The binary policy was unveiled by Anthony Crosland in a speech at Woolwich Polytechnic on 27 April 1965 and refined in a speech at Lancaster University on 20 January 1967. The new policy was formally announced on a White Paper *A Plan for Polytechnics and Other Colleges* (London, 1966).

8. *The Development of Higher Education into the 1990s* (London, 1985).

9. *Higher Education: Meeting the Challenge*, paras. 1.2–1.7.

10. The Robbins committee expected there to be 558 000 full-time and sandwich course students in higher education in 1981. In fact there were 533 000 in that year.

11. *Higher Education: Meeting the Challenge*, paras. 2.4–2.13.

12. Ibid., para. 2.15.

13. Ibid., para. 4.6.

14. In the report of the steering committee for efficiency studies in the universities, under the chairmanship of Sir Alex Jarratt and published in April 1985, it was recommended that there should be an investigation into the role of the University Grants Committee. As a result, a committee was established under the chairmanship of Lord Croham which published its report, *Review of the University Grants Committee*, in 1987. Some, but not all, of its recommendations were incorporated in the White Paper published in the same year.

15. Public expenditure on universities was reduced by an average of fifteen per cent between 1981/82 and 1983/84. These cuts were made worse by an earlier decision to require universities to charge 'full-cost' tuition fees for overseas students but mitigated by special funds to pay for the restructuring of departments and the recruitment of younger lecturers under the 'new blood' scheme.

16. After the 1981 cuts, universities reduced their intake of students. Many of the displaced students found places in polytechnics and colleges, which, although they had not had their budgets cut, were forced to accept less favourable staff/student ratios. Between 1981 and 1987 their productivity increased by twenty per cent, so widening the gap between the average cost per student in universities and polytechnics and colleges.

17. 'Save British Science' is a pressure group formed by scientists in Oxford, St Andrews and other universities worried about the declining international competitiveness of British science.

18. In 1985 the Committee of Vice-Chancellors and Principals established a Universities Information Unit designed to promote the collective image of the universities and to coordinate the efforts of individual universities in the public relations field. A little later a similar initiative was taken in the polytechnics and colleges when the Higher Education Information Services Trust (HEIST) was established. But as a result of institutional rivalries it has been less successful.

19. The Council for Industry and Higher Education is a forum in which senior academic leaders and businessmen meet to discuss matters of common concern. It has produced policy papers on issues such as the need for expansion and student support.

20. The contrast between positional and non-positional goods is explored in F. Hirsch, *Social Limits to Growth* (London, 1977).

21. Martin J. Weiner's *English Culture and the Decline of the Industrial Spirit 1850–1980* (Cambridge, 1981) has already been noted. A less measured account of a similar thesis was offered in Correlli Barnett, *The Audit of War: the illusion and reality of Britain as a great nation* (London, 1986).

22. Few questions of higher education policy have been more thoroughly investigated than the relationship between demography and student demand. The pioneers were the Conference of University Administrators which established a group on forecasting and university expansion in the mid-1970s. This group produced an interim report (Glasgow, 1977) and a final report (Norwich, 1978). The investigation was then taken up by the Department of Education and Science and the Scottish Education Department which published two consultative papers, *Higher Education into the 1990s* (London, 1978) and *Future Trends in Higher Education* (London, 1979). Demography and demand were also the subject of one of the seminars in the Leverhulme inquiry into higher education. The proceedings were published as Oliver Fulton (ed.), *Access to Higher Education* (Guildford, 1981). Two further DES papers followed: *Report on Education Number 99: Future Demand for Higher Education in Great Britain* (London, 1983) and *Report on Education Number 100: Demand for Higher Education in Great Britain 1984–2000* (London, 1984). Further projections were published in the 1985 Green Paper and 1987 White Paper.

23. J. H. Newman, *The Idea of a University* (London, 1852).

24. Clark Kerr, *The Uses of a University* (New York, 1966).

25. The best description and advocacy of this open-door tradition are contained in Eric Robinson, *The New Polytechnics* (London, 1968).

26. The Leverhulme inquiry into the future of higher education was an unofficial attempt to revise the Robbins report of twenty years before. The inquiry was funded by the Leverhulme Trust and its director was Professor Gareth Williams. Between 1981 and 1983 eight seminars were held. The following monographs were published:

Robert Lindley (ed.), *Higher Education and the Labour Market* (Guildford, 1981)
Oliver Fulton (ed.), *Access to Higher Education* (Guildford, 1981)
Leslie Wagner (ed.). *Agenda for Institutional Change in Higher Education* (Guildford, 1982)
Geoffrey Oldham (ed.), *The Future of Research* (Guildford, 1982)
Kenneth Robinson (ed.), *The Arts in Higher Education* (Guildford, 1982)
Donald Bligh (ed.) *Professionalism and Flexibility for Learning* (Guildford, 1982)
Donald Bligh (ed.), *Accountability or Freedom for Teachers?* (Guildford, 1982)
Alfred Morris and John Sizer (ed.) *Resources and Higher Education* (Guildford, 1982)
Michael Shattock (ed.), *The Structure and Governance of Higher Education* (Guildford, 1983)
In addition, a final report was published signed by the chairmen of the seminars, *Excellence in Diversity* (Guildford, 1983).

27. 'Development of a strategy for higher education into the 1990s', a circular letter from the University Grants Committee to vice chancellors and principals, November, 1983.
28. University Grants Committee, *A Strategy for Higher Education into the 1990s* (London, 1984), 1–3.
29. Kenneth Minogue's *The Concept of a University* (London, 1973) contains an impressive account of the objections to practicality in the university.
30. Matthew Arnold, *Culture and Anarchy* ed. J. Dover Wilson (Cambridge, 1932), 6.
31. Ibid., 8.
32. The main writings by Arnold on education, apart from his inspector's reports, are 'The Popular Education of France' and 'A French Eton', in R. H. Super (ed.), *The Complete Prose Works of Matthew Arnold* (Ann Arbor, 1962), vol. 4; and 'Schools and Universities on the Continent', op. cit., vol. 4.
33. Matthew Arnold, *The Scholar Gipsy*, lines 203–6 in Kenneth Allott (ed.), *Poems* (Harmondsworth, 1954), 202.

NOTES TO CHAPTER 6

1. The increasing proportion of older people is shown in chart 1.3 in *Social Trends 18* (London, 1988).
2. James Boswell, *Life of Johnson*, 445 [22 July, 1763].
3. Thomas Hardy, *Jude the Obscure* (London, 1896).
4. The Education Reform Act 1988 made provision for English schools to opt out from the control of local education authorities, for a national curriculum and national tests, for the abolition of the Inner London Education Authority and the University Grants Committee and for the establishment of polytechnics and colleges of higher education as independent corporations.

5. *Children and their Primary Schools*, report of the Central Advisory Council for Education (England), (London, 1965).
6. The debate about whether standards have been rising or falling in schools has been long, complicated and inconclusive. Much of the British data depends on comparisons of examination results, which are not a properly objective measure. International comparisons have also encountered technical difficulties. The International Association for the Evaluation of Educational Achievements has carried out comparative studies of the mathematical ability of pupils in eighteen countries. The results are summarised in *Digest of Education Statistics*, Center for Education Statistics, United States Department of Education (Washington, 1987), 303, tables 248 and 249.
7. The proportion of pupils in independent schools has risen from 5.8 per cent in 1976 to 6.9 per cent in 1987. One reason for this increase is the assisted-places scheme from which 24 000 pupils benefit.
8. Public Schools Commission under the chairmanship of Sir John Newsom, first report (London, 1968); Public Schools Commission under the chairmanship of Professor David Donnison, second report (London, 1970).
9. In 1862 the Revised Code for the payment of grants to schools was introduced following the report of the Newcastle Commission on elementary education. Under the code, pupils were tested in reading, writing and arithmetic and the grants to schools determined by the results. The code was bitterly opposed by Sir James Kay-Shuttleworth, Matthew Arnold and many others but remained in force until the 1890s.
10. 'A French Eton', in R. H. Super, *The Complete Prose Works of Matthew Arnold* (Ann Arbor, 1962), vol. 2, 325.
11. Speech by the Prime Minister, James Callaghan, at Ruskin College, Oxford, 18 October, 1976.
12. *Better Schools* (London, 1985).
13. The Technical and Vocational Education Initiative, introduced in 1983, was a programme funded by the former Manpower Services Commission which attempts to develop and propagate examples of a more relevant curriculum for 14- to 16-year-olds unlikely to benefit from more academic study. At the start it was treated with great suspicion by teachers and local education authorities who saw it as an attempt to introduce a narrow training regime. In fact TVEI has acted as a seed-bed for important experiments in secondary education.
14. *History in the Primary and Secondary Years: An HMI View* (London, 1985) offers a good account of current thinking about the place of history in schools and the balance between content and method.
15. Jane Austen, *Northanger Abbey*, ch. 14.

NOTES TO CHAPTER 7

1. G. M. Young, *Portrait of an Age: Victorian England* (Oxford, 1953).
2. J. M. Froude [1864], quoted in Asa Briggs, *The Age of Improvement 1783–1867*, rev. ed. (London, 1979), 3.

3. Linda Colley, 'The Apotheosis of George III: Loyalty, Royalty and the British Nation 1760–1820', in *Past and Present*, 102 (February, 1984), 94–129.
4. A critical view of the role of the monarch was provided in Tom Nairn, *The Enchanted Glass: Britain and its Monarchy* (London, 1988).
5. Peter Hennessy, *The Good and the Great: an Inquiry into the British Establishment* (London, 1985).
6. Tom Nairn, *The Break-Up of Britain*, 2nd edn (London 1981).
7. G. K. Chesterton, 'The Secret People', line 60, quoted in Philip Larkin (ed.), *The Oxford Book of Twentieth Century Verse* (Oxford, 1973), 128.
8. David Glass (ed.), *Social Mobility in Britain* (London, 1954).
9. The Oxford social mobility project, based at Nuffield College, was responsible for two surveys, the 1972 national mobility inquiry with more than 10 000 respondents and a smaller scale in-depth follow-up two years later. The most substantial and synoptic of its many publications were John Goldthorpe (in collaboration with Catriona Llewellyn and Clive Payne), *Social Mobility in Modern Britain* (Oxford, 1980) and A. H. Halsey, A. F. Heath and J. M. Ridge, *Origins and Destinations: Family, Class and Education in Modern Britain* (Oxford, 1980).
10. George Orwell, 'The Lion and the Unicorn', in Sonia Orwell and Ian Angus (eds), *The Collected Essays, Journalism and Letters of George Orwell* (London, 1968), vol. 2.
11. Halsey, Heath and Ridge, op. cit., 201–219.
12. In 1971 just over eight million people were employed in manufacturing industry in the United Kingdom and 11.6 million were employed in service industry. In 1986 the first total had fallen to 5.2 million and the second had risen to 14.5 million. The most rapid increase had taken place in banking, finance, insurance and business services. These figures are taken from the annual labour force surveys conducted by the Department of Employment.
13. Gerard Manley Hopkins, 'Tom's Garland: upon the unemployed', lines 19–20, *Poems and Prose* (Harmondsworth, 1953), 64.
14. Patrick Wright, *Living in an Old Country* (London, 1986). Although written from a radical perspective, this book successfully captured the unacknowledged antiquity of many British political and social attitudes.
15. An attempt to combat the anti-utilitarian strain in British universities and, to a lesser extent, polytechnics was the Enterprise in Higher Education initiative launched in 1988. Under this initiative £100 million was given to institutions to develop courses which included enterprise studies.
16. The number of divorces increased from 27 000 in 1961 to 168 000 in 1986. Although Britain at 12.9 per cent, had the highest rate of divorces per 1000 existing marriages in the European Community it was closely followed by Denmark's 12.6 per cent. Lower rates in other European countries were said to reflect the greater difficulty in securing a divorce and so higher rates of cohabitation. In any case, the British rate was half the American. *Social Trends 18* (London, 1988), 43.
17. Public expenditure of all kinds rose from 35 per cent of the

gross domestic product in 1961 to 43 per cent in 1986 having
reached a peak of 48.5 per cent in 1975. Even during a period of
Conservative government expenditure on health and social
services increased from £19.6 billion to £22.2 billion between 1981
and 1987, and, on education, from £17.9 billion to £18.8 billion.

18. Between 1971 and 1981 the number of people employed in the
professions and in management increased by a third, while the
number employed in manufacturing declined by 24 per cent.
Census 1981 (Office of Population Censuses and Surveys),
quoted in *Social Trends 15* (London, 1985).

19. In 1951 defence took up 24 per cent of public expenditure
compared with 6.8 per cent for education. In 1985 defence
accounted for 12.6 per cent and education for 13.4. But Britain
still spends a higher proportion of its GNP on defence than
other members of the European Community. These figures are
taken from the Government's annual public expenditure
surveys.

20. Fernand Braudel, *Civilization and Capitalism: 15th–18th Century*,
volume 1, *The Structures of Everyday Life* (Paris, 1979 and
London 1981, translated by Sian Reynolds), 435.

21. Matthew Arnold, *Culture and Anarchy*, ed. J. Dover Wilson
(Cambridge, 1932), 165–201.

22. Speech by Dean Acheson at the West Point military academy
on 5 December, 1962.

23. Alan Bullock, *Ernest Bevin: Foreign Secretary 1945–51* (London,
1983) and Alan Bullock, *The Life and Times of Ernest Bevin*, vol. 1
(London, 1960); vol. 2 (London, 1967).

24. T. S. Eliot, 'Little Gidding', line 220, *Four Quartets* (London, 1944).

25. T. S. Eliot, ibid., lines 232–3.

26. Robert Darnton, 'What Was Revolutionary about the French
Revolution?', *The New York Review of Books*, 19 January, 1989, 10.

27. Matthew Arnold, *Culture and Anarchy*, 62.

INDEX